THE
IMPROPER
BOSTONIAN

THE IMPROPER BOSTONIAN

DR. OLIVER WENDELL HOLMES

by EDWIN P. HOYT

WILLIAM MORROW AND COMPANY, INC.

NEW YORK   1979

Library of Congress Cataloging in Publication Data

Hoyt, Edwin Palmer.
    The improper Bostonian.

    Bibliography p.
    Includes index.
    1. Holmes, Oliver Wendell, 1809-1894—Biography.
2. Authors, American—19th century—Biography.
3. Physicians—Massachusetts—Biography.   I. Title.
PS1981.H64   818′.3′09   [B]   78-21275
ISBN 0-688-03429-2

BOOK DESIGN   CARL WEISS

Printed in the United States of America.

First Edition

1   2   3   4   5   6   7   8   9   10

For Punky

CONTENTS

((8))

THE
IMPROPER
BOSTONIAN

1

THE END OF
A LITERARY LION

OCTOBER 7, 1894. DR. OLIVER WENDELL HOLMES WAS DEAD IN BOSTON. His son, Judge Oliver Wendell Holmes, Jr., informed Dr. Edward Everett Hale, the family minister, and King's Chapel was reserved for the services. When the word reached the undertakers, it was flashed to the press, and in minutes the news began coursing the wires across America and the cables to all the Western world.

Next morning the messages of condolence began to arrive at 296 Beacon Street, the old brick house the Holmes family had occupied for many years. From near and far came hundreds of telegrams, cables, and letters.

The Boston *Transcript*, Holmes's favorite newspaper, placed the doctor in context—Boston context: "The death of Dr. Holmes extinguishes the last lingering star of what was a constellation of American genius. . . . He was, in the prime of his powers, the companion and associate of Hawthorne, Howells, Longfellow, Whittier, Bryant, Emerson, . . ." And the *Transcript* editorialist said much more, ". . . the centripetal force of genius, his life spanned the second great day of American literature."

That *Transcript* appraisal was accurate enough. By Holmes's own definition, he was "the last leaf" on the New England bough of the stately elm of American literature. Even in his final days, America's literary growth had taken root elsewhere, and New York had shown it most. The death of Dr. Holmes put finis to Boston's lingering literary pretensions. Boston would never be quite the same.

Holmes's death was lamented in Washington, in Richmond, in San Francisco, where soon an Oliver Wendell Holmes Society would appear to honor his memory with such magnificent banquets as Boston's Saturday Club and Holmes's Harvard class of '29 had regaled themselves in past years. At New York's Century Association, where Holmes was a favorite speaker, his passing was noted in quiet conversation at the tables. The London *Times* gave three columns to his obituary, which was as much space as would be devoted to the passing of a prime minister. In Paris, where he had studied modern scientific medicine and learned so well that he became its finest American teacher, *Le Temps* compared Dr. Holmes to Addison and Steele, those movers of British literature in the eighteenth century. He would have preferred to be compared to Dr. Johnson, his lifetime hero and model.

The French, had they been more conscious of his relationship to their own tradition, might have compared him to Pasteur. In his way Holmes was as important to the history of scientific medicine as that great French scientist whom Holmes crossed the Channel to see in his last years. But at the hour of Dr. Holmes's death, the full impact of his medical and scientific contributions was unrecognized even in America. It would not be until the second half of the twentieth century that the growing interest in the history of science and medicine would begin to bring Dr. Holmes the honors he deserved in his principal profession.

The trouble—if one might call it that—with Holmes was his eclecticism. *L'Independence Belge* of Brussels remarked on that phenomenon, likening the doctor to Joseph Ernest Renan, the great French philologist, historian, and critic.

Holmes was not a philologist, he was a poet. He was not a historian, but a biographer and novelist. He was not a critic, but a lecturer, and the greatest conversationalist in the English language since Dr. Johnson left the scene. Beneath all that, Holmes's scientific and educational achievements were buried in 1894. He had "discovered" the cause of puerperal fever and begun the move that would stamp it out. He had brought histology into American clinical teaching, and microscopy into the classroom. He had done more in his lifetime than any other man to end the time-honored American medical practices of bleeding, dosing, and shocking a patient who might otherwise recover through the forces of nature.

As a poet and novelist Holmes was, at his death, more highly regarded by literary communities abroad than at home. As he had long forecast, time had passed him by. He did too many things and did them too well, and his critics blamed him. For the most part professional critics accepted the transcendental judgment laid down years earlier by Bronson Alcott. "Holmes knows too much," said Alcott—therefore Holmes could not be among the truly great.

Dr. Holmes's three novels, *Elsie Venner*, *The Guardian Angel*, and *A Mortal Antipathy*, aroused the interest of the American public in the then-unnamed fields of psychology and psychiatry. Holmes wrested man's personality from the environs of religion and gave it back to mankind. In the 1940s medical historians began to recognize Holmes's contributions, but it was twenty more years before their acceptance became general. And even then, few in the literary world saw his three novels for what they were. S. I. Hayakawa and Howard Mumford Jones pried at the edges of the truth in their critical study of Holmes written in 1939. They called his novels good examples of the "novel of purpose." But it was left to critic Edmund Wilson to place Holmes firmly in the literary community as the major developer of the psychological novel, and to recognize his contribution to this form of prose literature as well as to science. Wilson's findings were never generally broadcast, but they appear in his letters, published in 1977. This "discovery" may even lead to a reevaluation of Holmes's place in American literature. In 1979, he has hardly a place at all, as he, being an intensely practical man of the world, had strongly suspected would happen. Holmes is recognized for a handful of poems and a few references to the lasting values of *The Autocrat of the Breakfast Table*—which revolutionized the essay as thoroughly as Charles Lamb's work had done the century before. Fifteen years after his death, the *Times Literary Supplement* would say that Dr. Holmes was "the most complete American of them all," and that he, more than any other, had made England realize that America had its own traditions and American literature its own strong character.

But in that week of Dr. Holmes's death there was little thought of such matters in Boston, for the city was shocked. No longer would the small straight figure in a top hat and long coat walk the Common in the evenings to nod and smile at all who passed and greeted him. No longer would teachers and poets and aspiring writers stroll past 296 Beacon Street and look up the long flight of steps, hoping to catch a glimpse of the Autocrat. No longer would the postman be burdened with thousands of letters, manuscripts, and gifts delivered to 296 each year. Boston was remembering him as he was to Boston. Helen Keller, whose courageous victories over darkness and silence had buoyed the world, sent a bouquet of flowers for the funeral, saying: "I think he was more to me than to most people, because I saw through his eyes and heard through his ears." But Miss Keller underestimated there; the *Times* said the same: "One aspect of Holmes's genius was his ability to observe the commonplace and put the irrevocable stamp of common experience on it." The Pall Mall *Gazette* called this characteristic one of Holmes's "own peculiar whimsicalities."

Shortly before his death, Holmes had autographed a picture for writer William Winter's son, on which he expressed his view that he had already lived long past his allotted time and usefulness, and that each month for ten years had been an outright gift from God.

"Ten—twenty—perhaps even thirty years from now—" he had written, "somebody may be interested to hear you say that you received this picture from the hands of the original; sometimes writers are remembered even as long as that."

Was Holmes's statement, so often made, a conceit—the reverse argument of the man who longs desperately to be remembered? Perhaps it was, for Dr. Holmes was very much the egotist. The ego would have been perfectly content with the services held that week in King's Chapel, where Holmes had nodded many a Sunday in his side pew in the gallery.

Not that the church was crowded, for the funeral service was notable for the small size of the audience. The Holmes family were Brahmins—the doctor's own term for it—and without anything ever being said, all Boston assumed that the services would be private. In fact, Judge Oliver Wendell Holmes, Jr., had never given that matter any consideration, but the effect was the same. The privacy that Holmes had always sought for his personal life, as opposed to the literary acclaim that he loved, was granted him in his last earthly rite.

The service was simple, and Dr. Hale wasted no words in eulogy of this great friend. Harvard was well represented from every department, undergraduate, law, and medical. The Saturday Club was there. His publishers came. So did his medical colleagues, his fellows of the American Academy of Letters, his friends from the Massachusetts Historical Society, and his last two surviving classmates from the class of '29. The mourners formed a sort of panoply of all that Holmes had ever been and done.

The service ended. The coffin was taken to the cemetery at Mount Auburn and lowered into the ground beneath a great oak, one large enough for Holmes to have yearned to measure its girth. The earth dropped down, the mourners turned, and the forgetting process predicted by Holmes began.

The silence was interrupted fifteen years later by a wave of recollections that surged across the Atlantic Ocean. On the one-hundredth anniversary of Holmes's birth, the American communities of literature and public affairs, joined by their English colleagues, paused to pay him tribute. A new American biography of Holmes was issued in that year, 1909, a new "appreciation" engendered, and Holmes's acquaintances reached deep into their memories for anecdotes that suddenly added inches to the little doctor's stature. But the centenary passed, and literary tastes moved on.

Holmes's timing was not far off: thirty years after the doctor's death, boys and girls still learned to recite "Old Ironsides" and "The Last Leaf," and some brave souls even attempted "The Deacon's Masterpiece, or, The Wonderful One-Hoss Shay" for special school literary occasions. Harvard College honored Holmes's memory more than most, but even there Holmes's importance had waned by the 1930s, and in the 1940s Holmes's prediction came very nearly true. It would remain for a new generation to rediscover the delights of the poet, essayist, novelist, philosopher, wit, *bon vivant*, physician, scientist, and inventor, who was the most interesting Renaissance man produced by Boston or any American city.

CHAPTER

2

THE REVEREND ABIEL HOLMES'S
SON PREPARES
TO DISAPPOINT HIS FATHER

IN LATER YEARS, LONG AFTER OLIVER WENDELL HOLMES HAD SETTLED
in Boston, he was claimed as one of Cambridge's own by the Cambridge literati, along with James Russell Lowell, Henry Wadsworth
Longfellow, and Louis Agassiz. There was truth to the claim, of
course, for Holmes was Cambridge-bred, and he never lost his affec-
tion for his boyhood home, even after the house in which he was
born was torn down to make way for Harvard College progress.

Holmes was born on August 29, 1809, just after Harvard's commencement. The event seemed no more noteworthy to his father,
the Reverend Abiel Holmes, who noted both events on a page in
the *Old Farmer's Almanac*.

But the Reverend Mr. Holmes was a middle-aged man of forty-
six who that summer had many other matters on his mind. He was
the Congregational minister in Cambridge, and was compiling his

American Annals, which would be highly praised in Boston and New York as a major historical work.

It had been a "late summer" marriage for Abiel Holmes and Sarah Wendell. He was thirty-eight and she thirty-three when he persuaded her to become his wife. She was, by the standards of the day, an old maid, and it seemed lucky that she caught even this widower. Abiel Holmes was a handsome man, and so she was twice lucky. But he was equally fortunate, for the Wendells were a family of property and after Holmes married Sarah in 1801, Judge Oliver Wendell bought his daughter and son-in-law a big, yellow, gambrel-roofed house near Cambridge's Congregational church. It was a historic old house. Once it was the headquarters of Revolutionary General Artemas Ward. There, Benedict Arnold had received his colonel's commission and orders to hasten to capture Fort Ticonderoga and seize the cannon so badly needed by the rebels.

Wendell, as the boy was called at home, was the third child born to Sarah Wendell Holmes. The first two were daughters. His mother was in her forties when he was born, well past the blush of youth and busy in Cambridge church and social affairs. So as Wendell and his younger brother John were growing up, they were faced by a world of older sisters and a mother and father who were immersed in their own activities.

Wendell's earliest memories were of the house with its tiny yard in front. From his low room under the eaves he could see the Red Lion Tavern, the Cambridge common, and the "Washington elm" that towered over it. Under this tree the Commander in Chief of the colonial forces had rallied his troops on the way to defend Boston in 1775.

One of the boy's first remembered experiences was the day in the winter of 1815 that Cambridge learned of the signing of the Peace of Ghent. Holmes was then a student at Dame Prentiss' school, located not far from the house. Coming home from school that evening he saw the college all lit up, lamps burning in every room in celebration of the end of the War of 1812, the end of the hated blockade, the hope of returning trade to a Boston that had never wanted war at all.

At home the Abiel Holmes household was excited by the news.

The Reverend Abiel said prayers of thanks, and in celebration of the occasion young Wendell was permitted to stay up as long as he wanted.

He lasted until eight o'clock, watching the college lights and bonfires, listening to the singing on the campus. Then, excitement or no, he fell asleep in his chair, and he was carried upstairs and put to bed by his father.

The big old house was creaky and seemed full of ghosts that walked at night, reminding the boy of the sins of man and the punishments of a Calvinist God. Gingerly, he passed the bare spots on the green ground known as the Devil's footprints. He knew why nothing grew there. The Devil was very much alive in early nineteenth-century Massachusetts. Tales of the Evil One were told to fit almost every occasion, and some of the Reverend Abiel's flock said Harvard College was a particularly favorite haunt of Beelzebub. The students were even said to "raise the Devil" in their "unhallowed orgies."

Wendell's devils and ghosts lurked in dark corners. He never opened unfriendly doors in the big house. He never went into the garret. In back of the old house stood a shed, where old and broken furniture was stored. In New England such items were saved "for a rainy day." Wendell knew the place was full of devils, and he avoided it as if it were hell.

At night, when he awoke, perhaps with the full moon shining in the window onto his face, he could hear the wide pine boards of the house creaking.

Who was moving those boards?

The winter wind howled against the clapboards and rattled the shutters.

Or was it really the wind?

Dogs howled in the night.

Or were they dogs?

The small boy's imagination kept him awake many an hour, huddled beneath the bedclothes, his head buried in the pillow to protect him from the evil spirits.

It was not much help to go down to the kitchen in the morning and talk about his fears. Like many men of moderate means in

Cambridge, the Reverend Abiel Holmes hired young men and women from the farms to help with the chores, from splitting wood to washing dishes and carrying slops to the pigpen. Invariably, these youths and maidens arrived with wicked stories of the Devil's doing in rural Massachusetts and New Hampshire.

Wendell was particularly horrified by one tale: if, in order to secure an oath, as boys sometimes did, one wrote his name in blood, and the Devil found it during his nightly prowling (for it was he who shook the shutters and creaked the boards, the servants told him), then the writer, be it Oliver Wendell Holmes or any other, would thereafter become the slave of the Devil *forever!*

Intensified by the crude jokes of the hired help, such fears accompanied the boy into manhood. Even in later life he would not stay alone in a country house, even if someone offered him title to the place.

He also feared the broomstick masts he could see in clusters down along the Charles River. They represented the unknown, the unthinkable, vessels that might spirit him out to sea, or who knew where?

His other great fear was of going to the doctor. The family physician was an old practitioner, Dr. William Gamage. There were no medical schools in the American colonies where Dr. Gamage learned to practice. He learned as an apprentice, and his medical knowledge was extremely limited. His favorite approach to illness was apparently homeopathic: Wendell swore Dr. Gamage prescribed either rhubarb or ipecac for every ailment. And for the boy, with his various complaints, most serious of which was asthma, life in winter became one round of ipecac after another.

But life in the big house was not all ghosts and ipecac. As Wendell grew he sometimes played in his father's study, a heavy-beamed room lined with books that first made forts and castles, and then became ships to sail the seas of imagination.

The Dame school specialized in teaching young boys and girls their ABCs and manners. For enforcement Dame Prentiss kept a willow wand as long as a dog whip, with which the large, elderly lady could reach all her charges with a flick of the wrist. Young Oliver was an inveterate whisperer, confiding quick little jokes to his classmates. His hands and shoulders often felt the smart of the good dame's discipline.

Oliver went from Dame Prentiss' guidance to that of William Bigelow, a teacher fallen from the ranks of the instructors at the Boston Latin School. Bigelow was a large man with a red face and weak nerves. He was a good teacher, but his Boston boys drove him so that he sought the placidity of Cambridge village. There he had the shock of his life: boys were the same everywhere.

Bigelow was blessed with some literary skill. (He once wrote an ode in Latin verse celebrating Harvard's bicentennial.) He was also a punster. The latter skill impressed the young Holmes, although Bigelow did not last long in Holmes's life. The Cambridge boys were too much for his nerves too. He suffered from headaches so severe that they made him miss his classes. Finally, he quit teaching altogether to become a proofreader. All Oliver ever recalled were his puns.

Abiel Holmes then joined with other prominent citizens of Cambridge to send his boys to the Port School, located a mile from the common, over on Prospect Street in Cambridgeport.

Cambridgeport was a rough business community, and the boys from gentler Cambridge were regarded as swells who needed to be taken down a few pegs. So they fought. Every day or two the Cambridge boys battled their way home after school through the woods and the huckleberry patches. They were led by Richard Henry Dana, Jr., the best fighter of all. Finally, the Port-Chucks, as the Cambridge swells called the locals, tired of the struggle and accepted them.

At the Port School, the Reverend Holmes's boy was known to the masters as the boy who (1) read stories behind his mathematics texts and (2) whispered illegally in a steady stream. His hands were chapped by the masters' rules.

Wendell was a fair student, not brilliant, but above average. He might have been better than that, but his interests were too broad and too shallow for real scholarship. Margaret Fuller was the leading scholar of his day at the Port School. She was a strange, tall girl who put down her schoolmates with big words. She professed literary tastes that led her to talk about "novels," and to use such words as "trite." She had been fluent in Latin since she was six years old. To Wendell and his friends, Margaret Fuller meant intellectual snobbery.

When Wendell was old enough to sit still, his father began taking him on visits to other churches. It was the practice of the Congregational ministers to exchange pulpits from time to time, because men and women lavished upon the church the same loving attention that four generations later their descendants devote to the television screen. The church provided instruction and entertainment, as well as religious faith. A change in ministers was as good as a new series.

So once a month Abiel Holmes and his son would go out to the barn on a Sunday afternoon and harness the horse to the two-wheeled chaise. Their destination might be Dorchester, Brighton, Lexington, or Burlington, which was sixteen miles from Cambridge. The Reverend Mr. Holmes preached the evening sermon at the exchange church as the trading minister preached at Cambridge. The distance was too far for a round trip, so each minister would spend the night in the house of the other clergyman. Wendell was exposed to new sounds, new smells, and new sights, as in the house that had a sanded floor instead of a carpet. He also came into contact with a number of ministers of varying degrees of Calvinism, most of them "weak in the theological joints" (whom he liked) and some of intense puritanism (whom he disliked instinctively).

Only a handful of houses stood around Harvard College, but the whole village reeked of history. The Reverend Abiel Holmes's church was as much the center as it had been when it was the meeting place of the First Provincial Congress for nearly two months in 1774, when John Hancock had led the delegates in debating the crimes of their British governors and the remedies that might be sought. There, too, the Committee of Safety met when affairs came to a head, and then the Second Provincial Congress convened there in February 1775 as the crisis was reached. Wendell was told these stories so often they grew tiresome. It was much more interesting for Wendell and his friends to play out the battle of Bunker Hill on grass-covered redoubts built by Washington's troops during the siege of Boston. The old batteries still stood sentinel on the revetments. He found a "King's arm," a flintlock, stored in a kitchen closet, and an old pistol. He brought these to pretend with young Dana and the others at defending the grassy walls.

Men still walked the rutted roads of Cambridge in three-cornered cocked hats, knee breeches, and silver-buckled shoes. In the village Wendell passed the Craigie House where General Washington had stayed and where Longfellow would live. American history for these youngsters was not a collection of dull facts from books, but came alive in almost every building in their town.

Many a character living in Cambridge struck awe into the heart of a small boy. One was Professor Levi Hedge, Harvard's instructor in logic and metaphysics, whose wife's father had been Cambridge's most notorious Tory, so hated by his fellow townspeople that the British had protected his house with sentries. The professor had an umbrella, the first Holmes ever saw, a heavy implement that took five minutes to spread. It was a treat to see the old man escorting his wife on rainy days.

Young Holmes was a curious boy and a tinkerer. With his jack-knife he carved a ball in a cage, but it was not so smartly done as those of other boys. As he said in later years, "My tendency was to hasty and imperfect workmanship." Before he had finished the ball and cage, his eyes were already elsewhere. He made a wooden skate, and he learned to skate on the ice in "the ditch" that ran near the house.

One wintry day Wendell was confined to the house with a touch of the asthma that would trouble him all his life. So that the day was not wasted, Abiel Holmes set for his son the task of writing a verse to illustrate the theme:

Perdidi diem (A lost day)—Tiberias.

When his father had left on his pastoral duties, Wendell settled down to work and produced a verse:

> I've lost a day: old Tibby said,
> Then sighed and groaned and went to bed.
> The monarch, as they said of old,
> Knew time was worth much more than gold.

> I'm of his sage opinion too,
> And think the man judged pretty true.
> But now my friends, I'll bid goodby,
> For you are tired—and so am I.

The verse was received well enough by the Reverend Abiel Holmes, but in seeing it many years later, the author shuddered. It was hardly worthy of an "educated" scholar of twelve years.

From time to time Holmes wrote lines for his sisters. They were quick with their praise. When asked later about these verses, he said, "So far as I know, no vestige of talent is found in any one of them. . . ."

Holmes's first exposure to poetry was derived from recitations in Latin, Greek, and English from his school books. He liked Gray's "Elegy Written in a Country Churchyard" and William Cullen Bryant's popular works. His favorite was Pope's *Homer*.

In these earliest days he wrote very little. Wendell Holmes was too busy with the world for introspection. He undertook, briefly, the study of the flute. He read books, but he found it hard to keep going. When he read a whole book through, he considered it a feat. His method was to flip through, find a passage or paragraph that pleased him, and then skip to another. The Reverend Mr. Holmes had a large library for the times, perhaps two thousand volumes. The books were mostly English classics, histories, poetry, and sermons. Holmes never read sermons. "I had enough from the pulpit," he said.

And of all the books, the one that caught his sustained attention was Rees's *Encyclopedia*, to which he could turn and dip and delve to his heart's content. Thus, Holmes acquired a smattering of knowledge in many fields.

At that time he was laboring with mathematics, Latin, Greek, and grammar. He did well enough in most subjects, but mathematics gave him a good deal of trouble, perhaps because of those other books tucked behind the volumes of theorems.

His father hoped his elder son would follow him into the ministry, so it was established that Wendell would go to Phillips Andover Academy, the seat of Calvinist orthodoxy, to prepare for college. But the Holmeses' family life made it almost certain Wendell would never become a preacher.

First of all, his mother's family, the Dutch Wendells, were more lively and worldly than the English Holmeses. The Wendells were a closer family, too, and so Wendell saw more of his Grandfather Wendell, who had a happy laugh and properties in Boston and off in Pittsfield, than he did of his Grandfather Holmes, who had a Yankee frown and seldom came up from Connecticut.

His mother's more liberal background and leanings preserved the household from the gray preoccupations of Calvinism. Sarah Wendell Holmes wanted a pianoforte, and she had the resources to buy one; her daughters would have piano lessons. So music rang throughout the house, particularly after Wendell finally gave up on the flute. The children also learned to dance—a decision that caused much whispering among the older ladies of the church congregation.

Sarah Holmes wanted good marriages for her daughters, and she got them. First, Mary married Dr. Usher Parsons of Providence. Then Ann married Charles Wentworth Upham of an old Salem family. In their teens Wendell and John were left in the house. John was two years younger, hampered by a lame leg and later by living in the shadow of his famous brother.

When Holmes was about ready for Phillips Academy, his father made it a point to take him on the excursions to other pastorates more frequently. He met pleasant men like Dr. Forster of Brighton, who impressed him because he smiled on Sunday, as if it were just another happy day of the Lord's week, rather than the "Sabbath." But he met too many who preached, as he said, "as dying men to dying men," and there was too much life in Wendell Holmes for him to take to them.

The Wendell heritage was the sort of influence that had impelled him at the age of seven to play hooky from Dame Prentiss' school and drag little John along across Cambridge to see the last public hanging that was ever held in the town. His father always tried to prevent such shocking laxity, and supervised his reading. He tore out certain pages from Dryden's books so that the boy would not be corrupted by them. But when pushed into John Bunyan's *Pilgrim's Progress*, all Wendell could remember was that "it seemed to me more like the hunting of sinners with a pack of demons for the amusement of the lord of the terrestrial manor than like the tender care of a father for his offspring."

So, although the elder Holmes did not know it, in the summer of 1824, when Wendell went up to Phillips Academy, the ministry was already a lost cause.

Young Holmes left for the sterile atmosphere of Andover with many misgivings. The old house near the common pulled at him. In the last year he had become good friends in a new way with the "help" in the kitchen. The young men exposed him to cider and wine. Cordial had its place in the kitchen, too, and a good deal of rum flowed there. The young women flirted with him. Wendell was more worldly than his father suspected.

From the beginning of his education he had been told of man's wickedness in the *New England Primer*:

> In Adam's fall,
> We sinned all.

Wendell did not believe it.

And then one day someone installed a telescope on the common, only a few yards from the Holmes house. It was at a time of a transit of Venus, and the charge was ten cents a look. Wendell took a dime from his youthful hoard and paid to have a peep. What he saw changed his whole view of the universe. There was a planet, as large as Earth they said, and yet it was no larger than a marble. Was not the compliment returned? Would not Earth, as seen from Venus, be an equally insignificant sphere?

And if that were true, contradicting all the emphasis on earthly importance that he had learned, then what else was true about the universe?

Such questioning did not make a theologian, at least not a Calvinist theologian. And so at that moment, if it were not ordained before, the church lost all chance of securing the services of Oliver Wendell Holmes.

A world that contained cigars, wines, cider, and women was much to be preferred to one that was dominated by the works of Jonathan

Edwards, a Calvinist who hated children as little vipers and welcomed the coming of death.

What Oliver Wendell Holmes knew he wanted was a taste of
life, even as he was driven up to orthodox Andover.

His father lectured him on the twenty-mile drive, and later by
letter, to remember that he had more advantages than most boys,
and thus more would be expected of him. It was a heavy burden
for a fifteen-year-old, but he was not alone. Most boys in his class
labored under similar conditions.

At Andover Holmes was again exposed to poetry in translating
Virgil's *Aeneid*, which he had to render into English verse. He also
experienced the torture that bigger and older boys inflicted on
younger, smaller ones, he being the smallest in his class. But he was
fortunate to have a big roommate, Nathaniel Dodge.

Holmes also made friends with Phineas Barnes of Maine, and they
spent many afternoons in fair weather climbing to the top of Indian
Ridge or swimming in the Shawshine River.

Wendell still came under the beady gaze of his teachers for his
habit of whispering. One day he aroused the irascible Jonathan
Clement, who was famous as a "beater." Clement came down on
the boy's hand with a ferule with such ferocity that the hand turned
black and blue. Holmes never forgot or forgave the teacher for the
brutality. Years later Clement was the one man in the world that
Holmes truly hated.

One teacher, Samuel Stearns, suggested that Wendell seemed to
have some talent for poetry, and that he ought to pursue it. Quite
possibly that encouragement was the most he got out of Andover.
His year there was not a success. In later life, although Andover
claimed him joyfully, he had little to say about the place, except in
asides in letters to Barnes.

At Andover Holmes did achieve some distinction. He was elected
to the Social Fraternity, a literary club, where he became loudly
famous for his debating ability. The club members raised such
heated questions as the tariff, the morality of history, and Queen
Elizabeth's treatment of her cousin, Mary, Queen of Scots.

Holmes endured the puritan orthodoxy of Andover for a year,
but he detested the "bigoted, narrow-minded, uncivilized" attitudes

of most teachers. Yet the year at Andover put the finishing touches on his youthful education and repaired his deficiencies in mathematics. Just a few days after his Andover year ended, on August 29, 1825, he appeared before the examiners at Harvard College and was passed for matriculation.

As Holmes noted with pride in a letter to Barnes, he and one other were the only Andover men admitted to Harvard that year without conditions.

It was a nice birthday present for a boy of sixteen.

CHAPTER

3

COLLEGE DAYS

As Oliver Wendell Holmes prepared for Harvard College in the early months of 1826, that institution's faculty was facing dismaying problems. The class of 1828 had been restless all year. In chapel on January 8, someone kicked the back of a pew. Other young men responded. Soon the chapel resounded with the knocking of feet against seats until the service was disrupted. Afterward, at dinner in the commons, the freshmen made so much racket the proctors were routed, and then, when the students adjourned to Harvard Yard, they continued the commotion.

Several professors appeared. The freshmen scattered. One troublesome fellow, Hall, was identified. When Hall was called up, he told so many lies that President Kirkland decided he should be "rusticated" for a year. That meant he would be sent down, but could come back to Harvard at the end of the punishment period on a pledge of good behavior.

Next day more serious disturbances erupted. Warren led half the class in an assault with rocks and sticks on the windows of Massachusetts Hall. The vandals broke nearly every window. Warren was "rusticated" for two years; Hagan, his lieutenant, was suspended for six months.

With that spate of punishment the freshman enthusiasm seemed to subside, but the difficulties continued, as if the freshmen had lighted a fuse. In April, six older students were suspended for wrecking furniture and one for beating up a college servant. In May came the most serious breach of discipline that had occurred in many years: someone planted a bomb in room 4 of Massachusetts Hall. When the device exploded, college officers came rushing to investigate. As they did, someone water-bombed the teachers.

In the investigation, Thacher was accused of setting off the bomb. Worse than that, the professors said, he lied when he denied it. He was dismissed—which meant forever. Crowninshield (2), as opposed to Crowninshield (1), his brother, was identified as the water-bagger, and rusticated for a year. Even when Crowninshield's father pleaded for leniency the faculty stuck to its guns. This was a crisis. Harvard might deteriorate if life continued on as it had been going that year.

Thacher proclaimed innocence. The faculty began to worry. There could be a lawsuit. The president warned the students that unless all those concerned with the "bomb" came forward, he would turn the matter over to the civil authorities. That meant the "bombing" could be seen as a real crime. President Kirkland was as reluctant as any educator to bring in politicians. But he was so worried about the discipline of the college that when no one confessed he called the solicitor general of the Commonwealth of Massachusetts. The solicitor general announced that he would come to Cambridge on June 8 to investigate. He would take the names of witnesses, and they would be called before the grand jury in Concord the next week.

The threat of outside official action unnerved the Harvard student body. It was one thing to bedevil the faculty; it was another to face the law. One student came to President Kirkland's office. What would happen to anyone who might confess to the crime?

Would he be turned over to the authorities?

No, said President Kirkland. Harvard would deal with its own. So that day John Samuel Prescott marched over to Massachusetts

Hall to admit that he had made the "bomb." He had stuffed a pound of gunpowder into a glass bottle and led in a paper fuse. He hadn't meant to do any wrong—he wanted to "create a little bustle."

Well, Prescott had his bustle all right.

But President Kirkland and the other teachers were so relieved to learn that there had not been a plot against their lives that they let Prescott off with three years' "rustication," and Thacher, absolved, was returned to good standing. There were no prosecutions and there were no lawsuits.

Hardly had that affair passed by when a senior assaulted Dr. Popkin, the professor of Greek. Popkin was a hard taskmaster. Still, one could not have students assaulting professors. Ten students were warned that they could be called by a grand jury. The college meant to prosecute the teacher-beater.

The student body took this declaration as an official breach of faith. In September, when Oliver Wendell Holmes's class of 1829 arrived at Harvard, tension was high. The resentments quickly infected the freshman class.

Holmes lived at home in the gambrel-roofed house across from Cambridge common, so he missed the evening hours in college, and also much unpleasantness. He was really a happy-go-lucky youth, pleased with himself and beginning to write a bit. One sunny day just after the semester began, Holmes was sitting out on the lawn of the house in the shade, reading a newspaper, when a tramp came along asking for something to eat.

Holmes stopped reading. He took a pencil, tore off a scrap of the newspaper, and wrote:

> Charitable Ann—
> Give this poor man—
> As much as you can—
> A little meat,
> And bread to eat,
> And a shady seat—

And he signed it O. W. Holmes—which was more than he would

the poems he would later write for publication. Then he handed the rhymed message to the tramp and directed him to the kitchen door.

Across the common each day he faced more serious business. Each morning he dressed in black trousers, black boots, a black single-breasted jacket, a waistcoat that was either black or white linen over his white shirt, and a black necktie; then he walked to Harvard Yard.

The curriculum was unyieldingly classical for the first year. That year the courses were more rigorous than usual. Spurred by the events of spring and summer, the college authorities had decided to keep the students occupied from morning until exhaustion.

The young men went to class to recite until one o'clock; then dinner was served in the commons. After gulping down their food they could wander about the Yard until two o'clock, when afternoon study and recitation hours began.

This regimen continued until six o'clock, when the students were called to chapel for evening prayer. Then Holmes and the other "townies" were freed, while the boarders ate supper and then went to their rooms to study.

Social life was officially confined to weekends. That life was never unified, for the class of '29 was not. Samuel May, class secretary, called his class "the most discordant material which ever entered." The seventy-one freshmen came from such divergent points as Louisiana and Maine. They were all of the privileged class, although of very different backgrounds. A dozen (including Holmes) began to meet together to smoke and talk. Others, who did not smoke, called them "Aristocrats," "Exclusives," and "Puffmaniacs." Soon "Puffs" and "Anti-puffs" virtually ignored one another outside class. The split lasted during the entire four years of college life.

Perhaps it was more than just smoking cigars or not smoking. Holmes was always a lover of the good things of life and it was in character for him to have joined the indulgers, while the more Calvinistically inclined looked on with sharp disapproval.

But because Holmes was a town student, and the son of a minister, he managed to move on several levels in college life. As a local boy he knew and was known to far more students than most of his classmates. Charles Sumner entered the class of 1830 and they were friends. The next year Holmes's cousin, Wendell Phillips, came. So did John Lothrop Motley, who later became a historian and diplomat. Motley's friendship with Holmes lasted all their lives.

Another college friend who had a great influence on Holmes was Charles Chauncy Emerson (brother of Ralph Waldo), who was a year ahead of Holmes. Charles Emerson loved rhetoric. He was one of Professor Edward Tyrell Channing's best students. But while Channing almost completely disregarded the new trend in English literature and the predominance of poets such as Samuel Taylor Coleridge and William Wordsworth, Emerson was immersed in them. He introduced young Holmes to Hazlitt's *Lectures on the English Poets*. Holmes went on from there.

Harvard just then was feeling the effects of a rebellion that had begun to change American society, and the college was in some ways a center of it. Harvard tended to liberalism. It was manifest in less brimstone in chapel and in such revolutionary ideas as allowing second-year students to study modern foreign languages. The ortho- dox among the ministry, not forgetting that Harvard had been founded to train men of the cloth, began to complain about the liberalism. In Holmes's second year, as he began the study of French under Professor George Ticknor, the orthodox-established Am- herst College was founded for the specific purpose of combating this Harvard backsliding.

The class of '29 was subjected to a new system. Students were arranged in sections by their class rank in a given subject. The bottom half of the class resented the "unrepublican" nature of the experiment. The students in the lowest sections said the quality of their education was inferior to that offered the more apt scholars. The system did not bother young Holmes. In his second year Holmes rose to the top tenth of his class, and stayed there.

In 1827 the same criticism that troubled Harvard also faced Holmes with a ticklish situation at home. His father became involved in the bitter controversy over the direction of the Congregational religion that had led to the establishment of Amherst.

The Reverend Abiel Holmes came from a strict background; his grandfather and his father never deviated from the old path. But Abiel's marriage to Sarah Wendell had tempered religion in the household, and not one of the Holmes children would accept the old doctrine that held they were "a set of little fallen wretches." So Holmes had grown up in an atmosphere of toleration of the family's vagaries. But in these later years, his father had been forced by the schism in the church to choose one path, and he had elected to follow the Reverend Lyman Beecher, apostle of orthodoxy, who held the pastorate at Boston's Hanover Street Church. Beecher became a leading figure in the strict movement, largely through the pages of the Boston *Recorder,* the newspaper of the orthodox, whose wide readership included the Reverend Abiel Holmes.

The *Recorder* fulminated regularly against "liberalism" of the sort that seemed endemic in the Cambridge atmosphere. The Reverend Abiel Holmes took then to curtailing his exchanges with pastors of a broad turn of mind, and brought to the First Church a succession of stern Calvinists. The Reverend Lyman Beecher appeared a number of times.

Some parishioners of the First Church objected to Beecher's style and to his "hell-fire" messages. In July they drew up a memorial message to the Reverend Holmes asking him to return to his previous policy of exchanging pulpits with ministers of many differing views, including Unitarianism, which had a foothold in Cambridge.

But convinced by Beecher and the *Recorder* that Congregationalism was headed for "moral desolation" unless it returned to the narrow road, the Reverend Abiel Holmes refused the request of his parishioners. He was supported—more, urged—by Deacon William Hilliard, a Cambridge bookseller whose orthodox views were far stronger than Abiel Holmes's. So Abiel Holmes refused to make any compromises.

The parish began to disintegrate. Even family members turned against one another. It was a difficult time for Wendell Holmes, who did not share his father's views. Yet he could not be disloyal. He kept going to church, a small, lonely figure, avoiding the congregation.

Luckily, Wendell Holmes's world was not his father's, and the activities and excitement at Harvard College kept him away from most of the controversy.

At Harvard President Kirkland was suddenly out and the intellectually liberal Josiah Quincy, mayor of Boston for several years, was chosen to succeed him. Wendell Holmes and his fellow students prepared to celebrate. They considered holding a ball, but could not find a ballroom. So they planned a feast to show their joy in the victory over orthodoxy, and celebrated with "the eating of meat, the drinking of wines, the smoking of segars [sic], and the lighting of tallow candles." Young Holmes expected that for this "the whole college will be gibbeted in the next week's *Recorder* for the immorality and impiety of a public dinner," but he did not care.

In his second year at Harvard, Holmes learned that he had to prepare to make his own way in the world. He was undecided between law and medicine, the two options reasonably open to him. Nothing could drag him into the pulpit, and although by 1828 he had written much prose for Professor Channing, and some poetry for the amusement of Emerson and other friends, he also had no illusions about writing as a way of making a living in America. If there was a clue as to the future, it was that he had done well in chemistry and mineralogy. Yet even he did not then recognize that leaning.

In Holmes's junior year he was no more settled. His rank in the class, in fact, fell that year because he did not do well in Spanish, which he chose to take along with Italian and French as an escape from mathematics and the classics.

In the autumn of 1828, as Holmes's senior year began, he moved into Harvard's Stoughton Hall. For the first time he was involved in the total life of Harvard.

Already he had been elected to Harvard's Hasty Pudding Club. He also joined a club called the "Medical Faculty," a mock society dedicated to burlesqueing the faculty, and another club called the "Notables" (*Diaphemizomenoi* in Greek), which staged debates. He was elected to Phi Beta Kappa.

Holmes, John Osborne Sargent, and Park Benjamin combined efforts to produce a little book, *Poetical Illustrations of the Athenaeum Gallery of Painting,* a sophomoric collection of satirical poems that poked fun at the new Boston art gallery.

Holmes's last year at Harvard was a successful one. It was marred, however, by the continuation of the struggle in his father's church, so upsetting to him that he confided to his old Andover friend, Phineas Barnes, that he was sometimes "as cross as a wildcat."

After months of increasingly astringent argument, the liberal element in the Reverend Mr. Holmes's church finally decided to terminate its relations with the minister who had served the parish for thirty-eight years. The Reverend Abiel preached his last sermon in the First Church on June 7, 1829; then he and Deacon William Hilliard led in the formation of Cambridge's Second Congregational Church.

Oliver Wendell Holmes went to the new church punctiliously, as befitted a minister's son, but without enthusiasm. The others scarcely knew him, nor would the congregation have approved of his behavior. At Harvard he had achieved a reputation as a punster and something of a wit; he was known even then as a remarkably able and lively talker. He wrote racy poems for the Hasty Pudding festivities, which usually ended at Porter's, where the tavern keeper was famous among Harvardians for his rum flip.

With maternal blessing Holmes gave parties in his room. The most extensive of these was held during the April exhibition of 1829, when Holmes read a poem of his own, "Forgotten Ages." The work was praised inordinately and unsteadily for several days in Holmes's "digs" in Stoughton Hall, over many rounds of claret and cider.

In July, at the class valedictory exercises, Holmes poked fun at himself in a poem he had written about the woes of a short fellow with too tall a lady. On the basis of the success of that venture, he was asked to provide a poem for commencement on August 26.

The men of the class of '29 put aside their petty differences that day to produce an exercise that was generally serious—except for the poem by Oliver Wendell Holmes.

The dignitaries processed into the meetinghouse in full regalia. President Quincy presided over speeches, addresses, orations, and a "philosophical discussion." The commencement exercises had been going for two hours by the time Holmes's turn came. It was very nearly one o'clock. Stomachs were growling and the benches got harder every moment.

Then Holmes rose, and for eight minutes delivered a "light and sarcastic" poem addressed to the ladies that ended:

> One classic tribute shall at least be thine
> The deepest bumper of the brightest wine.

The brevity, the jokes, the youthful appearance, and what a newspaper reporter called the "childlike innocence" of the poet made him the success of the occasion. He sat down in a hail of applause.

Then came dinner, and tea dancing with the ladies, and finally in the evening, the major celebration, the class supper.

College days were ended. Now came the serious problem of choosing a way of life that would enable Holmes to support himself.

CHAPTER

4

THE SAD END
OF A BUDDING POET

GRADUATION FROM HARVARD COLLEGE HAD FAR LESS IMPACT ON THE life of Oliver Wendell Holmes than on most of his classmates. It meant only moving out of Stoughton Hall back across the common to the big yellow house, where he could live until he completed his education. That fall, for reasons that were never entirely clear to succeeding generations, Wendell chose to make law his profession, and enrolled in the Dane Law School to study under Judge Joseph Story and John Hooker Ashmun. He had considered going away, perhaps to Yale, to study law, but was persuaded by the coming of Judge Story and Professor Ashmun that Harvard was the place to be. Perhaps because the law school was located just next to the big yellow house, Holmes felt altogether sequestered there. In a matter of weeks it became apparent that the law did not suit him, and by winter he was thoroughly disgruntled, admitting as much to Phineas Barnes, although he did not mention the reason.

By way of amusement he produced poems for a literary magazine called the *Collegian*, published by Harvard friends. The poems gave him more pleasure than Blackstone, by far. By spring he had published fifteen poems in the four issues of the *Collegian*, and they had been copied by various other newspapers and literary journals around New England; but since they were unsigned, they brought him little more than self-satisfaction.

The *Collegian*'s "admirable comic poetry" became known to Frederick Hill, editor of the *New England Galaxy*. Hill made it a point to learn the name of the poet. He was particularly taken by "The Height of the Ridiculous," Holmes's simplest and most professional work to date. It brought him new commissions from editor Hill.

So in the summer of 1830 the poet labored and the advocate slumbered. From this period came "The Ballad of the Oysterman":

It was a tall young oysterman lived by the riverside,
His shop was just upon the bank, his boat was on the tide;
The daughter of a fisherman, that was so straight and slim,
Lived over on the other bank, right opposite to him.

It was the pensive oysterman that saw a lovely maid,
Upon a moonlight evening, a-sitting in the shade,
He saw her wave her handkerchief, as much as if to say,
"I'm wide awake, young oysterman, and all the folks away."

Then up arose the oysterman, and to himself, said he,
"I guess I'll leave the skiff at home, for fear that folks should
    see:
I read it in the story book, that for to kiss his dear,
Leander swam the Hellespont,—and I will swim this here."

And he has leaped into the waves, and crossed the shining
    stream,
And he has clambered up the bank, all in the moonlight gleam;
Oh, there were kisses sweet as dew, and words as soft as rain,
But they have heard her father's step, and in he leaps again.

Out spoke the ancient fisherman,—"Oh what was that, my
    daughter?"

"Twas nothing but a pebble, sir, I threw into the water."
"And what was that, pray tell me, love, that paddles off so fast?"
"It's nothing but a porpoise, sir, that's been a-swimming past."

Out spoke the ancient fisherman,—"Now bring me my harpoon!
I'll get into my fishing boat, and fix that fellow soon."
Down fell that pretty innocent, as falls a snowwhite lamb,
Her hair drooped round her pallid cheeks, like seaweed on a
    clam.

Alas for those two loving ones! She waked not from her swound,
And he was taken with the cramp, and in the waves was
    drowned;
But Fate has metamorphosed them, in pity of their woe,
And now they keep an oyster shop for mermaids down below.

This poem achieved instant fame at Harvard. It was put to music
and sung in taverns and restaurants where men made merry. But
only a handful knew the name of its author, for again these verses
were unsigned. Holmes, then, by his twenty-first birthday, was an
accomplished creator of humor, although still unknown outside a
select circle.

Then came a change.

The morning of September 14, which should have found Oliver
Wendell Holmes deep in his case studies, instead found him deep
in the pages of the Boston *Daily Advertiser*. There he read a short
news item reprinted from a New York newspaper:

Old Ironsides—It has been affirmed upon good authority that the Secretary of the Navy has recommended to the Board of Navy Commissioners to dispose of the frigate *Constitution*. . . .

          —New York Journal of Commerce

When the young poet Oliver Wendell Holmes saw those lines, his
Massachusetts man's soul flamed up. If a New York editor lamented
the fact that the Secretary of the Navy was considering scrapping the
famous frigate, the matter was of far more interest in Boston and
its suburbs. The *Constitution* was Boston's own ship, built in Boston

harbor by Massachusetts men and sailed by Massachusetts men, by and large, in wars against the French, the Barbary pirates, and the British.

She was an old ship now, her timbers were rotting and her refurbishment would cost the navy a pretty penny at a time when Congress was complaining about expenditures. The pressure was on in Washington to break up the ship and stop the rot. But as the editor of the *Journal of Commerce* suggested, public pressure should stop the attempt.

Holmes took pen in hand and dashed off three rousing stanzas of sardonic poesy, and hastened by horsecar to Boston to offer them to the editor of the *Advertiser*.

OLD IRONSIDES

Ay, tear her tattered ensign down!
Long has it waved on high,
And many an eye has danced to see
That banner in the sky;
Beneath it rung the battle shout,
And burst the cannon's roar;—
The meteor of the ocean air
Shall sweep the clouds no more.

Her deck, once red with heroes' blood,
Where knelt the vanquished foe,
When winds were hurrying o'er the flood,
And waves were white below,
No more shall feel the victor's tread,
Or know the conquered knee;—
The harpies of the shore shall pluck
The eagle of the sea!

Oh, better that her shattered hulk
Should sink beneath the wave;
Her thunders shook the mighty deep,
And there should be her grave;
Nail to the mast her holy flag,
Set every threadbare sail,

> And give her to the god of storms,
> The lightning and the gale!

The editor read, and knew a sensation when he saw one. It was indignant, damning, patriotic, and loving all at once. Next day the *Advertiser* ran the three-stanza poem. A few days later it was picked up in New York, and then in Philadelphia, and in Washington; and soon it had traversed the nation, north and south, east and west. Everyone knew something of the saga of "Old Ironsides," and she represented the finest tradition of America. So the protests began to arrive at the navy yard, and if there had been any serious thought of actually junking the old frigate (which is debatable), minds were changed and a warning was issued for the future: nineteenth-century Americans did not like government meddling with their traditions.

"Old Ironsides" was signed only with a timid *H*. So while the poem became a national institution, its author continued to be unknown outside the literary circles of Boston and Cambridge.

In his work for the *Collegian* Holmes was joined by a number of young men whose paths would cross his constantly in future years. C. C. Felton would become professor and then president of Harvard. Chauncy Emerson would die, but his brother Ralph Waldo would carry the family name to literary greatness. James Freeman Clarke, often Holmes's rival as class poet, would become his steadfast friend.

In a few months Holmes had written a number of poems for "gift books." A gift book was precisely what the name indicated: a volume of lighthearted miscellany, printed with care on fine paper, handsomely illustrated, and bound in morocco. Its purpose was the same as that of the "coffee-table books" of a later generation; almost all the sales were for gifts, usually from a man to a woman. The gift book *Token*, published in 1831, contained Holmes's "The Lost Boy," and two prose pieces by an unknown writer from Salem, Nathaniel Hawthorne.

Already the Boston area was attracting figures who would make it the literary center of the United States.

Holmes wrote only a few more poems that year. They were nota-

ble for their excellence and originality, a major step above his sophomoric collegiate work. Those poems of 1830 and 1831 rank among
his best, and among the best work produced anywhere in America
at the time.

That might not be saying much. In the 1830s American literature
had not yet found itself. Cambridge's Richard Henry Dana had
written his *Two Years Before the Mast*; New York's Washington
Irving was busy with his stories; and James Fenimore Cooper was
weaving his tales of the northeast frontier. But Cambridge's Henry
Wadsworth Longfellow was as yet no more known than Hawthorne;
John Greenleaf Whittier was just beginning his writing. James Russell Lowell was a schoolboy. Ralph Waldo Emerson was still a Boston preacher.

When Americans talked about "literature," their minds turned
to England. As far as America was concerned, it was the age of the
orator, and books were more likely to contain extracts from a speech
of Daniel Webster or Edward Everett than a story by an American
writer. New York's William Cullen Bryant was the most famous
poet of the period, yet he was primarily a newspaper editor.

So while Holmes dearly loved writing—"the intoxicating pleasure
of authorship," he termed it in a serious moment, and "lead-poison-
ing" when in a jovial mood—he felt he needed a profession. And
tiring of the law, he considered only one alternative, medicine.
Others who would become famous in the world of letters put their
hands to occupations close to the pen, but not Holmes.

Perhaps it was the family background that kept him from considering journalism, perhaps it was the influence of Harvard College. But he might have given thought, as did Longfellow, to
teaching in the literary field. He did not. He turned from law to
the harsh mistress of medicine, a field even more difficult in America
in the 1830s than now, principally because there was so little knowledge of scientific medicine.

For years most of Holmes's intellectual efforts would be devoted
to his new profession. And when he resumed poetry it would be on
a different basis than before. The promise of this short early period
would never be fully realized; the genius that had produced "Old
Ironsides" would be concentrated elsewhere, not even concentrated,

some said, but scattered so widely that the full effect would never be felt in any field.

Holmes wrote one more major poem in the next year, "The Last Leaf."

> I saw him once before,
> As he passed by the door,
> And again
> The pavement stones resound
> As he totters o'er the ground
> With his cane.
>
> They say that in his prime,
> Ere the pruning-knife of time
> Cut him down,
> Not a better man was found
> By the Crier on his round
> Through the town.
>
> But now he walks the streets,
> And he looks at all he meets,
> Sad and wan,
> And he shakes his feeble head,
> That it seems as if he said,
> "They are gone."
>
> The mossy marbles rest
> On the lips that he has prest
> In their bloom,
> And the names he loved to hear
> Have been carved for many a year
> On the tomb.
>
> My grandmamma has said—
> Poor old lady, she is dead
> Long ago—
> That he had a Roman nose
> And his cheek was like a rose
> In the snow.

But now his nose is thin,
And it rests upon his chin,
Like a staff,
And a crook is in his back,
And a melancholy crack
In his laugh.

I know it is a sin
For me to sit and grin
At him here;
But the old three-cornered hat,
And the breeches, and all that,
Are so queer.

And if I should live to be
The last leaf upon the tree
In the spring,
Let them smile, as I do now,
At the old forsaken bough,
Where I cling.

When Edgar Allan Poe saw this poem, in his capacity as literary critic he acclaimed it as one of the finest works in the English language. Holmes would scribble other verses, and many of them would be printed. But for all practical purposes, when Oliver Wendell Holmes left his childhood Cambridge home in the autumn of 1830 to move into a boardinghouse in Boston and study medicine, he cut not only his close family ties, but his literary ties as well.

Neither the man nor his writings would ever be quite the same.

5

THE MEDICAL STUDENT
LIVES IT UP IN PARIS

WHEN OLIVER WENDELL HOLMES WENT INTO HIS FIRST DEMONSTRA-
tion room in the Boston Medical College, he found a dozen other
young men crowded around a table beneath a suspended skeleton.
Bones were scattered about. The place smelled of carbolic acid. He
was nearly paralyzed—and a grave doubt struck him. Could he face
the grim reality of his chosen profession? But soon enough he was
studying in his rented room, a stethoscope on the desk, a copy of
Wistar's *Anatomy* before him, and his scalpels on the table, blood-
stains on his sleeve. He spent his days in dissecting room, lecture
hall, and hospital ward, amid the smells of sickness and death, and
got so he never noticed them.

Medicine was a thoroughly respectable American profession, but
medical study was not. Massachusetts still forbade dissection of the
human body, and so corpses for study were secured by stealth, sometimes by grave-robbing. Holmes and his teacher broke the law every
day that they worked on dead bodies.

The doctors taught only five subjects: medicine, anatomy and surgery, obstetrics, chemistry, and materia medica. The Americans did not use microscopes (although they were used in Europe). There was virtually no knowledge of pathology (diseases) or histology (tissues) in the United States.

A student did not need a college degree to enter an American medical school. All that was required were Latin and elementary physics. Classes were held at the Boston Medical College from November through January only, and the student was required to attend only two terms of lectures. Holmes's real training would come as an apprentice to a doctor; after three years' apprenticeship he could take an oral examination and, when passed, be granted a license. Harvard had its own medical school (which for some reason Holmes did not choose to attend), but once graduated from that institution, a student need not even take an examination. The Harvard degree alone was sufficient for a license.

As for visits to the hospital, it took a strong stomach to be a practicing physician. Anesthetic—even the name—was unknown, and surgical operations were bloody, grisly spectacles of pain. The people in the wards were mostly the poor; hospitals were still regarded as charnel houses, and because of ignorance about the transmission of disease, many persons who came to Massachusetts General Hospital for one complaint, died of another, perhaps even one given them by the hand of the physician.

But in spite of the gore and the human suffering all around him, Holmes responded to medicine's challenge. He saw pneumonia, typhoid fever, syphilis, infantile paralysis, scarlet fever, and smallpox. Some fevers none of his teachers were able to diagnose; medicine was an uncertain art at best. Most doctors still followed the precepts that led old Dr. Gamage of Cambridge to dose the young Holmes with gallons of ipecac over the years. To adults they gave similar dosages of calomel and semipoisonous drugs. They bled and blistered and calomeled their patients half to death. A sick patient who did not die of his disease might succumb to the treatment.

Most of the medically educated men in America in the early nineteenth century had taken their training at Edinburgh or in London. But times had changed, and in 1830 Paris was acknowledged to be the seat of modern medical culture. Indeed, at the Boston Medical College that Holmes attended, Dr. James Jackson, Dr. Walter Channing, Dr. George Otis, Dr. John Ware, and Dr. Winslow Lewis gave lectures and trained students in the French methods.

Holmes soon came under the special tutelage of Dr. Jackson, perhaps because he became friends with Jackson's son, a fellow student. Living away from his own home, Holmes was a continual visitor at the Jackson house. In one way, Dr. Jackson was a substitute father to whom the young student could come for advice. Holmes was not close to his father; he never had been close, but the growing differences in their religious views obviously had created new strains. Holmes followed Dr. Jackson about on his hospital visits. He worked as a chemist in the hospital dispensary. He also continued to write verses, none of them particularly notable. Far more significant were two essays he wrote for *New England Magazine* about life as seen from the breakfast table of his boardinghouse. One was published in the November 1831 issue, and the other in February 1832, under the heading, "The Autocrat of the Breakfast Table."

But Holmes scarcely had time for any literary efforts those days, so consuming were his medical studies. At the end of his first year in Boston, his friend, young James Jackson, Jr., Dr. Warren's son, Jonathan Mason Warren, and Henry Ingersoll Bowditch, son of the mathematician who perfected the American system of navigation, all left Boston to complete their medical studies in France. Holmes wanted to follow them, and he asked his parents if they would support so expensive an extension of his education. He could, after all, profitably spend only one more year in medical school in America, and then begin to practice. But he wanted the best, and his parents agreed he should have it. The Wendells still had property in Boston and Pittsfield, and so the Reverend Abiel Holmes and his wife could manage the expense. The Reverend Mr. Holmes had some serious reservations about Paris, but Dr. Jackson added his weight to the argument. After his second year, Holmes had his way.

Near the end of March 1833, Oliver Wendell Holmes carried his luggage to the stagecoach terminal in Boston, boarded a coach for Providence, and took the snorting steamboat to New York. He had passage for England on the sailing packet *Philadelphia*. After a brief visit there he would go to Paris and undertake his further education.

When Holmes boarded the *Philadelphia* on April 1, he shared a state-room with Robert Hooper, who would be a fellow medical student in Paris. They were twenty-three days from Sandy Hook to Portsmouth. There the ship's passengers parted company, with Holmes and Hooper joining forces to travel together to France. Stormy weather prevented them from crossing the Channel for several days, so they went sightseeing. They visited castles and rode a "fly" drawn by two mules to the ruins at Stonehenge on Salisbury Plain. They went to call on the son of J. L. McAdam, the inventor of the macadam road process, whom Holmes christened "the colossus of roads." They went to the theater twice, passed themselves off as Englishmen to gain admission to the forbidden Portsmouth naval docks, and rowed a boat out to see the Isle of Wight.

When the storm ended, they took the Channel boat to Le Havre and there, when they identified themselves as Americans, saw their luggage passed over with virtually no inspection, while the agents went through the bags of their fellow English passengers apparently with combs.

Hooper and Holmes took a *diligence* to Paris, a journey of two days across roads so rough they had to get out and walk on some of the hills. They greeted that experience in the spirit of adventure. But in Paris they met with shock: they believed they spoke French. Had not Holmes labored three years under the direction of Professor Ticknor? Hooper had the name of a hotel written down, and the taxi driver they engaged took them there. Holmes began to address the hotelkeeper in his best Cambridge French. The *hôtelier* hated the English, and that detestation rubbed off on all foreigners who did not speak the language of Voltaire. So the young Americans, having been greeted so effusively in Le Havre, now found themselves isolated, facing the cold perusal of Parisians. They were turned away from the hotel.

The driver took pity on the young Americans and drove them to l'Hôtel de la Bourse, where they were accepted. They sent a message to Warren, Jackson, and Bowditch, who had been in Paris for a whole year. These old hands took the greenhorns in tow, and out to breakfast. That day they sampled *café au lait*, *brioche*, and *flûte*, and Holmes pronounced it all *magnifique*.

After a few days in the hotel, Holmes moved to lodgings at 55 Monsieur-le-Prince, on the Left Bank, near the Luxembourg Gardens. The room was large and airy, with a tile floor and high ceiling, a marble-topped mahogany bureau, cheap prints on the wall, and a green rug on the floor. He had two armchairs and two tables. The room was very bourgeois, but Holmes thought it luxurious, for he also had the services of the porter who awakened him, made the bed, cleaned his boots, and ran errands. All this cost ten dollars a month.

Thomas Appleton, son of a wealthy cotton manufacturer, had settled in much finer quarters near the Louvre. He and Holmes began to go around the town under the guidance of Appleton's valet, François. They dined at the café Les Trois Frères Provençaux, then one of the most famous (and expensive) eating establishments in Paris. They went to the Place Vendôme, the Louvre, the Luxembourg, and Frascati's. They went to see the Gobelin tapestries. They went to the Panthéon and saw Rousseau's tomb.

They dallied at the Café de Paris, and went to the Opéra Français. One evening they visited "the most Parisian of *fêtes*, Tivoli," in the woods outside the city. Appleton wrote home about it:

> Laughing groups of well-dressed Parisians lounged under the trees, or to the music twinkled their pretty feet. Here it is that the fair milliner, the fairer goddess of the café, and the nonchalant do-nothing meet in common revel. A boat in full sail, holding a laughing party, whirled . . . on a circular cruise in the air. Quadrilles were performed on the turf, and lovers turned aside to the darker alleys of the wood. A man put a pistol in my hand; I pulled the trigger, a rocket shot through the skies, and as it hit a metal bird, a shower of fire fell around. . . . Pantomime rules the moment. Harlequin eats whole puddings at a swallow and plays a thousand tricks. Café blazes before me in many colored letters. A party is watching a game in which a Frenchman strikes his ball into a hole and wins—a flower.
>
> *"Blanche ou rouge?"* asks the winner of a pretty girl at his side.

"Blanche," whisper her rosy lips. *"Excellent, c'est l'image d'inno-cence et de vertu,"* he replies, and fastens the rose to her bosom with an insinuating bow. . . .

Such adventures as these did not find their way into Holmes's letters to his parents. These stories would have convinced the Reverend Abiel Holmes that Paris was all the Calvinist world said, "the city of wickedness." So the new medical student was circumspect in concealing his adventures from his father.

Holmes had to decide what to do about language and study. Typically, he leaped in; shortly after his arrival he presented himself at seven-thirty in the morning at Hôpital de la Pitié, to follow Pierre Charles Alexander Louis on his rounds. Holmes knew all about Louis from Bowditch and the others; once in Boston they had spent half an evening arguing about the merits of this man, who seemed almost godlike to the young Americans. Holmes was there to observe and to learn. He would learn medicine and French at the same time.

Louis was one of the premier physicians of the day, a practicing scientist, particularly a pathologist, teaching practical approaches to disease as yet unknown to most American physicians. It was hard at first, because Holmes scarcely understood a word of the rapid Franch. The notes he took were in English.

He also began to study French grammar under M. Delaraux, who had been recommended by earlier generations of American students. He began taking his dinner at Mme. Morel's pension, with a guarantee that nothing but French would be spoken at the table.

Holmes studied so intently that soon he was attending lectures and following the work of several other prominent French doctors.

He wrote letters of discovery to his family. He walked in the streets and visited newsstands. After three weeks he wrote to his brother John, back in Cambridge, that he felt as if he had known Paris from his childhood. That rank exaggeration concealed his fumbling with French. He also told his brother that with the rate of learning in Paris, he could return in two years with more knowledge and skill than many an American physician of sixty.

Much of this ebullience could be put down to the values and judgments of a twenty-three-year-old. But each day new vistas were opening for him.

It was up in the morning at six, off to the hospital to begin rounds, and then over to the Café Procope for breakfast with the other Americans. These sessions helped his medical studies, as the more experienced young men explained and amplified what the newcomers had missed. But they did nothing for his French; the young men chattered in English.

The lectures quickly gave him the medical French. The social and dining vocabularies came from Mme. Morel's. The literary vocabulary and the language of the salon were longer in arriving; it would take the theater and readings in French literature, plus the newspapers and an appreciation of all going on around him, to perfect the impression that he had known Paris from his childhood.

Holmes was entranced with everything French. Coming from a culture in which the standard recipes still featured hogsheads of beef and demijohns of rum, he learned that a five-course dinner was far more delectable than five helpings of stew. He learned that wines were to be sipped, not quaffed, that the aperitif was superior to the tot, that one could drink and enjoy oneself and not get falling-down drunk as had been the lamentable habit of too many young men in Cambridge.

At first Holmes was lonesome and bemoaned the absence of letters. But within three weeks after his arrival, a stream of visitors began to arrive. Ralph Waldo Emerson dropped in one day, and Holmes effusively greeted his old friend Charles Chauncy's older brother. Then came James Russell, from a Cambridge family. He had the news. It was almost as if Wendell had not left home.

In July the American medical students domiciled in Paris suddenly scattered. It was the month of holidays. Some went off to Switzerland. Some went to England. Some traveled to Italy. Holmes, having just arrived, felt no need for a change. He was busily adjusting to a new life.

He learned fast. "I love to talk French, to eat French, to drink French every now and then. These wines are superb, and nobody gets drunk except as an experiment in physiology." So he wrote to his Calvinist father.

But these slips were seldom. His letters home told of hard work and public affairs, very little about his private affairs.

On the Fourth of July the Americans in Paris held a dinner. The guest of honor was the Marquis de Lafayette, America's friend in need in 1776.

At six o'clock the group assembled at Frascati's. The members of the committee in blue sashes stood at the door to welcome them. In a few minutes Lafayette, his son, and grandson entered and shook hands all around.

After some small talk the party adjourned to a long table set with plates and glasses, to begin a feast for which each of them paid seven dollars, or almost as much as it cost Holmes for his lodgings for a month.

The table was decorated with red, white, and blue bunting. Behind, a band played from time to time, loudly but badly—"stunned us at intervals," Tom Appleton said.

The Boston group sat together near one end of the long table; Holmes was between Appleton and James Russell, who was dressed in his best Boston finery and had waxed his moustache for the event. Soon the talk became spirited, flavored by wines poured by a stream of waiters. The Americans ate soup, partridge stuffed with truffles, vegetables, fish, and fruits. The band played what the bandmaster said was "Yankee Doodle." The company helped by banging their glasses with silverware.

Then came the toasts. First, of course, was the toast to the President of the United States, the most Honorable Andrew Jackson.

It might have been that the cheers the Massachusetts contingent gave for Old Hickory were less enthusiastic than they ought to have been. But the next toast was to Louis Philippe, king of France, and the din seemed considerably greater at Holmes's end of the table.

At the other end of the table sat a United States naval officer in his high-collared blue uniform, his face red from drink. Suddenly the naval officer lurched to his feet and faced the head of the table.

"Mr. President, I would like to know if this is a meeting of the

Hartford Convention, or of citizens of the United States?"

The officer referred to a meeting eighteen years earlier at which an assembly of New Englanders had opted to read themselves out of the federal union in dissatisfaction over the War of 1812. The plan had come to a sudden end with the peace of Ghent, but since that time a symbol of New England federalism had been the Hartford Convention. There was no easier way to start an intersectional quarrel among drinking companions than to mention it.

The drunken officer pointed toward Holmes's end of the table. Some at the table hissed and booed.

James Russell leaped to his feet. "Gentlemen," Russell shouted, his moustache quivering, "I propose that we cut the buttons from that man's uniform and turn him out the door for the scoundrel that he is."

The officer lurched back. Russell sat down.

"Do you know that man?" asked a diner across from Holmes.

"No."

"Well, he is about the best shot of the Americans in Paris. You had best be ready to defend yourself tomorrow."

Holmes blanched. Russell was no marksman. Young New Englanders did not learn the use of foil and saber.

But even as Holmes worried, another American took up the argument with the naval officer.

"By God, sir, my seconds will call on you," said the officer.

"You are a blackguard, and I would not do you the honor of dueling with you," said his opponent.

The officer rose, looked around, found no support, and left the room. The table erupted with a general sigh of relief. The wine passed around once more. From that moment the toasts were noncontroversial but fervent.

A duel? It was an activity common enough in Paris within the social framework in which Holmes moved. Napoleon was on St. Helena, apparently safely sequestered, and Louis was on the throne. But Napoleon made all royalists nervous simply because he was alive, and the young Americans in Paris, as no one forgot, were republicans. As foreigners they were safe as long as they minded their manners and refrained from political hyperbole. Yet the danger was real enough: during Holmes's stay in Paris, one of his fellow lodgers at Mme. Morel's pension was arrested and jailed as a dangerous republican revolutionary. Holmes was lucky that he was not politically inclined.

By August Holmes's command of French was such that he began "thinking French" and could take his notes in French. Dr. Louis became aware of this particular young American when Holmes delivered to him a small medical instrument sent by Dr. Jackson. The contrivance pleased Louis, and he began to take a special interest in Holmes. One day, seeing him busily inscribing notes on clinical procedures, the doctor stopped by his side.

"Vous travaillez, monsieur. C'est bien, ça."

Holmes nearly blushed. Such attention from the great one was unusual.

If Holmes in Boston had considered his friend Bowditch "mad" in his enthusiasm for the French clinicians, Holmes in Paris contracted the madness. He became one of Louis' most ardent disciples. At the Hôpital de la Pitié the doctors grouped their cases according to diseases and similarity of complaints. Thus, in his rounds behind Louis, in a few months Holmes saw more variations and more cases of a given disease than he might have in years in America. Further, the French doctor was totally empirical; he returned constantly to nature and cited the physician's obligation to allow the healing processes to take over without undue interference.

Holmes also attended the lectures of Auguste François Chomel, head of the Hôtel Dieu. He followed Chomel on his rounds of the wards and then assembled—with hundreds of others—in the hospital amphitheater for Chomel's talk.

He studied surgery under Alfred Louis Velpeau and Jacques Lisfranc, whom he called "that great drawer of blood and hewer of members."

He studied physiology with Baron Alibert and gynecology with Philippe Ricord, an American-born specialist in venereal diseases, whose abilities were surpassed only by his cynicism about human morality. Holmes called him "the medical Mephistopheles." But from Ricord Holmes learned the vital distinction between gonorrhea (readily curable) and syphilis (often permanent and fatal).

He also studied obstetrics under a woman, Mme. La Chapelle, who gave him an unusual appreciation of the role and possibilities for women in science.

The French had none of the Anglo-Saxon queasiness about working with dead bodies; no more treading on the fringes of the law. In Boston he had journeyed as far as Providence to dissect. But in Paris one simply went down to the morgue and for fifty centimes took his choice of the bodies of the suicides and other unfortunates whose corpses lay unclaimed on the slabs. Consequently, Holmes could examine the human body in all its parts more thoroughly in one year than many American practitioners did in their whole lives.

He learned three new principles: First, distrust duly constituted authority and search for facts. Second, never guess on a diagnosis. Third—what most American and English doctors of the time never learned—don't think a man must take medicine because he is sick.

Gradually, Holmes became involved in life in France. He met Englishmen as well as Americans; he read French newspapers, catholic in their attention to politics. He began to learn European history. He discovered where Portugal was, and what was occurring there. He observed a growing repression of the people by Louis Philippe.

By the time he had been in Paris six months, Holmes had made French acquaintances and had begun to learn to live less like a foreigner. He discovered that he had been paying his servant twice the standard wage and he stopped. He learned to ride omnibuses instead of cabs. He learned why the French valued the *à la carte* menu—a diner could eat as little as he wished, instead of stuffing himself.

Occasionally Holmes went to the theater or out for an evening. Since his father continued to be concerned lest he fall into the fleshpots, Holmes's letters to his brother and mother noted that some ideas were best not transmitted to the Reverend Abiel. But going to see Mlle. Mars, France's first lady of the theater, in Molière's *Tartuffe* was something he would not apologize for, be his father an orthodox Calvinist or not. If there had been any doubt that Holmes was forever lost to the strictures of his father's religion, it was dispelled in his insistent letters to the family.

But he studied. In that second summer others, including Hooper, who had traveled with him from America, went off on vacation to see the sights in other lands. Holmes remained in Paris and reviewed his work of the spring. In the winter series of lectures, which would begin in November, he proposed to undertake a course of visits to the Jardin des Plantes to acquaint himself with the medical values of botany. He bought books and medical instruments to take home.

By that time the expenses had begun to press on the Reverend Abiel Holmes, or he indicated that they had. The student felt impelled to write several letters defending his position. None of his friends even tried to live on less than twelve hundred dollars a year, he said. It took at least six or seven thousand francs (five francs to the dollar) to live decently.

"I can go home if I must, but while I am here I will not eat a dinner for twenty-five sous, and drink sour wine at a shabby restaurant."

In the winter term, four mornings a week Holmes went to the Hôpital de la Pitié for clinical observations and then to the Chomel lectures. He learned that Chomel was far more entrenched as a member of the French clinical teachers than Louis, although not possessed of the same tender spirit for humanity or love of nature that made Louis the superior instructor. With Chomel's large following, with perhaps three hundred students in attendance, it was hard to have a feeling of personal contact. In Louis' classes Holmes participated. The teacher examined the patient with his stethoscope; so did the students. They compared findings. But with Chomel it was lecture and note; the professor talking, the students writing furiously.

The difference was that between scientist and practitioner, and Holmes found himself irresistibly drawn to Louis, the scientist who always wanted to know why, rather than Chomel, who was more interested in what—how the doctor could bring the best practices of current medicine to his patient.

In this adherence to Louis among all the teachers to whom he was exposed in Paris, Holmes made a choice. As a budding medical scientist, what most appealed to Holmes in France was the scientific approach, an atmosphere that did not exist in the United States. Even in Boston Holmes had felt that American doctors fell far short of the standards they might have achieved. After a few weeks in France his view of American medicine was even more negative, yet he had begun to understand why the Americans lagged. They did not have responsible education in the field. This concern tugged at Holmes's conscience, and made him, even as a student, approach medicine with a responsibility to improve the standard when he returned home.

He wrote and talked now almost like a teacher, building his library, preparing himself to pass along in America what he had learned in France. For if French medicine, as he said, was half a century ahead of England's, then how much more needed to be done to bring American medical practices up to the best European standards? The thought was with him constantly, and emerged repeatedly in one way or another in his correspondence home. Holmes did not know it then, but he already talked and wrote more like a teacher than a doctor.

THE MEDICAL STUDENT RELUCTANTLY GOES HOME

THE CORRIDORS AND BULLETIN BOARDS OF THE ÉCOLE DE MÉDICINE were covered with notices of meetings and lectures to which all serious students were invited. The amphitheater and dissecting rooms were filled with young men watching the masters of anatomy and learning. Among the busiest of them was Oliver Wendell Holmes.

After months of hard work Holmes's interest had not flagged. Each day he was up and out at seven hurrying to find M. Louis and join the handful of students who tagged after the master as he made his morning rounds at the Hôpital de la Pitié. Then at breakfast with his fellows at the Café Procope, Holmes would bask in the reflected glory of the celebrities of the university world who gathered there: the mathematician Denis Poisson; the medical lecturer Gabriel Andral; and his predecessor, François Broussais, who had devised the new theory of "irritability of tissues." After this came another clinical lecture at one of the three hospitals Holmes attended, and then at noon he would hurry to the dissecting pavilion a mile from his rooms on Rue Monsieur-le-Prince. In the afternoon he would sit at another lecture—maybe two. There would be time for an aperitif, and then dinner with half a bottle of wine. Afterward he went to his room and his books.

Holmes was sometimes invited to attend the meetings of Le Société Médicale d'Observation, which had been organized by Louis' brightest students two years earlier. The admission requirements were brutal; an applicant had to have at least a year of Paris work behind him, and then pass a competitive examination and give a distinguished lecture on a particular disease. Once elected, he had to attend the Saturday evening meetings faithfully or be dropped.

It was far too early for Holmes to expect attention from the Société, but he began to aspire to it.

The normal term for a youth studying in Paris was three years. It seemed unlikely that the Holmes family would manage the extra expense for so long. He was forever writing home about how hard he worked, how much less he spent than his fellows, how he remained Paris-bound as they traveled. But he continued to insist that he would not live like a drudge, even if he would work like one. He said he could not cut expenses.

Holmes took little part in the expatriate life of Paris; like his fellow medical students he was too busy to be bothered with travelers and resented having to cross the Seine to dine with someone who bore a card or a letter to him, when that person had no part in his daily life. In January 1834 the American community organized a grand ball, but Holmes did not even attend, "because I did not choose to spend seventy-five francs for a parcel of folks of whom I knew little more than that they were raised on the same side of the Atlantic that I was."

He was totally immersed in medicine. When two members of the French Chamber of Deputies, M. le General Bugeaud and M. Dulong, dueled, and the latter was shot in the head and killed, Holmes was only interested in the autopsy report—"the ball striking on the external part of the orbital process. . . ."

As much as any intelligent resident of the French capital, Holmes was aware of the political currents, the rise of republicanism, and the approaching crisis of the restored monarchy. But politics was no more than an academic interest to him. Even the Christmas holidays found him at the École de Médicine.

In the early months of 1834 Holmes began going to the St. Louis Hospital to follow the lectures and clinical observations of other famous men, Laurent Biett on skin diseases, in particular. He heard surgeons and microscopists, specialists in all sorts of diseases.

In those few months he had also dissected so many cadavers that he could not remember how many—and had become an expert in human anatomy. This was one result of his adherence to M. Louis.

In April, after a full year of backbreaking work, Holmes was exhausted. He felt so much in need of a change that in spite of the knowledge that his family would think him wasteful, he joined Hooper and Jonathan Mason Warren on a trip to Strasbourg, Belgium, Holland, and then England. On the defensive as usual, he wrote to explain, half belligerently ("I have lived comfortably, liberally if you please . . ."), half placatingly ("My aim has been to qualify myself . . . not for a mere scholar . . . but for the character of a man who has . . . arrived at his own conclusions. . . . I hope you do not think your money wasted . . .").

But whatever the family back in Cambridge thought about his behavior, Holmes was bent on vacation. The three young men took a *diligence* all to themselves (a real luxury), and traveled for three days through the champagne country, refreshing themselves liberally with bubbly wine at thirty sous a bottle.

They went sightseeing in Strasbourg, visiting churches as was recommended and respectable. They went on to Germany, to Baden, Heidelberg, Frankfurt, and Metz. Where possible, they stopped at hospitals and universities to see exhibits and learn something of the condition of medicine in the area. Holmes was impressed by the cleanliness of the German hospitals, as compared to the French (and American).

At Metz they took a riverboat to Rotterdam down the Rhine, then considered the most romantic river in the world: its undulating, steep banks carpeted with vineyards, the castles sitting on the crags in the spring sunshine, and the red- and brown-roofed towns sprawled along the river's edge.

They spent a week in Holland, during tulip time, but they were as interested in anatomical museums as in windmills. They always dined well, and spent the evenings entertaining themselves at operas, circuses, and recitals.

From Rotterdam they sailed across to England, arriving in London on a dreary Sunday. They lodged at St. Paul's Coffee House on the advice of a Dutch acquaintance, not knowing that it was an establishment too rich for their student purses. After two days there, they moved to a cheap bed-and-breakfast house, where the three of them had a room for £2.10 a week.

They saw the sights, the most impressive of which to Holmes were the Thames bridges. They went to a meeting of the Royal Society. The English surgeon Edward Stanley got them into the amphitheater at St. Bartholomew's so they could observe some operations.

The young students mixed visits to hospitals with walks through Westminster Abbey and St. Paul's Cathedral. By July Holmes was sick of sightseeing and worried about money. He was spending more than his family would like, and he knew it, and he worried about what they would say when the day of accounting finally came. He did not stop indulging himself, however. He bought clothes. He went to the theater night after night. He went to the races, and specifically made it a point to take the expensive journey to Epsom Downs on Derby Day. It was a gray, windy, dusty summer's day, and as was the fashion, the young Americans took seats on the outside of the coach, so the dust of the road half smothered them before they arrived at the track. But they were soon revived. They saw royalty and nobility in their finery (King William IV looked to Holmes "like a retired butcher," the queen reminded him of "the wife of the old Cambridge milkman").

All England, in fact, brought negative reaction from Holmes. He found the country squalid, its politicians and churchmen stupid, its shopkeepers grasping. He, who had studied at the feet of M. Louis, was contemptuous of the unscientific ways of the best English doctors, and the quackery of the worst.

Hoping to find more of interest, he and a Philadelphia friend from Paris set off on a tour of the Midlands and Scotland. They stopped at Stratford-on-Avon, and went through the lake country. They stayed two weeks in Edinburgh, the capital of Scottish medicine. Then it was Liverpool, Birmingham, and London again, all on the outside of the coach. A few more days in London, and he headed for Dover and across to Calais. On September 3 Holmes was back in Paris—"*Me voilà revenu*"—back in the City of Light, his scientific, social, and cultural capital of the world.

As Holmes had feared, his "extravagance" of the summer's travel had once more raised the specter of money back in Cambridge. But the aspiring doctor was well armed to argue against cutting in half the ordinary stay: he had just been elected to membership in the exclusive Société Médicale d'Observation. M. Louis had granted him free access to his two wards in the Hôpital de la Pitié—a privilege given only a handful of his most promising students. Holmes wrote to his family, flatly refusing to come home. He had so much more to study. He promised to try to be "more moderate" in his spending. After all, he wrote, if "you think it necessary to have clean waiters, good honest cooking, and not to have stale articles given you to eat" —why one must spend at least 150 francs a month for dinners.

He did not, however, mention to his father his love for the theater, for dining out in style, for the racetrack. He did dwell on the need for the constant replenishing of his supply of boots—"I trot to pieces at a terrible rate on these streets. . ."—and he stoutly defended his spending for books "for professional uses." He knew his father could not gainsay him those. His letter was effective. The complaints about expenses stopped.

By the autumn of 1834 Holmes's command of the language was such that he could take a case, write it up, and lecture on it success-fully in French.

Mornings he still went early to La Pitié—earlier in fact than even Louis. And he moved into the Louis wards to "examine and pound and overhaul" the patients before Louis arrived to see them. This aspect of his training Holmes found the most valuable of all, and he was proud and grateful—proud of his position and grateful to Louis and to James Jackson, Jr., son of Holmes's Boston professor, who had led him to Louis.

Young Jackson had fallen ill in France that last year, and had gone home and died, a matter that saddened Holmes and made him feel even more obligated to the whole Jackson family. His letters home were interspersed with inquiries about the Jacksons.

Throughout 1834 Holmes continued in a fever of medical dedication. His Cambridge friend, John Sargent, who had edited the *Collegian*, had bought into the *New England Magazine*, and wanted Holmes to resume writing for that publication. But the young doctor refused. He had, he said, turned from popular literature forever. He was, he said, the "Cincinnatus of Science" and he had to struggle and slave ("how hard I must work") in the footsteps of Aesculapius. His efforts left him no time for levity, or for the relaxation of mind that alone could produce a literary and poetical view of the world.

Holmes was spending five hours a day visiting patients. Then it was off to lectures and three or four hours to study the books. The Société Médicale d'Observation made heavy demands on him: in two months he was called on for as many papers.

The complete confidence of M. Louis was flattering, but also brought new obligations. Louis spoke little English, and he asked Holmes to give him a thorough report on a work by the English physician, Dr. Marshall Hall. Holmes did so after considerable time spent on reading the work and writing a careful review of it.

Always in the air hung the question from Cambridge: when are you coming home? Every letter referred to it in some way, and as he ended his second year the approach became more strident. He indicated that he planned to repay his indebtedness, but the requests did not cease. The family professed itself worried about "war in Europe." In May 1835, when the danger of war seemed to have ended, came new plaints.

But Holmes brushed them aside. He had just turned his attention to "operating." Dissection was the stripping down of an organ of the body to reveal all its parts to the student so that he might familiarize himself with those elements of the living body. "Operating" was the simulation of surgical procedures. He and a Swiss student named Bizot together bought a set of surgical instruments and carved away at the cadavers available to them from the mausoleum of Clamart cemetery.

By the summer of 1835 Holmes had been studying medicine for five years, and at the age of twenty-five he probably knew more than most of the doctors in the United States about the practical and scientific treatment of disease. He was, in other words, an accomplished physician. But he was not yet a doctor. The private school run by Dr. Jackson and his associates depended upon the Harvard Medical School to give the degree, and Holmes had not bothered to take his before he went to France.

So he was still a student, but a most competent one. One day on the way to the Hôtel Dieu he encountered two women hastening to the charity hospital, but one of them obviously was in pain. He heard her cry out, and then hurried to her side to ask what was the matter. But by the time he covered those few steps there was no need to ask: she sat down on the curb and almost immediately delivered a baby. Holmes used his pocket knife to cut the apron string of the woman's companion, and used that string as a ligature to tie off the umbilical cord and then cut it with the knife. He picked up the child and took it into a wine shop and washed it off in the wine merchant's sink before the man's astonished eyes; he bundled it up in the apron and sent them all off to the Hôtel Dieu with the aplomb of a fifty-year-old practitioner whose habit it was to deliver babies in the street.

The pressure from Cambridge was now unremitting. In every letter he was asked to come home. Further, all extra funds stopped coming, and by summer 1835, Holmes had run out of his money and had to borrow to maintain himself in Paris against his family's wishes. American banker in Paris, Benjamin Welles, accommodated Holmes, but it was a wrench for a well-born Cambridge man to go into debt.

The matter came to a head: he replied finally that if his father ordered him to come home, he would abandon his studies and seek passage on the next ship. But if they did not intend to order him home against his judgment, they must leave him alone to work out his affairs in his own fashion. He offered three alternatives: to come on receipt of the next letter, to wait for July and come home when Hooper did, or to spend two months in Italy (which he wanted to do) and then come home in the fall. He bullied his parents unmercifully in that last letter, citing his intense labors "for your honor and happiness," reminding them that old Dr. Channing of

Harvard College had been years in debt for his European education that had opened for him the gates of that college. He pulled out all the stops of his emotional organ: "Were I a parent . . . I should consider no sacrifice too great . . . and I should hesitate long before I would say to him, pale and fatigued with study—leave Europe forever, the only one among your companions who has not been beneath the dome of St. Peter's. . . ."

If that was putting it on a little thick, Holmes desperately wanted to enjoy those last months in Europe. He sensed that he might never be back, that his role once he reached the United States would be to settle down and practice medicine, which meant he would seldom leave Cambridge or Boston. "Pale and fatigued with study" he was not. Eager for a last fling he was. He needed four thousand francs.

Holmes got the money from home. He paid off Mr. Welles and had enough to make the trip to Italy. He packed up his books, a pair of skeletons, a microscope, some other instruments, a few engravings, and shipped them home.

Holmes's friend Bizot had told him the way to see Switzerland was to walk, so in Geneva they bought knapsacks, filled them with necessary clothing and toilet articles, and sent their heavy baggage on to Milan by freight. They hired a guide to take them around Switzerland.

In the first week of September he was in Rome, rushing from the Colosseum to the Vatican. He had shorted all else to "do" Rome properly, and he did. He tramped to the Pantheon, and stood in proper awe before the Laocoön, and the Apollo Belvedere, and the Dying Gladiator, but he said nothing about food or drink or any entertainment his family might find unseemly.

Then, having spent all the time he dared, he traveled to the Mediterranean coast and booked passage for Marseille. His journey to that point had been by carriage and by foot; it would be another twelve years before the railroads made their impact on European travel. So, by far the fastest and most pleasant way to travel back to France was by ship. After an uneventful voyage, the ship reached Marseille, only to come under the strictures of French bureaucracy. The vessel was detained in quarantine, and Holmes was kept an unwilling prisoner aboard the ship anchored in the outer harbor.

He could see the bustle of the city so close by, but could only sit on deck and wait.

When the ship was cleared, he went ashore to hasten to Aix and then up the Rhone to Lyon, finally to reach Paris early in October.

The sad process of disengagement then began. In summer Holmes had finally become resigned to leaving, although he knew he had not exhausted the fonts of scientific knowledge opened to him. The family pressure had grown too strong, the letters too demanding, and he had to yield. Now he did so graciously, saying good-bye to his friends and mentors. He attended a meeting of the Société Médicale d'Observation, and packed up the rest of his books, including some rare "finds" he had made on his tour. At the end of the month he gave up his lodgings and took the coach to Le Havre, where the *Utica* was waiting. The ship sailed on November 1.

7

YOUNG DR. HOLMES
SETS UP SHOP

TEN DAYS BEFORE CHRISTMAS HOLMES ARRIVED IN NEW YORK, "DE-lighted to see my own country again." He stayed over for a few days to regain his land legs. Then he took the steamboat north to New England.

It was a joyous Christmas in the big yellow house in Cambridge, with the prodigal son home at last, safe from the dangers of foreign climes and the moral threat of wicked Paris.

So it was not until after Christmas that Holmes was faced with the reality of homecoming.

Harvard was no respecter of foreign educational institutions. Like all others, Holmes would have to fulfill Harvard's own requirements for the medical doctor's degree. He would have to take the medical examination. Four weeks before he wanted to take the examination he would have to apply to the dean of the faculty and at the same time deliver a dissertation on some subject connected with medicine.

If the dissertation was approved, the faculty would give him a general oral examination. In 1836 the examination was to be held on the first Wednesday of February, so Holmes had very little time.

Holmes was confident—cocky—enough to wait until after New Year's to begin his paper. In four days he wrote "A Dissertation on Acute Pericarditis." On February 4 the essay was approved and he appeared before the faculty. A week later he was granted the degree of Doctor of Medicine.

In the month between, Holmes had been renewing acquaintances with old friends. John Sargent had accepted with good grace Holmes's refusal to write verse from France for the *New England Magazine*, but Holmes was not forgotten. Three months before he came home, Park Benjamin, reviewing a literary annual in the *New England Magazine*, had lamented the lack of any verses in it from Holmes. Actually, that mention was for many the first identification of the author of "The Last Leaf," "The Ballad of the Oysterman," "The September Storm," and above all "Old Ironsides." Without asking, Holmes was receiving his literary due. Benjamin lamented, but he also indicated that Holmes was so deeply immersed in medicine that no more could be expected from him, and that Holmes really did not care whether his large body of readers in America and England knew his identity or his poems.

Benjamin must have been baiting the young poet. He had taken over the *New England Magazine* from Sargent, and proposed to change its name to *The American Monthly* magazine and extend its purview across the continent. He needed help of the sort that Holmes could give him.

Holmes succumbed. Well, why not? In Paris he had promised only to refrain from poetry as long as he was studying for his profession. Here he was, idle. Why not write a verse or two?

He did. "An Evening Thought" was published in the February issue of *The American Monthly*. The poem concerned the weariness of the world traveler, ending: "My youth's bright flood ebbs, not to flow again." The author was twenty-six years old.

The next month the philosopher who had, in his flaming youth, attained such heights of poesy, lamented the dying of his talent. This poem seemed to be intended as an end to versification. He called it

"The Last Reader." When he received a copy of the magazine, he turned to the page. There it was, in its glory:

> I sometimes sit beneath a tree
> And read my own sweet songs . . .

His eye traveled swiftly down the page to the fourth verse:

> What care I though the dust is spread
> Around those yellow leaves.
> Or o'er them his corroding thread . . .

"Corroding thread?" Corroding thread indeed! That was not *his* adjective; the editor had altered his poem. He rushed to find his copy. Yes.

> What care I though the dust is spread
> Around those yellow leaves.
> Or o'er them his sarcastic thread . . .

That was how the verse should have been. Was there, then, more meddling? He went on.

No more meddling at least. And, there would be no more meddling again, ever. Dr. Holmes set his small mouth firmly, picked up pen and paper, and scribbled a note to Benjamin. Never again, he said, was Benjamin or any other to touch his verse except to render it into type. He would write no more until Benjamin would promise that the poet's words were to be inviolate.

Benjamin yielded, and the poet's anger subsided. He forgot that he had said farewell in "The Last Reader," and continued to write for *The American Monthly.* Once again, Oliver Wendell Holmes was infected with "lead poisoning."

Again, why not? As a doctor he had a long, hard road to travel. M. Louis had served an apprenticeship of fifteen years, and had indicated that his young men ought to prepare under the same regimen before they could properly regard themselves as finished doctors. In America no such delusions existed; in Massachusetts a Harvard degree alone gave a young man the right to pry and probe and dose and even cut up patients to his heart's content. But Holmes knew that establishing a medical practice was another matter, and although he was preparing to go back to the loneliness of the board-inghouse at 2 Central Court, where his landlady suited him and he was regarded as a respectable gentleman, still it was good to have an avocation that brought respect and pride.

In that spring of 1836 Holmes wavered; he wrote his classmates and competing class poet James Freeman Clarke dramatically that "The Last Reader" experience had quite turned him off to writing. In the next paragraph he told Clarke that he had accepted the task of producing the Phi Beta Kappa poem for the coming founder's day dinner. It was called "A Metrical Essay," heroic verse for a heroic occasion. He recited the poem himself before the Harvard audience, and repeated it later at Brown. It was published and his name was attached as its author. He said he did not at all care for renown as a poet, medicine was his meat. But then he collected his favorite poems that had appeared under "H" or "O.H." or no name at all, and sought their publication. In writing the introduction he claimed that it would be his last bow before the public, because he was "already engaged in other duties. I can sleep quietly after closing the last leaf of my little volume," he said.

If Holmes had set forth to tempt and lure editors, he could not have chosen a surer method than to continue quitting, declaring his intention of fading away from the literary scene. It seemed to take him longer to die than it had Desdemona. Benjamin wrote frantically to him to demand more poems. Reviewers as far away as New York suggested that he must not commit "literary suicide." The *North American Review*, New England's prize publication, scolded Holmes. No profession could be so all-engrossing as to leave no time at all for poetry. If Holmes thought so, then "he had a most unmanageable mind and certainly was not fit for the practical busi-ness of life." No poet, no doctor.

Holmes pretended to ignore the criticism. Actually, he was quite practical when he said he must turn his whole mind to the serious business of earning a living and establishing himself in a hard pro-fession. In the 1830s doctors were even more independent, less mutually cooperative, than they are today. No older doctor asked Holmes to share a practice. No hospital offered him a post. He hung out his shingle at 2 Central Court, and he waited.

"Small fevers gratefully received," he wrote. But the fevers were smaller and farther between than he would have liked, and, as if to emphasize his unimportance, one night a vandal smashed the night-light that illuminated the shingle. Holmes might then have followed the road that Dr. Arthur Conan Doyle chose forty years later. Waiting, as did Holmes, Doyle took to scribbling tales. Out of them came the famous Sherlock Holmes series.

But Holmes chose another path to relieve his boredom. He joined the Massachusetts Medical Society. He joined the Boston Medical Society. He became a force in the Boston Society for Medical Improvement, an organization of young doctors, most of them Paris-trained. All this because it was necessary, and also because a young doctor could go further faster if he had the attention of his elders.

It was a hard life and there were many disappointments, although successful physicians with Cambridge connections tried to help. One day a friend of the family's, Dr. Walter Channing, took Holmes on a visit to one of his patients, an invalid lady. When she saw young Holmes come in as her doctor was about to examine her, she half rose from her bed, protesting, "Dr. Channing, why do you bring that little boy in here? Take him away! This is no place for boys."

For at twenty-six, having grown to his full height—five feet three inches in his elevator shoes—Holmes still had the fresh look of a schoolboy about him.

Higher elevator shoes could raise him up to five feet five. Long sideburns helped conceal youthful features. But the cure lay in achieving success. Holmes had seen an announcement in the *Boston Medical and Surgical Journal* for the Harvard Medical School's 1836 Boylston Prize dissertation, offered for the paper deemed the best contribution to medical literature. He was well enough aware of the importance of the Boylston Prize in New England medicine; his brother-in-law, Dr. Usher Parsons, had won it four consecutive times, and was now an eminently successful practitioner in Providence.

Before April 1, the announcement said, competitors were to submit a paper on the question, *How are the external means of exploring the conditions of the internal organs to be considered useful and important in medical practice?*

Dr. Holmes's father,
the Reverend Abiel Holmes . . .

. . . and mother,
Sarah Wendell Holmes

Holmes subordinated his literary
interests, particularly writing poetry, to
the study of medicine at the
Tremont Medical School

During the 1840s, his eclectic nature
again led him to dabble in areas
outside of medicine

By 1860 Dr. Holmes was an established
Boston Brahmin, with a medical
practice, a professorship, and a wide
reputation as a major literary figure

The Holmeses' yellow,
gambrel-roofed house in Cambridge

The familiar figure of
Dr. Holmes strolling
in front of 296 Beacon Street

Ralph Waldo Emerson's religious and political views may have differed from those of Holmes, but shared literary interests made them frequent companions at the Saturday Club and the Old Corner Bookstore. Dr. Holmes wrote the first biography of Emerson, just a few years after the transcendentalist's death

Dr. Holmes delivering his farewell address as Parkman Professor at the
Harvard Medical School, November 28, 1882

At work in his book-lined study, 1886

Dr. Oliver Wendell Holmes in 1892—"the last leaf upon the tree"

Oliver Wendell Holmes.

It was not a place for poetry. The subject indicated the state of American medicine. Doctors did not have electrocardiographs; indeed, they did not have electricity. They did not even have sphygmomanometers to measure blood pressure by pulse strength.

Even given such equipment, the doctors would not have known what to do with it; medicine was not cognizant of blood pressure. Nor could a physician dose a patient with chalk and then trace its passage through his organs on a screen, or X-ray a broken bone.

There was no safe way to make a person unconscious. All surgical procedures were intensely painful and accompanied by shock that could kill the patient if the surgeon did not. How, then, did doctors discover what was happening inside the sick person's body?

In Paris Holmes had learned two new techniques, "percussion" and "auscultation," the processes of listening to sounds within the body through a stethoscope. Most American doctors had never heard of stethoscopes. When the "new-fangled contraptions" were introduced, the reaction of the American medical journals was almost uniformly negative. Thus Holmes's spirited defense of the technique and the tool came at just the proper time; the father of Holmes's Paris schoolmate, Dr. Warren, and other Harvard professors favored the stethoscope, but their arguments needed shoring up.

So having delivered his paper, Holmes turned to other matters. The decision on the Boylston Prizes would not be made until almost Harvard commencement time in late summer.

Holmes began to take a hearty interest in professional problems. Such a course was recommended by successful physicians, another of the ways to attain recognition. But there was more to Holmes's interest than that. Those writings from Paris about the primitive nature of American medicine and the need to bring it up to the European standards were serious. Holmes came home imbued with evangelistic zeal, youthful innocence, and the contempt he had registered against charlatans.

In 1836 the Massachusetts Medical Society investigated "quackery." Among its members, Dr. J. S. Bartlett was accused of conspiracy with one of the most notorious quacks in the commonwealth, a manufacturer of patent medicines promoted in the Boston *Ad-*

vertiser as "curing" everything from bunions to cancer. Dr. Bartlett was brought up before a meeting of the society and expelled. The Boston Medical Society then decided to do the same, and in June called a meeting to hear charges. Dr. Holmes attended the meeting where Dr. Bartlett was expelled by voice vote. Bartlett demanded a right to defend himself. The president of the society said in the interests of justice the doctor could make a speech.

Dr. Bartlett rose, pale and grim. It was true, he said, that he had been "indiscreet," but he was far from the only member of the medical society to do what he had done. He could mention by name, he said, a large number of members of the society who had committed far greater wrongs. Some of those doctors had advertised quack remedies of their own making in the press!

Did the members doubt? He would, he said, proceed in a moment to name them and delineate their crimes. Should they not be ejected from the society for their greater crimes as he had been for his lesser ones? Dr. Bartlett asked.

As Dr. Bartlett paused for effect, the meeting was ready to erupt. Gray-bearded doctors looked at one another out of the corners of their eyes. Several figures moved in the gloom. Doctors were suddenly called elsewhere in a great hurry.

The president of the medical society stood, gavel in hand, not quite certain what to do.

Then, a slender, short figure stood to full height. It was Dr. Oliver Wendell Holmes, in a neat black suit and dark flat bow tie, begging for attention.

"Doctor Holmes?"

"Mr. President. I submit that according to Roberts' Rules of Order, this discussion is a waste of the society's time. Doctor Bartlett is no longer a member of this organization and has no right to speak here."

"Hear, hear," came enthusiastic shouts from the audience.

The president of the society so ruled. Dr. Bartlett was shut off without another word. None of the ancient and honorable members were embarrassed.

Dr. Bartlett left the hall furious. He went to see his lawyer and announced that he intended to sue the Massachusetts Medical Society, the Boston Medical Society, and some of the people involved. He was thinking of the young whippersnapper who had prevented him from having his say.

At least the young whippersnapper thought that was the case, for he hastened to write the editor of the *Boston Medical and Surgical Journal.* His letter appeared on June 22:

> As the remarks attributed to me in the report of the proceedings of The Boston Medical Association have been considered by Dr. J. S. Bartlett as a personal attack, it may be well to say that my observations were intended by myself, and understood by the reporter, to apply to Dr. Bartlett only in his capacity of member of the Association, for the common privilege and intercourse of which he had been declared unfit by expulsion, and in which his character as a member had been forfeited, he could no longer be restrained by a proper responsibility in preferring his numerous accusations.
>
> Respectfully yours,
> O. W. Holmes

It had a nice ring to it. "Common privilege and intercourse," "proper responsibility," a good, solid bit of writing, nothing wildly poetic about it, the sort of letter that would build confidence among men of affairs. Holmes had, on that occasion, established himself firmly as a young man to be trusted by the defenders of the status quo.

So the summer of 1836 was altogether a triumph. Who cared if only a handful of patients made their way to his dispensary? The fewer the patients the more time he had to devote to his Phi Beta Kappa poem. It was not to be just a poem, but a literary exercise. It was a great honor to be asked. The presentation of the Phi Beta Kappa poem was an event in Harvard life, and the poet received the laurels of the Harvard community in a way not to be compared to writing a ballad that appeared in a commercial magazine. The poem was delivered at Harvard commencement, celebrating the college's bicentennial year. In the end the occasion grew even bigger: the college authorities scheduled so many activities that a special day of celebration was set aside a week after commencement.

It began with church services in the First Church, a dinner in the Yard, and exercises in the afternoon. Holmes performed twice.

Holmes's poem was the longest he had yet written, and when he had committed it to memory, it took an hour and ten minutes to deliver. The presiding expert in "Harvardiana," the Reverend John Pierce of the class of '97, who had attended forty-six consecutive commencements, declared Holmes's poem "beautiful" and "uttered with charming ease and propriety."

That work, repeated at Brown, the song he sang for Harvard's two-hundredth anniversary celebration, and the song he wrote and sang for the reunion of the class of '29, provided a fitting climax to the career of the "retiring" poet.

He won the Boylston Prize for his medical paper. Then his collection of poems was published in book form.

It was a marvelous year. He acquired a one-horse chaise and an indifferent nag to draw it. He loved driving up the Charles to Cambridge and into the northern countryside. He had a slowly growing list of patients, but he had also realized that the life of the general practitioner was not for him. The teachings of M. Louis kept reminding him of the need for constant observation and reporting of cases, an art generally neglected in the United States. If he were going to have cases, he had to practice in some public institution. In the fall of 1836 Dr. Warren and Dr. Jacob Bigelow, another of his old instructors, undertook to secure Holmes a post at the Boston Dispensary, where he would have a string of charity patients to observe. The appointment would guarantee him income that he needed to be independent of his family, and the work was far more in keeping with his interests.

The intervention of these two respected figures secured the post for Holmes, and soon he could be found thumping patients and writing mysteriously in his black book as he sat at their bedsides.

He had been home from Paris but a year, and already he was a famous person in Boston.

8

THAT BUDDING TEACHER,
DR. HOLMES, SUCCEEDS

IN BOSTON DR. HOLMES HAD ALREADY BUTTED UP AGAINST ONE UN-
pleasant attitude: his renown as a poet worked against him as a
private physician. Who wanted to say that he was treated by "young
Holmes—you know—the poet."

Medical Boston did not much care for funny doctors either. When
his *Poems* was published, Holmes had an uncomfortable time
among his medical colleagues. Most of *Poems* had a humorous
touch; he amused the literati, but his words might discomfit the
sick. It was so often brought to his attention that medicine and
poetry did not mix that he determined to sublimate his literary
talent even further.

Dr. Oliver Wendell Holmes's medical appointment at the Boston
Dispensary assigned him to care for the people of the Broad Street
slum district. Under the dispensary system each patient presented
a ticket that had been given to him by someone who patronized
(paid) the organization. At first, Holmes spent a good share of his

time running around Boston to beg tickets from friends and acquaintances for his poor patients.

From the moment he set foot on the shabby premises, he saw a need for reform. He did not like the way the dispensary worked, or how many of the doctors behaved, and these matters concerned him more than money or a successful practice.

Practice at the Boston Dispensary involved many house calls, and Holmes maintained careful records in each case, in his neatest handwriting. He was appalled by the filth of the clinic. M. Louis had taught him that in health care cleanliness is at least next to godliness, an aphorism that seemed totally unknown to the attendants who carried infection on their pus-stained garments wherever they went. If anybody got well at Boston Dispensary, Holmes observed years later, it must have been that they were saved by "the rough and tumble constitution which emerges from the struggle for life in the street gutters. . . ."

The conditions under which Holmes worked and the patients suffered lent credence to M. Louis' contention that more patients got well in spite of bleeding and ipecac than because of them. Holmes carried on a year-long battle against the abuse of medicines by his fellow doctors, many of whom still followed the old practice of giving heroic dosages to shock the patient's system into good health. The best the dispensary could do for its patients, he wrote the directors, was to provide them with decent food and warm clothes.

Holmes called for the establishment of a clean consulting room, modeled on the French system. He said doctors appointed to work at the dispensary should be chosen by competitive examination, not at the whim of physicians and teachers of Boston and Cambridge.

Dr. Holmes did not accomplish what he set out to do. His youthful exuberance and forthright criticism offended the powers that operated the dispensary. His last suggestion threatened to get Holmes into serious trouble. The members of the Massachusetts medical profession did not care to listen to a young doctor, with his foreign ways, who questioned the entire basis of their program.

But Holmes was not a reformer in the usual sense. He lacked

the zeal to pursue a course of action against social pressure. After he made his suggestions for reform of the dispensary, he turned his attention elsewhere. When the *Boston Medical and Surgical Journal* announced that the Harvard Medical School would award two Boylston essay prizes in 1837, Holmes decided to compete for both of them.

The subject assigned for the first of these dissertations was "intermittent fever" (malaria), a disease that worried and confused American doctors because they could find no rhyme or reason for the recurrence of attacks.

It was known that people came down with high fever that developed very suddenly. Either they died or they recovered, almost equally suddenly. But months later, whatever the season, they would come down with the same fever. The cause of illness could not be isolated as catching a chill, or eating hot peppers, or any other source. It struck man, woman, and child, white and black. Intermittent fever thoroughly confounded the doctors, who had never heard of microbes or viruses and who had no idea that mosquitoes carried disease.

In 1834 the Massachusetts Medical Society appointed a committee to undertake a study of intermittent fever, but nothing came of it. The task was time-consuming, and the doctors were too busy to go back to beginnings to study the history of the disease in New England.

Holmes began at the beginning. He visited libraries and town halls, and leafed through the pages of the town records. He pored over histories of New England and the memoirs of educated men. Phineas Barnes helped him from Maine. His brother-in-law, Dr. Usher Parsons, collected information from Rhode Island. Holmes wrote doctors all over New England for accounts of their experiences with intermittent fever.

The result of the investigation was a concise and accurate history of the disease in New England.

Having finished that paper to submit for one Boylston Prize, Holmes undertook a second dissertation on the best methods of treating neuralgia.

The second paper was not as difficult for Holmes as the first. He was able to draw on a large body of clinical experience, including his own. He also had much modern material from his Paris studies. In Paris he had assembled that impressive collection of the most modern European medical works.

These papers were delivered to the Boylston Prize committee at Harvard in April. Then Holmes waited.

In that spring of 1837 Holmes continued to practice at the dispensary, but he did not nag his contemporaries about reforms. He wrote a few poems, and he mingled easily in the literary society of Boston—perhaps more easily than in the medical society. The center of literary Boston was located at the Old Corner Bookstore on Washington Street. There Park Benjamin, Edward Everett, and Henry Wadsworth Longfellow came to buy books, to discuss books, and to talk to one another about the literary scene. George Ticknor, the proprietor of the bookstore, welcomed them all. He had already begun to publish works by some of them. His assistant, young James T. Fields, dusted the books, and made sales, and listened in awe to the erudite talk of these literary lights.

Sometimes Holmes and his old Harvard friends, John Sargent and John Lothrop Motley, visited Park Benjamin's house at 14 Temple Place. Soon it became a Sunday ritual to drop in at Benjamin's, but not entirely for Park's company. He had two attractive sisters, and they brought most of the eligible young men of Boston and Cambridge to the house at one time or another. Holmes was smitten by Mary Benjamin; he had mentioned her name in his Phi Beta Kappa poem, but she looked over the top of his head at John Lothrop Motley, to whom she became engaged later that year.

Polite Boston society was akin to, but not entirely the same as, the literary group. Holmes attended soirees, concerts, readings, and receptions, where he encountered important, well-bred people, the famous and near famous. There were Quincys and Adamses, and Phelpses and Cabots, Lowells, Appletons, and Bigelows. Daniel Webster came to these affairs, so did Charles Sumner and Holmes's cousin, the Reverend Wendell Phillips.

That spring of 1837 Mary Benjamin married Motley, and there were more rounds of parties. Some of the joy went out of the season in June, when the Reverend Abiel Holmes died in the big, yellow, gambrel-roofed house in Cambridge. The house was almost completely surrounded by Harvard University by that time, and the corporation, which had made several offers to Abiel for the property, made another, but Abiel had always refused to sell, saying it was a home and refuge for his wife and children. And so it remained.

Oliver Wendell Holmes was scarcely more than a weekend visitor those days, but John Holmes lived in the house with his mother after Abiel's death. Sarah would keep the place as long as she lived, and John stayed on with her.

In early summer there were rumblings within the Boylston committee. They reached the pages of the *Boston Medical and Surgical Journal*: there would be strange doings in relation to the Boylston Prizes that year. In August the secret was revealed; young Dr. Oliver Wendell Holmes had won *both* Boylston Prizes, setting a record to challenge his brother-in-law's.

It was almost enough to wipe out the stigma of his poetry. To help that trend along, at the end of the year Holmes had his three Boylston Prize essays put together into a small book. The volume was reviewed in all the major medical journals, and if the essays were not uniformly praised (the intermittent fever study was by far the most important), at least the essays extended the author's reputation to the broader American medical community.

Such praise was useful just then, for Holmes was embarking on another venture. He joined his old teacher from the Jackson school, Dr. Jacob Bigelow, who was also Harvard Medical School's professor of materia medica, and two others, to form the Tremont Medical School in Boston. Dr. Bigelow and Dr. Holmes had some particular ideas as to the manner in which medicine would be taught. They did not altogether follow the Harvard way. Their major innovation was the arrangement of the curriculum as an orderly discipline, rather than the hodgepodge of lectures that was offered at Harvard. The first year a student would learn anatomy, chemistry, physiology, and pathology. The second year he would begin clinical work, following the professors in the wards as Holmes had followed M. Louis. In the third year the student would continue clinical work, and was expected to recognize his own weaknesses in the fields taught and remedy them by extra efforts.

Dr. Bigelow, the senior teacher of the school, would teach materia medica and the practice of medicine. Dr. Edward Reynolds, who had substituted for Dr. Warren at Harvard when that teacher took a year off, would teach anatomy and surgery. Dr. David Humphreys Storer, another bright young doctor who had become a friend of Holmes's, would teach midwifery and chemistry. Holmes would teach pathology and physiology.

For Dr. Bigelow's benefit, and to assure the wholehearted support of Harvard, the Tremont school year was organized to dovetail with Harvard's. Tremont would operate when Harvard shut down, and Tremont would offer what Harvard did not, so a student could conveniently take courses at both institutions.

The Tremont Medical School was successful from the outset. It had good reports in the medical journals. Harvard approved. Boston accepted the school, and the courses were satisfactorily filled.

One reason for its success was the growing prominence of Dr. Oliver Wendell Holmes, and the recognition by the medical profession in New England that he was more than ordinarily knowledgeable in his fields. Pursuing pathology, for example, he followed his terminal cases to the end, and if possible secured permission to perform an autopsy.

The Tremont school was located upstairs at 35 Tremont Row. The doctors rented a large room from an apothecary named Metcalf, who had his shop below. There, in this cramped space, they lectured and gave examinations. The clinical work was done at Massachusetts General Hospital, the Lying-In Hospital, and the Eye and Ear Infirmary, where the doctors had credentials. In addition to his formal courses in pathology and physiology, Holmes taught the French system of auscultation by the use of the stethoscope, and a course in surgical anatomy. Later he would teach the first course in the use of the microscope.

As a scientist, Holmes was already among the foremost American doctors; as a lecturer, in 1837 he left much to be desired. He had halting speech and was easily distracted from his point by chance remarks, his own or others'. His affinity for puns and wordplay sometimes got him off the track altogether. He went faster through the course of study than his young men could follow. Bigelow, who was not given to overstatement, told him he could use some "sharp-ening" in the lecture department.

Fortunately, the opportunity to do so came just then, although from outside. Holmes was asked to contribute a song for the Phi Beta Kappa dinner at Harvard. The speaker of the occasion was Ralph Waldo Emerson. This chance meeting was to change Holmes's life. The year before, Holmes had devoted a stanza of his long elegiac poem to the memory of his classmate, Charles Chauncy Emerson. The older Emerson had not forgotten the mention of his brother. He renewed his acquaintance with Holmes at the dinner. Shortly afterward, Emerson suggested that the doctor-poet would be an apt candidate for the Boston Lyceum circuit.

Emerson was an important man in literary affairs. In 1832 he had lost his faith in organized religion, had resigned his post as second minister of the Second Unitarian Church in Boston, and had gone to Europe. It was during that sojourn that he had stopped in to call on Holmes and the other Harvard students in Paris; Emerson had returned just a year before Holmes to take up residence in Concord and begin writing. His first major work, "Nature," had confounded the conservative community and brought Emerson much unfriendly criticism, but it had also established his reputation as a strong, if controversial figure. With his ministerial presence and undeniable message, he was a natural find for the growing lecture circuit, and had that year begun to support himself by lecturing around New England under the auspices of the Boston Lyceum.

So Emerson's recommendation to the Lyceum committee was not taken lightly. Holmes was approached.

Lecture on general subjects? It would bring in welcome money and need not in any way interfere with his teaching duties. It was a more fitting avocation for a doctor than poetry.

So, in the late months of 1837, Holmes became a public lecturer. His first appearance was at the Boston Lyceum, where his subject was "Cities." He compared the merits of his beloved Paris to those of squalid London and bedraggled Rome. Soon, he added to that subject a lecture on English versification, which seemed so much more successful that he gave up the "Cities" lecture altogether.

By the beginning of 1838, then, Holmes was a busy man. His

writing brought him a little money, his lecturing brought more, and his teaching was the mainstay of his income. He had few private patients, but he could not have guaranteed the time for a private practice with all his obligations, even if he had wanted to.

The young doctor was also taking an active part in the affairs of the Boston Society for Medical Improvement. As with the old Société Médicale d'Observation of Paris days, the doctors discussed cases. Attendance was obligatory, and nonattendance over a period caused a member to be ejected from the club. Every member had to submit a paper at intervals, and if he did not conform, he also was dismissed.

Holmes gave the society all the papers the members could ever want. He dealt with M. Louis' work and the habits of French medical lecturers. He discussed the history of medicine and medical literature. He was probably as responsible as any member for the harsh membership requirements, so similar to those of his Paris group, for later, when Holmes became less active, the stringent rules faded and finally disappeared altogether.

But while Holmes believed in the highest standards, he was far from a sobersides. He was secretary of the club, and his humor crept into the minutes. At the annual dinner of the society he delivered a poem so anatomical—even scatological—that it could not be repeated in a family newspaper or set down in a nineteenth-century book. The subject was "the two scourges of the human race"—malaria and syphilis. His descriptions were rhymed references that titillated his audience. Such behavior could be countenanced among gentlemen doctors sequestered in a private dining room. In those circumstances Holmes was always quick with the anatomical pun.

So, already, within the bosom of his profession, he was a leader, a wit, a much-heralded speaker, and a notable dinner companion.

Holmes knew a number of society's young women, but after Mary Benjamin escaped him, he had no particular romantic attachment. From Maine his friend Phineas Barnes wrote that he was engaged and about to be married, and recommended the same course to Holmes.

Holmes agreed. He told his friend that at age twenty-nine he felt "domestic and tabbyish," and that he feared if he did not marry in the next year or two, he would be too old to do so.

"I have several very nice young women in my eye, and it is by no means impossible that another summer or so may see my name among the hymeneal victims."

In the summer of 1838 he went to Harvard commencement, as usual, and then to the reunion of the class of '29 at the American House in Boston. The occasion was notable for the singing of his classmate Samuel F. Smith's new patriotic ode, set to the tune of "God Save the King." They called it "America," and it began, "My country, 'tis of thee . . ."

Holmes brought news to his classmates. In the spring of 1838 he had learned that Dartmouth College was seeking a professor of anatomy for its medical school. He was approached, asked if he would be interested in such an appointment, and he said he would. So the trustees of the college met, and found the candidacy of Dr. Holmes eminently acceptable. Shortly before the class of '29 meeting, he had received an official announcement of appointment, although his duties would not begin until August 1839.

However, there were a few problems. His predecessor at Dartmouth had left Hanover and taken his personal collection from the museums of special and morbid anatomy. In a day when there were virtually no visual aids to medical education, dried, bottled, and pickled specimens of viscera and other bits of the human anatomy were essential for the orderly dissemination of knowledge. So Holmes had to begin rounding up a collection. He wrote to France. He wrote to England. He scouted around Boston and sent the word to New York, and all that year the pieces of the new collection came in.

That autumn another change came into Holmes's busy life. While he was seeking a proper wife, a young lady named Amelia Lee Jackson was summering in the country with her family, awaiting with restlessness the Boston social season.

"We shall soon be in town and then for parties and dissipation . . . ," she wrote her cousin. She had met no one who interested her. Life was a dreadful bore.

Amelia Lee had been properly educated in all the homely virtues of the New England maiden. She had come out into society, and now she had nothing to do but await a suitable offer of marriage. She waited, but not patiently. Amelia's eyes flashed and her temper burned when she contemplated the lot of women in her world— sitting and waiting. Sometimes her thoughts were downright revolutionary: she said she would even accept being *poor* if it meant she would have to exert herself.

Amelia was anything but poor. Her father was Judge Charles Jackson of the Massachusetts Supreme Court, a man of probity and property. He was the brother of Dr. James Jackson, Holmes's old mentor and good friend, who had been at least partly responsible for many of the young doctor's recent successes.

Holmes met Amelia, and their mutual dissatisfactions triggered an electric impulse. From Holmes's point of view, Amelia was eminently marriageable. She was shorter than he. She was vivacious, self-contained, and as respectable as any Harvard man and medical practitioner might want the mother of his children to be. From her point of view, the young doctor was a good catch. He was related to the Forbeses, Phillipses, and Wendells. He had no money, but high professional expectations. Her uncle spoke highly of him. He was almost handsome. He was funny. Everyone she knew liked him.

So the winter for Amelia was not quite as desolate as she had feared it would be.

Early in 1839 came a new opportunity for Holmes. The publishing partners, Little and Brown, had recently secured American rights to Marshall Hall's *Principles of the Theory and Practice of Medicine,* which in England was labeled a "major work." But Little and Brown said the book would not do for the American market as it stood. There were too many differences in American botany and pharmacology, and the book needed editing and annotation.

Little and Brown approached Dr. Bigelow. They learned that Holmes was acquainted with Dr. Hall and had even dined with him in Paris (after M. Louis had asked Holmes to translate the book into French). Dr. Bigelow agreed to revise the sections dealing with some of his special fields of knowledge, such as botany and self-limiting diseases. Little and Brown asked Holmes to annotate the work, in view of his experiences in Paris and with due recognition of developments in that medical capital of the world.

Holmes, then, was teaching at the Tremont school, chasing down his medical specimens for Dartmouth, lecturing on the Lyceum circuit, writing on the Hall book, courting Amelia Jackson, and seeing occasional patients. It was an eminently satisfying life. But just as he was enjoying it, came another flattering offer that could change his entire career.

In the 1830s the University of Maryland's medical school had fallen into an unhappy situation in a quarrel between legislature and educators, and most of the professors had quit, among them the school's professor of surgery. Dr. Nathaniel Potter, former dean and founder of the medical school, had agreed to try and put things right, so he undertook to hire a new faculty. Holmes's name had become so widely known through his three Boylston Prizes and Little and Brown's announcement of the Hall work that Potter chose him as his first candidate for the professorship of surgery. ("The reputation you have acquired, seems to designate you as a proper person to be united with us. . . .")

Potter bragged about Maryland's physical plant (". . . not excelled, if equalled in the country") and about the anatomical museum (". . . the best collection in America.").

The opportunity seemed tremendous. There was only one surgeon of any capacity in Baltimore, to serve one hundred thousand people, and he was about to leave for Kentucky. There was one other, Dr. William Nelson Baker, the new professor of anatomy, but he was only twenty-eight years old, "rising very rapidly, but too young to acquire public confidence."

How the thirty-year-old Holmes must have chuckled at those words, too young indeed.

The Dartmouth job would last only fourteen weeks a year, through August, September, and October. Holmes considered that he might be able to take on the Baltimore post in addition to all else he was doing. He went to his old friend, Dr. Jackson, for advice.

"Don't take it," said Jackson.

But, he said, if Holmes did decide to take it, he ought to plan to move to Baltimore, because he certainly could not teach surgery and become a good surgeon otherwise. And at the moment, Dr. Holmes was not a surgeon, as they both knew. He was far more the medical man. "I should be sorry to see you desert what I regard as your calling," said Dr. Jackson.

But Holmes was still interested in the new challenge.

Dr. Potter wrote that it would certainly be possible for Holmes to keep his residence in Boston and teach in Baltimore. The course began in late October and lasted through February. With a little juggling then, Holmes could teach at Dartmouth three months, and then hurry down to Baltimore for four months. He would get $400 for his whole Dartmouth stipend, and Potter said he would get at least $180 a week in Maryland. And then, having amassed such a fortune, he could come back to Boston in windy March.

But then came the catch: if he took the Baltimore job, he could not hold a chair in any other medical school. He would really have to move to Baltimore. It meant giving up Tremont and Dartmouth. On the other hand, he might expect to earn three thousand dollars for his teaching, and there would be at least that much again in operating fees if he practiced surgery. What was offered, in comparison to Dartmouth's four hundred dollars, was virtually a key to fortune.

On the negative side, he would be moving into a society as different from Boston as was that of Paris or London. His entire world would change. What would Amelia say?

Yet there was all that money. Holmes was intrigued. He asked many questions. How often would he have to lecture? Would there be conflicts with other professors if he taught surgical anatomy, too, as he believed necessary?

Perhaps he would come down and see them.

But he delayed. He pleaded the pressure of the Hall book, although that was not quite true.

His associate at Dartmouth, Dr. Dixi Crosby, warned Holmes against going: Holmes would arrive in a burst of glory, but how long would it last? Holmes listened to Dixi Crosby and Dr. Jackson. He was a Massachusetts man. The lure was great but . . .

In the end Holmes refused this promise of easy fortune and elected to stay in New England.

He went to Dartmouth in August. It meant missing commencement at Harvard and the reunion of the class of '29, but there was nothing else to be done, except to send a letter to the class to be read at the banquet. There would be no song for them that year. Holmes's literary and medical skills were to be devoted to Dartmouth. He had been asked by the Dartmouth chapter of Phi Beta Kappa to give them a poem for commencement, and he could not very well refuse. So he wrote the poem "in great haste" and delivered it on commencement day. His performance came at the end of a long succession of determined orators, including Alexander Everett, the brother of Edward Everett, and the Reverend Calvin E. Stowe, husband of Harriet Beecher Stowe. The orations were soon forgotten, and Holmes wished the poem had been too, for he regarded it as a work too contemptible to publish. But others liked it; the critics of bucolic Hanover did not demand so much as those of Boston. The poem was hailed by the crowd (perhaps in sheer relief) and by the reporters when they wrote their accounts. The commencement was a grand success, followed by a joyous feast.

And then the young professor settled down to work.

CHAPTER

9

AND IN THIS CORNER,
PROFESSOR HOLMES

HOLMES WAS A MARVELOUS TEACHER. HE COMBINED HISTORY, CUR-
rent science, and a sense of the excitement of the medical pursuit
of truth in language so vivid it made the lessons unforgettable.
From his opening lecture on anatomy and physiology at Dartmouth,
Holmes set himself to interest his classes and thus to instruct them
by encouragement. Critics, such as biographer Eleanor M. Tilton,
remarked that Holmes did not improve on principles by his im-
ageries, and later some of his brightest students complained that
he spent too much time on the commonplace and not enough on
advanced detail. But the proof of the pudding was that no one liked
to miss Holmes's lectures.

At Dartmouth it was important that no time be wasted, for
Holmes in three months had to give the students background in
anatomy ("the wheels and levers of the machine which we are to
study") and physiology ("how they move when in operation"), plus

the more specific surgical anatomy and chemistry. He did not have "a chair" at Dartmouth, he said, "it was more like a settee."

The year ended, and he returned to Boston and Tremont school. In fact, when he came back, he moved into 35 Tremont Row. He was determined to devote his full efforts to teaching and consultative medicine. The quarters were anything but sumptuous, with Thomas Metcalf's apothecary shop below and the Tremont schoolrooms adjacent to his own, but they would do. He was not staying long. He and Amelia Jackson had decided to resolve their mutual problems by marrying one another. They were married in the King's Chapel across the street from the school on June 15. Judge Jackson gave his daughter and her new husband a furnished house at 8 Montgomery Street, not far from the school. His mother gave them a piece of the Wendell land in Pittsfield.

The newly married couple went out into Boston society, where Holmes's friends felt that he improved her style and intellect vastly, and her friends said she was quite properly toning down his irrepressible nature. Everyone seemed to agree that they were very happy.

Almost immediately Amelia became pregnant, and then retired to the bosom of her household, from which she would not emerge until the Civil War. For twenty years she put herself firmly in the background. She managed her husband's correspondence. She arranged his notes as well as his socks, and she remained in Boston when he went to Hanover to stay at the Dartmouth Hotel and teach his course in the fall of 1840.

That was not a happy arrangement for a pregnant wife, and at the end of the term, Holmes decided not to repeat it. His financial situation was secure enough that the four hundred dollars was not vital, and his professional situation was such that he no longer needed the prestige.

For several years, Holmes had been interested in a number of special clinical problems. He wrote medical journal articles about emphysema and diseases of the throat, heart disease, and acute hydrocephalus. He was constantly observing cases of puerperal (child-bed) fever. In Boston this disease seemed to afflict the Irish women, in particular, and it was frustrating to him that the Irish were in such horror of "desecration" of the human body that he found it difficult to secure permission to conduct autopsies.

He persevered, however. "Perseverance" had been the motto he had attached to his difficult paper on intermittent fever, which took so much original research. Now he concentrated on puerperal fever, as much as he could concentrate on any one subject.

Holmes mixed this medical study into his Lyceum lectures. He had begun to do so in 1840, after the first series on cities and poetry. His particular aversion was quackery, which had afflicted even the members of his family. His brother John read advertisements for the wonderful waters of Brattleboro, Vermont, and went off hoping to be cured of everything from a cold to his lame foot, in spite of Dr. Holmes's warnings.

Such blindness by relatives and friends caused Holmes to turn public attention to what he considered quackery. His new lecture was "The Natural Diet of Man"—a warning against vegetarianism. He added another lecture on scientific mysticism, which was about semi-scientific delusions, including homeopathy. A third lecture on frauds was "Astrology and Alchemy."

By the spring of 1841 Holmes was so popular as a lecturer that George Tyler Bigelow, secretary of the Lyceum, invited him to undertake a new course of lectures and promised him thirty dollars for each of them—a higher payment than the Lyceum made to anyone.

He was also asked to lecture by the Society for the Diffusion of Useful Knowledge, a group of Boston's social leaders. Socially speaking, in 1842 Holmes was very much a part of this group. His Harvard College background, his status as the son of the old minister of the puritan church of Cambridge, and his excellent marriage had done him well. He was even an active, highly respected member of the society. In fact, Holmes served as secretary for the 1841–42 season.

So in Holmes's thirty-second year he had a position in Boston. He was regarded as one of the learned men of the community. He had been forgiven his poetry by most, because solid medical accomplishments tended to overcome resentments. He behaved as a Boston gentleman should. His devotion to family and to duty was complete. He missed the class of '29 reunion in 1840 because he was at Hanover, but he was back with his friends in 1841. He joined the Wednesday Evening Club of 1777, a select group of Harvard College graduates. He was, then, in every way a member of Boston's intellectual and social elite, welcome in any drawing room and, by this time, in almost any consulting room.

Holmes's lectures of this period might be termed "medical public service." His primary concern, as a doctor and a citizen, was with good medical practices. He had never abandoned the conviction that American doctors dosed too much and observed too little. As for himself, he was more observer than doser. He spent one terrible twenty-four hours, not leaving the side of a poor woman who was dying of cholera, so that he might add to the body of knowledge of that dreaded disease. He was very much concerned about the welfare of poor, shy New England girls who were afraid to submit to the examination of a physician, and he worried often about what could be done to allay their fears.

He used a microscope to study disease, and he discussed microscopy with his students at the Tremont school, although the science of histology (tissues) was still in its infancy. Because of all this activity, some medical enthusiasts in the twentieth century would describe Dr. Holmes as "a man a hundred years ahead of his time."

A century ahead? In what way?

Holmes's impact as a doctor and scientist came through his abilities as an interpreter and popularizer, as in the lecture series, more than through any particular discovery of his own.

Holmes's first society lecture, on February 19, dealt with medical delusions of history. He spoke of scrofula, a tubercular disease of the lymphatic glands and joints, common in medieval Europe. He compared the old treatment (the touch of royal hands) with the ancient practice of "weapon ointment." This was a system used for healing wounds. The wound was washed and bandaged; the ointment was then applied to the weapon that had inflicted the wound.

The composition of the ointments varied, said Dr. Holmes, but they often contained portions of mummy, human blood, and moss from the skull of a thief who had been hanged in chains.

The secret of both treatments was inadvertent cleanliness. The victims of scrofula were washed before being brought to be touched by kings and queens. The wounds of soldiers, washed and left alone, had a chance to heal without infection, while the obnoxious medicines couldn't hurt the weapons. The "doctors" had done just right for the wrong reasons. Hygiene was such a simple, sensible approach.

Holmes told a tale about Bishop Berkeley, who produced tar water by stirring a quart of tar into a gallon of water, boiling the mixture, and then pouring off the clear water. This course was guaranteed (by the bishop) to cure anything from scurvy to gangrene, and was also touted for care of the teeth and gums. Pure, boiled water always had been useful, Holmes observed. The bishop died at the age of seventy. "He might have lived longer," Holmes said, "but his fatal illness was so sudden that there was not time enough to stir up a quart of the panacea."

In Holmes's second lecture he took up the "science" of homeopathy, which had been founded by Dr. Samuel Hahnemann, a German, around the end of the eighteenth century. The principle was that "like cures like"—diseases were cured by agents that produced the same symptoms as did the disease.

Hahnemann and homeopathy subverted all Holmes had learned and all he believed about medicine. Hahnemann denied that there was such a thing as the "course" of disease. Nature, he said, does not ever cure chronic disease. He set up a complex system of medication in which medicines were never mixed but "diluted."

Holmes proceeded to illustrate the dilution of a single drop of tincture of chamomile according to the Hahnemann principle. The first dilution would require one hundred drops of alcohol. The ninth dilution would take enough to fill a lake two miles in circumference.

Under this system, Holmes said, a single drop of tincture of chamomile, if given by the manual, would have supplied every human being who ever lived up to 1843 with more than five billion doses!

Holmes then told how a challenge was offered by prominent physicians to the best-known homeopathic doctor in Paris to pick any ten substances and test them publicly to prove the homeopathic contention. The challenge was never accepted.

What had upset and angered Holmes particularly was the effect the homeopaths were having on American public health. By promoting this "pretended science," the quacks drew people like his brother away from medicine.

The homeopaths were on an equal plane with the quacks around Boston who pretended to treat venereal disease, but who usually left their patients worse off at the end than they had been in the beginning.

He could not say that much, of course, to the Society for the Diffusion of Useful Knowledge. One did not discuss V.D. among the Quincys, Cabots, Phelpses, and Forbeses.

Dr. Holmes developed a respectable medical practice in this pursuit of science, and that success militated for his remaining in Boston. He was offered a summer post teaching at the Berkshire Medical School in Pittsfield, but he turned it down. There was no conflict with his other posts, but the Pittsfield job would keep him from his researches.

He continued these researches diligently, keeping careful case records of the patients he saw in his hospital rounds, where he also taught his Tremont students.

He had a way of making medical subjects more than usually interesting, even to medical men. His paper on medical characters in Paris—his teachers—before the Society for Medical Improvement, created such a stir that the doctors asked him to do it again for those who had missed it.

There was a reason for that enthusiasm: the society membership included Henry Ingersoll Bowditch, Jonathan Mason Warren, George Amory Bethune, Herman Brimmer Inches, George Cheyne Shattuck, Jr., and Robert William Hooper—all contemporaries of Holmes's from the Paris days.

Holmes loved medical oddities and displayed many before the society with the perspicacity of a showman. He and Dr. James Jackson discovered a dwarf, and took friends to see him, too. From the dissecting room, Holmes once brought two enormous toenails that were as tough as horns for the delectation of his fellow enthusiasts. On another occasion he brought a uterus showing large fibroid tumors, which he displayed with an appropriate impromptu lecture. Another time he prepared a paper on giants, and at the meeting produced "Mr. Freeman, the giant from the West," nineteen years old, seven feet four inches tall, and weighing 340 pounds. Mr. Freeman was a grand success; he showed the doctors how he could bend his elbows backward and sideways. So impressed were the members of the society that they gave Holmes a round of applause and Mr. Freeman a fee of five dollars.

But most of the society's studies were more serious. Holmes gave one report on a medical student who had contracted a case of syphilis in the course of delivering a child. Something about this study stuck in Holmes's mind, and nagged at him.

In the spring of 1842 puerperal, or childbed, fever became prevalent in the Boston area. A doctor from Salem reported that fourteen cases had occurred there within a few weeks. From Cape Cod came similar reports. In June Dr. Walter Channing, who taught obstetrics at Harvard, brought before the Society for Medical Improvement a study of thirteen fatal cases of the fever that he had seen in the Boston area. Two other doctors spoke up. One had encountered several cases of puerperal fever in Pembroke. Another had seen four cases in New York.

All that summer the subject kept cropping up at the society's meetings, and one doctor told of an "epidemic" in the little town of Bath, New Hampshire, where there had been eighteen deaths.

In October the doctors had a real shock, a report on the illness of a Dr. Whitney of Newton, that seemed to be directly related to puerperal fever.

Dr. Whitney and two medical students who lived with him had undertaken a postmortem examination of a woman who had died of puerperal fever. Dr. Whitney had a hangnail on one finger, but it did not seem serious enough to merit attention, so he went ahead with the examination. One of the medical students had recently burned himself and the scar on his hand was still raw, but not bothersome enough to prevent his participation.

The medical men cut up the corpse on Friday. Dr. Whitney pointed out all the evidences of "mortification" to his students. Then the medical student with the burn sewed up the incision.

On Saturday Dr. Whitney had to go to Boston on business. When he went home on the train, he felt chilly. He believed he must have caught cold in the city. That night he began to run a fever. The temperature subsided in the morning. He felt well enough to see a few patients and then he went to church. But that night he felt much worse. He dosed himself with physic.

Next morning Dr. Whitney was very weak, but he decided he must make his medical rounds. Going down to the bathroom to shave and dress, he felt his sore hand begin to tingle. When he reached the washroom and pulled up his shirt-sleeve, he noticed a red spot about the size of a pea, about halfway up his arm. A fine red line extended from the spot down to the hangnail. He supposed it would go away, but by that night many red lines had appeared on his arm and the arm had begun to swell. On Tuesday he had a high fever and vomited. His arm was twice its normal size.

That day Dr. Whitney stayed home. Next day he directed his students to blister the arm to bring down the swelling. It did not seem to help. That is when they sent for Dr. Fisher.

Dr. Fisher tried leeches and emetics. Nothing seemed to reduce the swelling or the fever.

On Friday Dr. Whitney's arm was as large as his thigh. By Sunday he was in bed, delirious. Dr. Fisher gave him wine and tonics. Slowly, Dr. Whitney began to improve.

The medical student who had sewn up the body had begun to feel sick on Wednesday and had gone home. Dr. Fisher went to see him too. The student's burned arm was sore, and he seemed to have a fever, but a lesser one than Dr. Whitney's.

Dr. Fisher left the student, satisfied that he would recover. But the student's condition deteriorated rapidly. On Friday he complained of soreness all over. On Saturday he turned purple and his belly swelled up. On Sunday he died.

The second student, who had no sores on his hands when they performed the autopsy, began to feel sick on Friday, and he went home to his family. He had a few days of illness, but he recovered.

This detailed report of cause and effect impressed all the members of the society with the relationship of open sores and infection. Throughout the fall months of 1842 they considered the prevalence and ramifications of puerperal fever, but they came to no conclusions.

January brought a new shock. Dr. John Jackson (a cousin of Amelia Holmes) told the members of the death of another doctor, in Lynn, after he had examined a case of puerperal fever. This doctor had several open sores on his hands at the time of examination.

At the next meeting of the society Dr. Jackson reported on the postmortem performed on the Lynn doctor. As expected, it showed he died of a massive infection. Then Dr. Jackson raised a point. What if the doctor from Lynn had not had any sores on his hands? Would he not anyhow have carried that infectious material around with him, and if he touched another patient's wounds, or sores, or the lacerated womb of a new mother, would he not perhaps infect that other patient?

That question started a lively discussion. That night Holmes went home thinking about it.

For the next three weeks Holmes devoted his spare moments to research on this subject. He perused his own extensive medical library. He borrowed every available book he could find that touched on the subject. He consulted his own records, and he begged case histories from acquaintances who had obstetrical practices.

And when Dr. Holmes was finished with his investigations, he was appalled at what they indicated: puerperal fever was obviously dangerously contagious, but the worst part of all was that the agents of death were none other than those whose task it was to succor the sick and deliver babies. Doctors, nurses, midwives, and ward attendants were the culprits. Having touched a contagious patient, they went on to help the uncontaminated—and brought them death.

"With passionate indignation," Holmes sat down to write the charge against his own profession.

On February 13, 1843, Holmes read his newly written paper before the meeting of the society. He began with reports of eighteenth-century England. Two gentlemen in one Midlands town divided the whole obstetrical care of the town between them. One of them constantly lost his patients to puerperal fever. The other never did. Why? One doctor always washed and changed clothes after a delivery. The other did not.

Holmes cited the findings of Dr. Gordon of Aberdeen, who in 1795 had become convinced that doctors and nurses who had touched women afflicted with the disease were the carriers. Dr. Gordon said that when he heard which women were to be delivered by which midwives, he could predict which women would be infected and which would not.

One doctor in Edinburgh had assisted at a postmortem examination of a puerperal fever victim and then carried the pelvic viscera in his pocket to his classroom to illustrate the case for his students. That night the doctor attended another woman in labor, without changing clothes. She died. The next morning he delivered a woman with forceps. She died. In the next few days he infected a dozen others and three more died.

Case upon case, Holmes piled up bits that had not been drawn together before; stories from both sides of the Atlantic; reports from every part of America, and especially from Boston. He pushed up a mountain of evidence.

Holmes ended the paper with his conclusions. No doctor preparing to deliver a child should ever take part in a postmortem on a puerperal fever case. If he did he was to wash thoroughly, change all his clothes, and wait twenty-four hours to attend another patient.

If a doctor discovered a single case of puerperal fever among his patients, he was to assume that he was the infectious agent and be wise enough to give up his obstetric practice for at least a month.

And all these precautions had to be extended to cover midwives and nurses who attended such cases.

Puerperal fever was a private pestilence of the medical profession, Holmes said. It had to be looked upon as a "crime" for a doctor to infect patients after the warning.

These were strong words. At the end of them, Holmes looked around. He had nothing but approbation from the members of the society. They clamored for him to have the paper published, and he did, in the *New England Quarterly Journal of Medicine and Surgery* in April 1843.

Here, Holmes had contributed something that he was uniquely

prepared to offer. He was a physician and an instructor in medical sciences; he was a writer of uncommon ability of organization and force of phrase, and a thorough student of his subject. In the paper on puerperal fever Holmes rose to a new height in his profession and in the world of science. He proved to all who considered his thesis that he was one of the world's great teachers.

10

HOLMES REFUSES
TO CONFORM

HOLMES'S CONTEMPORARIES, AND HIS BIOGRAPHERS AS WELL, ALWAYS had difficulty in categorizing him. The restless little doctor would not sit still long enough to warm the seat. He had foresworn poetry, picked it up again, announced his retirement, and emerged once more. Later, he would extend his literary efforts when his best friends told him to curtail them.

His world, and that which came after him, did not like people who could not be pigeonholed, and so Holmes has been regarded as shallow. But in his own day he lived comfortably in several worlds. The learned doctor was also poet laureate of Boston. In 1838 he was elected to the American Academy of Arts and Letters, then located in Boston. When Charles Dickens came from England to visit, Holmes was called by others of the social and intellectual elite to honor the visiting novelist. When Dickens arrived on a steamer, literary Boston went to the Tremont House to meet the famous young author.

Dickens came bounding up the stairs.

"Here we are," he cried, and hurried forward to his American greeters. They interrupted the talk for Dickens' supper—the ship had arrived late in the evening. It was midnight when Dickens finished, and then they went on a nocturnal tour of Boston.

But "the" event of the visit was the dinner of welcome given in Dickens' honor on February 1 by "the young men of Boston." They had enlisted Holmes to write and recite a poem suitable for the occasion at Papanti's hall, the biggest and most impressive hall that could be obtained. In other times Papanti's was a dance salon, where many of the young men had learned the fair art of ballroom dancing. But this night, it was a dining hall, filled with long tables covered in white damask, set with gleaming silver service and shining glasses.

Dickens sat at the head table with Washington Allston and President Quincy of Harvard, Dr. Holmes, and other important men. Publisher Fields was across from the honored guest. After Quincy and all the other orators had spoken, and Dickens had responded, Holmes got up to close the session with his poem:

> The stars their early vigils keep,
> The silent hours are near . . . ,

Four verses later, he sat down to applause. The poem was what was wanted for the "occasion," heavy with allusion to Britain's recent literary past, suitably admiring of Dickens, and a fervid proclamation of good fellowship to this writer from across the sea.

Just the proper touch, said everyone. The Dickens dinner put another feather in Dr. Holmes's literary cap.

Later in the year Elisha Bartlett gave Dickens a copy of Holmes's volume of poetry as Dickens was leaving on the ship back to England. Dickens straightaway read "The Last Leaf," as Bartlett advised. He was so moved he wrote next day to his friend, "There is something inescapably quaint and thoughtful in it."

Holmes was pleased. Not everyone got compliments from England's leading novelist. It was the same poem Edgar Allan Poe had liked so well. Such praise was enough to make a writer take himself seriously.

Holmes had written a few other "occasional poems" in the intervening years, although he had threatened several times that he would not. But Holmes was too genial. Occasional poetry was so undemanding, and it came too easily for him to refuse for long.

The heady growth of his literary fame continued. That year Rufus Griswold compiled an anthology, *The Poets and Poetry of America,* and included fifteen of Holmes's poems. This publication placed Holmes among the "leading literary figures of the nation." With such praise, with constant attention and invitation, it would have taken an iron will and a firm purpose to have eschewed literature.

Had the paper on puerperal fever reached as many doctors as Holmes had hoped it would and created the stir it would later, Holmes might have been given that sense of purpose, forsaken literature, and devoted himself entirely to scientific pursuits. But the *New England Quarterly Journal of Medicine and Surgery* lasted but a few months, and then suspended publication.

Some publicity was given the Holmes argument in the *American Journal of the Medical Sciences.* In July 1843 that magazine summarized the Holmes paper, but only in a two-page abstract that stated the conclusions and lost almost all of the arguments on which they were based.

What little discussion that abstract stimulated in America bogged down in heated argument. The progressives led by Holmes insisted that the profession must clean its own house of pestilence. The conservatives—old-line doctors—took a protective view: the doctor could do no wrong.

Holmes might have pursued the argument, perhaps hastening by a decade the control of puerperal fever in America, and established his incontrovertible leadership in scientific medicine. Why didn't he? He certainly had the faculty of indignation: one of his young, unmarried patients nearly died after she aborted. She had been taking the pills dispensed by a local "female specialist," Mme. Restelle. Holmes put Mme. Restelle out of the abortion business.

But Holmes did not seek extended scientific battles, and so his work on puerperal fever continued to be largely ignored in the profession, even in Boston. Dr. Walter Channing, who was certainly no enemy of Holmes, had not attended the meeting of the Society for the Advancement of Medical Knowledge the year before when Holmes had read his paper. Apparently Dr. Channing had never seen the printed version. At the society's February meeting he presented a paper denying the contagiousness of puerperal fever. New American medical textbooks said doctors were too pure to be contagious. And a large number of doctors, even in New England, agreed. Holmes did not rise to defend his thesis as he might have done. He did not abandon all other interests and fight the puerperal fever battle. If he had, his scientific reputation would have soared, perhaps, but that would have been out of character. Holmes was a Bostonian before he was anything else; a humanist, not a causist.

He was by this time one of Boston's most successful doctors. He was acting secretary of the Boylston Prize committee and he was a member of the medical staff of the Massachusetts General Hospital. He had all the private practice he wanted, among the best families. If in the 1830s he had set out to secure his position in the 1840s, he had done so.

On a morning he would be at Massachusetts General observing a mastectomy. In the afternoon he would visit the household of his brother-in-law to treat Lucy Morse, and while there look in on the sick cook. That evening he would see patients in his consulting room.

He was often called in on difficult obstetric cases, and he performed many deliveries. He was extremely careful in his own hygiene and insisted on similar precautions by all who worked with him.

Dr. Holmes was quick to respond to calls for help, but slow to medicate. A patient who came to him short of breath and red of face, expecting to be bled, would instead be advised to lay off meat and start walking or taking horseback rides (which is part of the therapy today).

Some went away indignantly to doctors who would give them the standard treatments that had killed their fathers.

As his undeniable truths about puerperal fever continued to be denied, so also his assaults on homeopathy never stamped it out in America. The doctor would have been shocked, and even the poet not amused, to have visited Harvard Square in the autumn of 1977, and seen there in the window of the Harvard Trust Co., a poster advertising homeopathy.

But in Boston the most progressive doctors sought Holmes's advice on many matters. Henry Jacob Bigelow, his former student and young friend, witnessed the first operations conducted under the effects of ether. Bigelow prepared a paper on the subject for publication, and came rushing to Holmes for approval. Holmes not only approved, he wrote a note to Dr. W. T. G. Morton, the dentist who invented the system, and gave him the name for it: *anesthesia.* It stuck.

Holmes was too much interested in everything around him to ever become a good causist. He kept a succession of notebooks, filled with his jottings. He noted down the name and address of the mason who had repaired his walk, next to the reminder that William Mitchell of Nantucket had promised him ten dollars and expenses for a Lyceum lecture if he would take the ferry to the island. Next to that was the girth of an elm he had measured and a note of a lecture to be delivered in Fall River. And next to that he noted the day that Dr. Whitney of Newton (who had survived the puerperal fever) had borrowed his lecture on alchemy—and the day it was returned. His notes were filled with parenthetical expressions and enumerations and fingers pointing at the parts most important to him, in the manner of circus posters. He penned tiny reminders along the margins: "Don't forget to write Mr. Strong. Write an essay as to popular mistakes as to the efficacy of medicines. There was intermittent fever in Castleton, Vermont, in April." His personal journals give no sense of priorities.

Any number of events and pressures combined to keep Dr. Holmes from deserting poetry, although he had the feeling that literature interfered with the orderly conduct of his profession. Sometimes he said as much. His doctor friends agreed with him. His poet friends did not. When he was immersed in the medical world, he said, he found it hard to switch over to the jocular frame of mind in which he composed most of his poetry. But he was able to do this often enough to continue to produce poems and songs.

In this period Holmes very nearly got into an argument with the transcendentalists of Concord. He had heard of the transcendental philosophy of the Germans, and privately had as much use for it as he did for homeopathy. He poked fun at the transcendentalists in his Phi Beta Kappa poem, "Terpsichore." But when a small noise of indignation emanated from Concord, Holmes backed off.

By 1845 Holmes's attitudes were fairly set, and many of them were revealed in the long poem "Urania," which he delivered before the Boston Mercantile Library Association that October. He opened with a description of himself: a doctor with a continued loyalty to the muse. The poem ranged in subjects from religious duty to human frailty. Holmes also laid the groundwork for a controversy that would cause him serious trouble. For the first time he spoke his mind on the subjects of slavery and Abolition.

Through the years, as Holmes had been struggling to secure his place as a doctor, a few of his friends, some of his relatives, and many of his acquaintances had been converted to the cause of Abolition. The word made Holmes shudder, for he saw in the movement no less than the disunion of the nation. It did not occur to him (as it did not to many another Bostonian) that adherence to the Union could be forced. Massachusetts had nearly attempted secession herself a time or two, notably at the Hartford Convention. Massachusetts men—the traditionalists among them—looked upon the Union as it had been constituted, a free association of sovereign states. Holmes was very much the traditionalist:

> If the wild filly "Progress" thou wouldst ride,
> Have young companions ever at thy side;
> But wouldst thou stride, the stanch old mare, "Success,"
> Go with thine elders, though they please thee less. . . .

Holmes had chosen the second road for himself. In London he would have been a Tory.

More important, "Urania" threatened to embroil Holmes in the fiery pit of the abolitionist struggle. The abolitionists had claimed a growing number of the intellectuals of Holmes's crowd and his peers in literature. Emerson was in the group with Longfellow and Channing, Garrison and Sumner, and James Russell Lowell.

In 1846, with the Mexican war in progress, the abolitionists were more vigorous than ever. Lowell wrote fiery articles for the *National*

Anti-Slavery Standard. An evangelist at heart, Lowell was an ardent believer who could not bear to see friends and acquaintances on the wrong side of the issue.

One of the meeting places of the literary people of Boston was the Mercantile Library Association. Lowell had been a regular there for several years, as had Holmes. It was at their meeting in 1845 that Holmes had delivered "Urania," and Lowell was there to catch every innuendo of that poem. When it was published, he took Holmes to task for his insensitivity and social failure to become imbued with feelings for the "right causes."

He did not like Holmes's apparent espousal of the glories of war; he did not like Holmes's attitude on slavery. Perhaps he did know that a quarter of a century earlier, poking about in his father's library, the young Holmes had come upon an account of an attempted slave uprising in the eighteenth century, that instilled in Holmes a fear of and contempt for blacks.

The letter prompted a reply, although perhaps it need not have. Holmes was Lowell's senior by ten years. Lowell's manners could be faulted for the attack. But Dr. Holmes was a gentleman, the Lowells were a Cambridge family, and he felt the younger writer deserved a reply.

Lowell had accused Holmes of warmongering. The abolitionists were opposed to the Mexican war. It was clear that the aim of the Texans was annexation to the United States, and the abolitionists did not want any more slave states in the Union.

Holmes tried to smooth Lowell's ruffled feathers without abandoning his views. He said he tended to agree with Lowell and with Charles Sumner, whose Fourth of July speech that year had been a diatribe against the Mexican war.

"But," said Holmes, "I cannot shut my eyes to the beauty of heroism and self-devotion which the battlefield has witnessed." After all, American revolutionaries had been justified in taking up arms in 1775.

In Lowell's mind the more important matter in his letter of rebuke had been Holmes's attitude toward slavery. Here Holmes gave his young acquaintance no satisfaction at all. He would not, he said, poke fun at the abolitionist cause now as he had done earlier, because it had grown too large. Too many of his friends believed in Abolition. He refrained from saying that he did not, and that he abhorred abolitionism as a radical nuisance that threatened to tear the United States apart.

Lowell had gone the whole way with the zealots of the period: against war, for the abolition of slavery, and against the demon rum. Holmes detested excess, and the abolitionists were nothing if not excessive in their zeal to free the black, sober the drunk, and uplift the poor. (Lowell had even accused Holmes of not caring about the poor.)

Considering what must have been the temper of Lowell's letter, now lost, the modesty and self-restraint of Holmes were remarkable. After he replied, Holmes, with his usual good humor, forgot the matter and let events take their course. Lowell realized then that he could not convert the doctor, and acted accordingly. No further rift developed between the two, and eventually they became good friends.

Meanwhile, Holmes continued to indulge in his literary "hobby." Even the doctors wanted poetry from him now; it was a mark of his standing that no one in the middle 1840s accused Holmes of being less the physician because he was capable of the humorous rhyme, the sentimental ballad, or the ringing patriotic ode. His very versatility, while not attesting to superior poetic skill, put him in constant demand.

He could travel to Pittsfield to recite "Lines," designed to help commemorate the Berkshire Jubilee, as he did in August 1844. It was an airy call to all the sons of the Berkshires to return and remember their birthplace. It was addressed to merchants, lawyers, clerks, city drudges, and even

> Ye healers of men, for a moment decline
> Your festas in the rhubarb and ipecac line;

One of the delightful aspects of Holmes's recitations was this ability to poke fun:

> Poor drudge of the city! How happy he feels,
> With the burrs on his legs and the grass at his heels.

Although Holmes was not Berkshire-born, and had no connection with the area at the time, the organizers of the jubilee had turned to him because his mother was one of the Wendells, who had originally held seventy-three thousand acres of Berkshire land and still owned a large chunk of it, and because Holmes's dinner-table and auditorium fame had so thoroughly permeated New England.

Holmes could also put his fellow practitioners to laughing until their sides hurt, as he did with *"Nux Postcoenatica"*:

> I was sitting with my microscope upon my parlor rug
> With a very heavy quarto and a very lively bug . . .

And he continued:

> I lost my focus—dropped book—the bug, who was a flea,
> At once exploded and commenced experiments on me.

This sort of verse was an antidote, or at least a palliative for oratorical excess. By the time the usual formal dinner neared the end, the diners might have been somnolent, or thoroughly out of sorts. Holmes's funning saved many a long, dreary dinner. In that respect, Holmes was certainly a delight to his peers. That is why he was, in addition, the most popular after-dinner "speaker" in Boston, this man who would not let himself be pegged.

CHAPTER

11

FAIR HARVARD SMILES
ON DR. HOLMES

WHEN HOLMES HAD SETTLED IN BOSTON HE ALREADY KNEW THAT HE wanted to be a teacher. In the 1830s the best medical school in the northern states was at Harvard. Philadelphia and New York might jealously dispute the claim, but it stood in the eyes of the majority of practitioners and teachers. For all sorts of reasons, what Holmes really wanted was to teach medicine at Harvard. But, even when Holmes's bona fides were firmly established, it seemed unlikely that he would ever achieve his ambition.

His old teacher, Dr. Jackson, was the senior professor on the Harvard medical faculty. He was only sixty-three and enjoyed good health. There was no pressure to retire on so exalted a figure as a Harvard professor, so if Jackson wished, God willing, he would continue to teach theory and practice of medicine for another ten years.

Dr. J. C. Warren, the father of Mason Warren, was professor of anatomy and surgery. He was sixty-two. Walter Channing, the obstetrician who had introduced the contradictory paper on puerperal fever to the Society for the Advancement of Medical Knowledge, was fifty-four and in mid-stride of his career. Jacob Bigelow, father of Holmes's young friend and the professor of materia medica, was fifty-three. George Hayward, the professor of surgery, was forty-nine, and John W. Webster, the professor of chemistry, was forty-seven.

None of them seemed in danger of giving out.

But in 1846, Edward Everett was chosen to become president of Harvard, and at the same time, Dr. Warren introduced ether into the operating room. Warren was so interested in the development of anesthesia (Holmes's title caught on) that he resigned his professorship. President Everett and the Board of Overseers decided to make some changes.

Holmes had recently returned from a convention of doctors who founded the American Medical Association (AMA). The new association advocated the enlargement of the American medical school curricula to seven subjects. Harvard accepted this idea. A new professorship of pathology was established. So was a new professorship of anatomy and physiology.

The latter was named for Dr. George Parkman, a wealthy physician who had just recently given Harvard land on which a new medical school building was being erected. And when it came time to fill the post, Holmes was considered for the position. His qualifications were good. He was active in the Massachusetts Medical Society and that of Boston, as well. He had been a founder of the AMA and head of a committee that surveyed medical literature. He was a respected diagnostician. He taught clinical medicine at the Tremont school. Further, he was a Harvard College graduate and had his M.D. from Harvard. President Everett was impressed. What more could one ask? Harvard appointed Dr. Oliver Wendell Holmes professor of anatomy and physiology.

Holmes could not have been more pleased. He had been busy in the past year—too busy. He was growing away from his wife and three children because he almost never saw them. The Lyceum lectures took more of his time than ever. So did meetings of the medical societies, the committee for the Advancement of Medical Knowledge, his chair at Tremont Medical School, his staff physician's job at Massachusetts General Hospital, his consulting work, and his private practice. He had managed in 1846 only a single week's vacation. This state of affairs could not continue.

Assumption of the Harvard post would mean Holmes would have to give up some of those activities, but he could afford to do so.

At least Holmes thought life would be easier. But when the new, young teacher came, Dr. Channing saw an opportunity to divest himself of a deanship he found irksome. Holmes was also appointed dean.

For that reason, and certainly because he was a most popular speaker, Holmes was asked to give the address at the opening of the Harvard Medical School when it occupied its new Grove Street building. Those present included President Everett and the Board of Overseers, and a number of important members of the intellectual community, such as the liberal preacher Theodore Parker.

If any in the crowd expected Holmes to amuse them, they had come to him at the wrong time in the wrong place. His lecture was inspirational. He had been much excited by the formation of the American Medical Association, and he told his listeners that here was evidence of the growth and maturity of the American medical profession. The purpose of the AMA, he said, was to monitor that profession, and it was a good purpose. What American medicine needed was leadership in medical education. Holmes dedicated himself and Harvard to the course he would pursue for the next thirty-five years.

The lecture was reported fully by the *Boston Medical and Surgical Journal*, whose editor called it "the best discourse ever given." That praise might be expected from Holmes's medical peers, but the daily newspapers said much the same, which was unusual comment on a relatively abstruse subject. The local praise was an indication of the stature Holmes had achieved in Boston in his thirty-eighth year.

At the medical school, Holmes was almost immediately plunged into controversy. Harriot Kezia Hunt, a young woman with an inquisitive turn of mind and more than adequate academic qualifications, wanted to attend Holmes's lectures. She wrote to Dean Holmes in December. But when it came to allowing a woman to attend anatomical lectures, which would certainly include "unmentionable" parts of the male and female bodies, in light of Victorian mores, it was obviously impossible.

Holmes's French education, however, was not Victorian. Some of the best anatomical lectures he had heard in Paris had been delivered by a woman. Why not let Miss Hunt attend? Holmes sent the request to President Everett, with his unqualified endorsement.

Everett was a college president whose antennae quivered in the presence of broad social changes. This, he said, was the sort of delicate decision that must be left to the overseers.

The overseers had no doubts about the proper course of action. Allow a young woman into a lecture room when the professor was discussing the penis and even the vagina? To what depths was Harvard sinking? The overseers were certainly not going to be the first to tarnish the name of womanhood. The answer was no.

Holmes had expected it. He had tried. That was all he felt impelled to do. As dean he was on record as favoring the angels.

He forgot the "issue" and turned to his teaching. As a teacher Holmes's enthusiasm was enormous. At Dartmouth, he had observed that the upper half of his class had little trouble. Those young men could probably have learned anatomy from anyone. But the lower half of the class was in constant difficulty, largely because of the abysmal differences in educational systems in various states and communities. Some of Holmes's students came with virtually no basic educational skills. Fewer than a quarter of them were college graduates.

At Tremont he had that experience, and at Harvard it was not much different: even the Harvard College graduates in the bottom half of the class had a difficult time grasping basic concepts.

Holmes concentrated on the lower half of the class. To do that he had to find ways to capture and hold the attention of the young men. He found the way was to "turn abstractions and catalogues of names into substantial and objective realities." Since he had no photographs or plastic models, he began to prepare exhibits. He sent to Paris for materials he had studied; he made up exhibits himself; he commissioned charts and wooden models. He raided the college anatomical museum established by his predecessor, Dr. Warren. He borrowed books and prints from his friends, and had copies made of anatomical drawings by Albrecht Dürer, Hans Holbein, Leonardo, and other masters who drew the human body. Harvard Medical School had no more money for such projects than Tremont or Dartmouth. Holmes ended up paying almost all of this expense from his own earnings.

Holmes was a showman. He used every device he knew to hold the attention of students and to teach them about the human body, from poetry to elaborate mechanical contrivances that made the opened lungs of a corpse appear to breathe.

Holmes would introduce his subject, and his demonstrator would unfold the tissues and reveal the organs as the professor spoke. Story, pun, poem, scatological joke—all of them had their uses. His techniques were successful. Young men seldom went to sleep in Professor Holmes's class. If they had, he probably would have exploded firecrackers.

That year all these lectures were given between November 1847 and the end of February 1848. Then Holmes began his clinical teaching at Tremont, which lasted from March through June and then September through October. That gave Holmes the greater part of the summer to himself. But for the children's sake, and for his own vacation from the cares of a busy medical life, Holmes needed to get away from Boston if he were to enjoy a vacation instead of a constant series of "emergencies." He learned that much in the summer of 1848. As long as he was available there was work to be done. In August he was supposed to be on vacation; instead he was negotiating with the Boston authorities for the use of bodies from the pauper cemetery on Deer Island.

Amelia had a two-thousand-dollar inheritance that year and Holmes had property in Pittsfield, inherited from the Wendells. The Holmeses decided that they would build a house on a three-hundred-acre plot there. They called the place Canoe Meadow. They built a house they called Holmesdale.

When winter came, he announced that he was giving up his entire private practice. It was time to have some fun.

12

DR. HOLMES
AND THE CRIME
OF THE CENTURY

AT CANOE MEADOW, HOLMES'S FAVORITE OCCUPATION WAS MEASURING trees. He would walk a mile to examine a big elm. He carried a tape measure and he reached up and wrapped it around the trunk at a height of five feet, took out his notebook and pencil, and noted down the location, the date, and the girth of that particular tree.

Some of Holmes's friends would josh him about this unusual hobby. He was never dismayed.

"I have a most intense, passionate fondness for trees in general, and have had several romantic attachments to certain trees in particular."

That was his answer. What more could be said to a man who planted a whole avenue of trees on the approach to his house, obviously for the purpose of letting them grow up so he could measure them?

For the first time in his adult life, Holmes had a chance to be lazy that summer of 1849. But he arose early. Sometimes he went for a long walk after breakfast, tape in his pocket. Sometimes he chopped wood for exercise, the kitchen stove, and the fireplaces, in that order. He took young Wendell fishing for pickerel. They went frogging. After he bought a horse and trap, he went driving. He was a prodigious admirer of fast horses, and often sneaked off to the trotting races.

He carried on a vigorous correspondence. James Russell Lowell had forgiven Holmes his sins of omission after his long letter of 1846. By tacit agreement, their letters dealt with life and literature—not politics. It was the same with others. He was asked to write poetry, comment on medical affairs, make dinner appearances.

He wrote a few verses, almost all of them to fit some occasion that had to be celebrated properly with a dinner, an oration, and end with a poem. He missed the reunion of the class of '29 in Cambridge that year. He was too busy enjoying himself in the country.

Most of what he wrote that summer he regarded as so inconsequential he never let it be published in other than the local Pittsfield newspaper, including such writings as a poem delivered to the Young Ladies' Institute. Early in October Holmes was asked to write and deliver an ode celebrating the anniversary of the Berkshire Agricultural Society. It was scarcely an occasion on which a poet could expect to move mountains. But one reason Holmes was so popular a public figure was that his listeners knew the poem would fit the occasion to a T. Always he threw himself into the task with enthusiasm, and the versification invariably delighted the listening audience, although often the words did not read nearly so well as they sounded.

On this occasion Holmes was as ebullient as always. He went to the meeting and, at the proper time, arose in his dark suit and wide bow tie:

> Clear the brown path, to meet his coulter's gleam;
> Lo, on he comes behind his smoking team
> With toil's bright dewdrops on his sunburnt brow,
> The lord of earth, the hero of the plough!

The meeting was adjudged a grand success by the local newspaper, and Holmes was, as always, the lion of the day.

Too soon it was time to close the house in the Berkshires and for Holmes to address himself to serious professional matters at Harvard.

One of them that began bothering Holmes that year concerned pressure within the American Medical Association to lengthen the lecture terms of the medical schools. Four months' study each year, said some, was not enough to give an aspiring doctor good grounding. That year the AMA's committee on medical education recommended that the AMA seek such a change. Holmes had been a delegate to the convention and he and Dr. Jacob Bigelow and Dr. John Ware, all of Harvard, had dissented vigorously. They preferred the system under which students heard lectures at Harvard four months of the year and then studied clinical medicine (if they could afford it) at such schools as Tremont. To lengthen the medical school lecture period would be to jeopardize Tremont's existence and leave the students without an opportunity to secure actual clinical experience.

Holmes plunged into his four-day-a-week teaching with his usual energy. He had contrived an office under the stairs of the amphitheater in the building on North Grove Street, and had cluttered it with papers, microscope slides, bone displays, and models of various organs, until the place was a cross between an apothecary's establishment and a curiosity shop.

He usually went down to North Grove Street around noon, and rummaged in the office for a while. He then stepped across to the dissecting room for a look at the day's corpse. Satisfied that all was well, he waited for the lecture hour, sometimes smoking nervously, for he never got over the tension that came before he was to appear in public.

His lectures to the public were meant to amuse and amaze. His lectures to his medical students were aimed, with a shrewd and yet compassionate warmth, at the common denominator of the class.

In the beginning of Holmes's tenure at Harvard, there had been some difficulty in obtaining cadavers, unlike the old days in Paris, where he and fellow medical students traveled down to the Rue Morgue and bought their bodies off the slab at fifty centimes a

corpse. But Holmes had ended the shortage two years earlier by securing permission to take the dead bodies from Deer Island. So he
had plenty of what in moments of levity he might refer to as "meat."

His opening lecture always set the tone for the entire year, a
combination of shrewd observation, indisputable fact, and racy
humor. He was given to anatomical and sometimes scatological puns,
and rhymes that were relished and remembered by his students. In
the beginning of his professorship, as junior man among the seven
of the medical faculty, Dr. Holmes on anatomy had been assigned
the least-desirable lecture period. The subject was regarded as the
dullest in the curriculum. By the time they reached the class the
aspiring young medical students had gone from one lecture to another all morning, from the hammering of Dr. Jacob Bigelow on
materia medica at nine o'clock, to chemistry at ten, theory and
practice at eleven, and obstetrics at twelve. They got to anatomy at
one o'clock in the afternoon, without a break since breakfast, their
brains ringing, barely able to mask the yawns.

Then came Professor Holmes. Holmes had an assistant; he had
to have one in order to both teach and carry out his administrative
duties as dean, and in fact he preferred it that way because he had
never much liked poking about in dead bodies. So in the morning,
knowing the subject of his lecture, his demonstrator spent four
hours dissecting, pulling loose the muscles, nerves, blood vessels,
and organs that were to be the subject of the day's discussion.

One day, the cadaver was that of a woman. The professor had announced he would use the body to acquaint his students with the
female reproductive anatomy.

Just before one o'clock, the lecture room began to fill with stamp-
ing, shouting young men, eager to have it done with and be off. The
professor came up the stairs from the street, and stopped by the
demonstrator's room, cutting his way through a cloud of smoke, for
his demonstrator puffed constantly to overcome the odors of carbolic
acid and death. He entered, small, smiling, and bouncy on his feet.

"What have you for me today?" He picked up a knife, muttering,
". . . plunging into the depth of the subject . . ." and laughed at
his own joke.

The cadaver was moved from the table to a board, covered by a sheet, and carried by the assistants onto a revolving table in the amphitheater. The professor would have it that way. "Show respect for poor humanity and admiration for God's divinest work," he told them.

The cadaver in, the professor followed, and as he came, smiling, the students began anew to stamp on the floor, threatening, as he often observed, the very underpinnings of Harvard medicine.

He acknowledged the applause, and then stopped and looked around until he had silence.

"My subject this afternoon is one with which I trust you young gentlemen are not familiar . . ."

And then he hurled back the sheet and began to lecture on the female genitalia. Every organ, every muscle, reminded him of a pun or a story. The fimbriated end of the Fallopian tube "is like the fringe of a poor woman's shawl."

No student in the room would forget the Fallopian tubes.

For an hour he held them enthralled, painting pictures of nature and humanity, outlining for them the glories of man—and woman— with many a wry aside.

And that is how it went all during the year. The one o'clock lecture was no longer the extension of torture that it had always been before. It was the highlight of the students' day. For as long as he remained at Harvard, Holmes lectured at one o'clock.

He adapted a microscope for use in his classes. The young men were invited to examine specimens, and while they were filing around and taking turns, Holmes would pass around some bones out of one of the ten skeletons he kept for instructional purposes.

The little professor stood tall, and handed the bones up to one of the students.

"Smith. Here, take the bone. What is the reason that the thigh socket is so much deeper than the arm socket?"

Smith looked at him and reddened. He said nothing.

"Because upon the leg rests the entire weight of the body, and it does not need much range of movement . . ."

Here Holmes kicked out a leg and did a sort of belly dance, and the students cheered.

He ignored the noise.

"But the arm requires to be moved in every direction, as for example, in knocking a man down . . ."

The little doctor delivered a ferocious uppercut at the air.

"Or in the oratorical gesture . . ."

He held up both hands and pointed a finger warningly.

They cheered him again through their laughter.

"Pass that bone along. . . ."

It was always that way. One day when he was explaining the function of the bile ducts to the class, he paused.

"I prefer mine broiled," came a loud whisper from the top of the room.

Holmes's eyes traveled upward at the laughter and he speared the offender with a glance.

"Young man, aren't you usurping my prerogative?"

The offender slumped in his seat, and others smirked.

"Now as I was saying, before I was interrupted . . ."

The routine of Holmes's teaching was disturbed that fall by a quarrel between Dr. George Parkman, that benefactor of the medical school for whom Holmes's chair was named, and Dr. John White Webster, the professor of chemistry. Holmes did not know it, almost no one did, but Webster had been borrowing money from Parkman for eight years.

The two were friends from college days, Parkman having graduated from Harvard College in the year of Holmes's birth, and Webster two years later.

Dr. Webster was stout, good-looking with curly hair, small steel glasses, and a ready smile. Parkman was tall and thin, "a long drink of water." Where Webster was bubbly, Parkman was deep and still.

Webster was the son of a wealthy apothecary and he was always openhanded. Parkman was close with his money. They could not have been more dissimilar in character or appearance.

In 1826 Webster was appointed professor of chemistry. His salary was only twelve hundred dollars a year, but that was augmented by the sale of tickets to his lectures. Webster did not worry about the low pay, he had plenty of money.

When his father died in 1833, Webster inherited fifty thousand dollars, which, if invested at 6 percent, would keep his family com-

fortable for life. Showing a remarkable lack of New England fru-
gality, Webster built a big house in Cambridge and entertained there
on a lavish scale. Dr. Parkman was a frequent guest.

Ten years later the fortune was gone, on the backs of Webster's
family and down the gullets of his friends. There was still the big
house to be kept up, but now only about two thousand dollars a
year with which to maintain it.

Webster began to borrow. He borrowed from everyone, but particularly from Dr. Parkman, his old friend, who had more or less
given up medicine when he learned his real calling was in making
money. He had quietly amassed a fortune by dealing in real estate.
In 1842 Dr. Webster borrowed four thousand dollars from Dr. Parkman, repaid some of it, and then borrowed more on the strength of
that payment. He repeated the loan procedure several times. By
1847 Webster's affairs were in such dreadful shape that Parkman took
a mortgage on his furniture, books, and his valuable mineral collection. Webster agreed to pay off slowly but surely.

That was the year that Holmes came to the Harvard Medical
School. He knew something about Webster's problems, but not
much, for it was not in his nature to pry into other people's business.

Matters soon grew worse. In the spring of 1848 Webster was
threatened by other creditors with foreclosure on his house. He applied then to Robert Gould Shaw, another friend, who was also
Dr. Parkman's brother-in-law.

Shaw was touched by Webster's account of his troubles, and found
twelve hundred dollars for him. Webster insisted on giving him a
bill of sale for his mineral collection, and Shaw showed it to Dr.
Parkman.

Dr. Parkman exploded. Webster had committed a breach of trust
in selling the collection that was already mortgaged to him. Whatever had been between them was shattered at that moment, and Parkman began to harry his old friend. He threatened: if Webster did not
pay up immediately, Parkman would expose his fraud to all Cambridge and Boston.

When Webster did not respond to letters, Parkman traveled up
to Cambridge and tried to catch Webster at home. He did not find
him. Back in Boston, he tried to persuade Mr. Pettee, who collected

the fees for lectures, to hold back Webster's fees to pay the debt. Pettee refused to become involved.

Dr. Parkman went to the medical school and found Webster in his laboratory. The school janitor, Ephraim Littlefield, recognized the storklike figure of Dr. Parkman in his long tailcoat and high silk hat. He heard the men raising their voices behind the closed door of Dr. Webster's laboratory.

Holmes heard about the trouble when Dr. Parkman invaded one of Webster's lectures insisting that Webster drop everything and come to terms with him right then. Parkman seemed somehow frenzied in his insistence that the money be repaid immediately.

But what was Holmes or anyone else to do? It was an extremely delicate matter: Dr. Parkman was a valued Harvard benefactor, responsible for the building of the school's physical plant. Dr. Webster was a respected member of the faculty.

So Holmes did what came naturally to him in times of trouble. He did nothing at all.

On the morning of Friday, November 23, Dr. Webster called on Dr. Parkman at his house on Beacon Hill.

Two boys who knew that strange figure saw Dr. Parkman walking toward the medical school at around one-thirty.

At quarter to two, janitor Littlefield saw Dr. Parkman approaching the school building, walking very fast, as he always did. Littlefield was on his way to his cottage next door for a little "lie-down" and he paid no more attention. Half an hour later, Littlefield came back and saw Dr. Holmes leaving the building after his one o'clock lecture. Littlefield cleaned up Holmes's exhibits and put them in the doctor's office, and then went to clear out Dr. Webster's laboratory. With the weekend coming, no one was likely to be about.

But Webster's door was locked, and Littlefield could hear the professor inside. He came back at quarter past four, and the door was still locked. At half past five he saw Dr. Webster going down the back stairs in the dark with a candle in his hand.

Littlefield made his final rounds at ten o'clock that night. Webster's rooms were still locked, although they never had been before. And the next day, Saturday, although there were no lectures, Dr.

Webster came to the school and spent several hours in the locked laboratory.

When Dr. Parkman did not return home Friday evening, his family worried. By the morning of the twenty-fourth, the Parkmans were sure some disaster had befallen the doctor. They knew he had had a one-thirty appointment with someone, but he had not told his family whom he was going to meet, or where.

That day Holmes became aware of the mystery. Robert Gould Shaw had hundreds of handbills distributed about Boston and Cambridge, offering a three-thousand-dollar reward for the discovery of Dr. Parkman.

The two boys told the police where they had seen Dr. Parkman, and the police searched the Charles waterfront. The medical school building was located on the river, on pilings, and the tidewaters washed in underneath—a neat way of disposing of the unwanted bits of tissue and viscera removed from Dr. Holmes's dissection rooms and also, of course, Dr. Webster's noxious chemical compounds. The police searched beneath the building and they made a rapid inspection of the school, along with Massachusetts General and other buildings. No Dr. Parkman.

Over the weekend Webster told a number of people that he had seen Dr. Parkman at one-thirty at the school, had paid him some money, and that Parkman had then gone rushing out, and he had not seen him again.

The police came to the school again on Monday and Tuesday, but Holmes said he had not seen any signs of Dr. Parkman, and the others said the same.

That being Thanksgiving week, there were no classes scheduled, and the other professors stayed home. Holmes came once or twice to attend to some administrative details. Webster came in every day, but he kept his rooms locked. Through the wall janitor Littlefield felt heat in the furnace in Dr. Webster's laboratory. That furnace had never been used before.

In the search of the college, one area had not been touched, and that was a private lavatory in Dr. Webster's laboratory. The lavatory was of the chemical sort, emptying into a vault that dripped dissolved materials into the tidal basin. Littlefield decided he would open the vault with a hammer and chisel. On Friday he secured the reluctant permission of two of the other professors, who insisted, however, that Littlefield not tell Dean Holmes what he was doing. Holmes, they knew, would never accede to such an invasion of another professor's privacy. That day Dr. Webster came to the college and told Littlefield that police were interested in a strange woman with a blood-stained bundle who had taken a cab on the afternoon that Dr. Parkman disappeared.

Friday evening, after many interruptions by Dr. Webster and others, Littlefield finally broke into the sewage holding tank and there found the pelvis of a man and two pieces of leg.

They could hardly have been parts of one of the corpses dissected in the college. One of Littlefield's tasks was to sew up the corpses and inject them with embalming fluid, so a single cadaver might be useful to the school for as long as six weeks. Then, according to the city of Boston's contract with Dr. Holmes, the cadaver had to be given a decent burial. Holmes would never have permitted one of his cadavers to be cut up and thrown down the lavatory chute.

So Dr. Webster was arrested and charged with the murder of Dr. Parkman. Immediately, he took a dose of strychnine he had concealed in his pocket, but the dose was not sufficient to kill him.

The authorities combed every inch of the school. They found bones and ashes in Webster's furnace, and a thigh, a thorax, and a hunting knife covered with tanning solution in a tea chest. They were bits of a body all right, but was it Dr. Parkman?

Dr. Holmes offered one clue. At the opening of the new medical school building, when he had made his celebrated speech, Holmes had noticed that Dr. Parkman had a shiny new set of false teeth. No one else seemed to know that Parkman wore false teeth. Among the oddities found in Dr. Webster's laboratory was a fused set of what had obviously been false teeth. Dr. Parkman's dentist was discovered, and he confirmed Holmes' observation, and identified the teeth as ones he had made for Dr. Parkman. But the identification could be no more than tenuous, for the heat of the furnace had nearly destroyed the dentures.

In the second week of December the medical school resumed

classes. There was no one to teach chemistry, so Holmes called a meeting of the faculty, and they voted to appoint a committee to consult Professor Webster about filling the vacancy "occasioned by his absence," as Holmes put it delicately. Holmes and Dr. Ware had the awkward task, and they called on Dr. Webster in his cell.

Holmes made it clear that he was speaking only of a temporary appointment. Webster suggested that Professor Horsford of the Lawrence Scientific School take his place. So Horsford came. If he did not anticipate remaining, then he was not betting with the majority of Boston. Cambridge doubted that a Harvard man could be guilty of so heinous a crime, but Boston was not so sure.

The reverberations were felt all across America, wherever Harvard's men had gone. Holmes's Dartmouth friend, Dr. Elisha Bartlett, wrote in anguish from Woonsocket.

"What is the meaning of this appalling and incredible horror?"

Holmes did not know. It was almost impossible for him to believe that his colleague, a *Harvard professor,* would commit so dastardly a crime, *and against a Harvard man!* But on January 26, 1850, a grand jury indicted Dr. Webster. The trial was set for March 17.

Harvard, particularly the medical school, was virtually paralyzed by the scandal. At any social gathering, one subject always held the floor, and Dr. Holmes grew thoroughly sick of it long before the trial.

Holmes hoped desperately for a miracle. Ned Sohier, one of his classmates, was one of the defense counsels for Dr. Webster, and one day Holmes sent him a letter from a Dr. Galloupe in Lynn, who said that a respectable woman he knew had seen Dr. Parkman after the time that he disappeared into the medical school building.

A few days later Holmes had another letter from Mississippi saying Dr. Parkman had been seen in Georgia. And there were many more. Holmes turned others over to Sohier, and then had fits of conscience—or legal advice—and hastened to write the attorney general of Massachusetts telling what he had done.

Weeks before the trial, reporters began to descend on Boston. In addition to representatives of the eleven Boston papers, there were correspondents from the New York *Globe,* the New York *Sun,* the New York *Christian Inquirer,* the Philadelphia *Sunday Globe,* the

Philadelphia *Saturday Gazette,* the Pennsylvania *Inquirer,* and many others. From the beginning the *National Police Gazette,* the most sensational weekly of the day, devoted enormous space to the case.

Nothing could have been more abhorrent to Dr. Holmes than this sort of publicity for the medical school. He fended off reporters, and refused insolent offers. But he could not stem the flood. No one could. Newspapers in France, England, Germany—all over the world—seized upon the Harvard murder case with glee. A young Harvard student, Horatio Alger, helped some reporters gather information and ran errands during these exciting weeks.

When the trial began on March 19, thousands of Bostonians crowded around the courthouse, hoping to get through the great bronze door. But the marshals had raised a chain waist-high around the building. The galleries and the courtroom were packed by eight o'clock that morning. The crowd was kept outside.

The newspapers had suggested that with so much interest in the trial, the court ought to move it to the Tremont Temple or some other large building. But Chief Justice Lemuel Shaw and his three associates said no, they would hear the case in their usual surroundings. Their one concession to the enormous public interest was to change the gallery every ten minutes, which could be accomplished without upsetting the proceedings in the courtroom below. Otherwise, the 130,000 people of Boston and all who came from far and near to see, had to take their chances.

Down on the floor of the courtroom were seated the participants, the witnesses, and celebrities, such as Daniel Webster and Rufus Choate.

When Professor Webster (no relation to Daniel) was led in shackled, the crowd murmured.

"Hear ye, hear ye, hear ye. All those having anything to do before the Honorable, the justices of the Supreme Judicial Court, gather round, give your attention and you shall be heard. God save the Commonwealth of Massachusetts . . ."

The trial of the century was ready to begin.

The Webster trial lasted twelve days, and an estimated 60,000 of Boston's 130,000 people flocked to the courthouse at one time or another for a glimpse of the principals, if they could get it, or at least to be on the scene of all the excitement.

Holmes appeared in the trial in two guises. As a character witness for the defendant, he praised Dr. Webster as a professor and as a man, and attested to his skills, a reference that might have been unfortunate. Holmes was also called as a prosecution witness, and had to say that when he saw the fleshy parts of the remains of the body, "they very evidently showed a knowledge of anatomy on the part of the dissector. They showed that the person knew where to cut. I should say generally that there was no botching about the business."

Yes, he admitted, the parts might have been pieces of Dr. Parkman.

It was probably not the sort of praise Dr. Webster cared to hear at that moment.

In one of the understatements of the trial, Holmes noted mildly that he could remember the day of Dr. Parkman's disappearance. Remember! He had scarcely had a sensible day since.

But he had no indications on the fatal day of anything unusual. Webster's room was beneath Holmes's and the ceiling was very high. He had been lecturing at the time. He had never heard a thing.

Dr. Webster, protesting his innocence, was convicted and sentenced to be hanged and dangled from the gibbet on August 30, 1850. All the evidence was circumstantial; Parkman's body had never been definitely identified, and Holmes, among many others, believed that Parkman was still alive, having gone somewhere for reasons of his own. Only when Webster's appeals had been exhausted did he finally make a full confession of the murder, in which he told how he had hit Parkman on the head with a walking stick, dismembered the body in his sink, flushed all the blood into the tidal basin below the medical school, then burned some parts and hidden others in the tea chest and the lavatory vault to decompose.

13

DR. HOLMES,
THE PUBLIC FIGURE

THE PARKMAN MURDER CASE WAS A NINE-MONTH WONDER IN BOSTON, but after the hanging of Dr. Webster it soon was forgotten there. Not so with Cambridge and Harvard and all connected with the university. Harvard was long living down that scandal, and the greatest sufferers of all were the professors of the medical school, who had to entertain a stream of gawkers all during 1850, and a scattering of inquisitive visitors for years thereafter. When Charles Dickens made his second trip to America, he asked Holmes to take him to the scene of the crime. So Holmes showed Dickens the chemical laboratory where Dr. Webster had chopped up, boiled, and burned the clay of the late Dr. Parkman, and the lavatory into which the telltale pelvis had been thrust. As dean of the medical school, it was the sort of thing he was called upon to do, and he did it well, showing no sign of his own anguish over the entire affair. He managed with such aplomb that in the fall of 1850, Holmes was chosen to give a memorial lecture honoring Dr. Parkman.

He had just then returned from a successful summer in Pittsfield, where he made a few public appearances, wrote a few poems, and did a great deal of relaxing. It was the year the New York lawyer David Dudley Field held a memorable mountain-climbing expedition and picnic outing at Stockbridge.

Early on the morning of August 5, 1850, the little doctor arose early from his connubial bed in the square white house he had built on the edge of Pittsfield. He dressed swiftly while his wife Amelia went down to the kitchen to supervise breakfast for the three children. He, alone, was going on an outing, and although he was "in the country," he donned his usual clothing, black boots, a dark worsted suit, white shirt with high starched collar, wide, flowing silk tie done in a bow, white waistcoat with gold watch chain and Phi Beta Kappa key, and long tailcoat of the same material as the baggy trousers.

He stood five feet two in his stocking feet, a dapper, almost handsome man, with thick brown hair and a pleasant face, if perhaps a little long in the chin, as were the faces of his New England Calvinist ancestors.

But the impressive features were the eyes—deep-set, wise, and yet twinkling eyes that gave youth to his face, even in middle age —and the mouth—a small, prim mouth perhaps, on another man, but on this one turned up at the corners, with heavy laugh lines running from the corners of the nose deep into the lower cheeks. It was a relatively clean-shaven face; in a day when nearly all adult men wore beards, Dr. Oliver Wendell Holmes sported no more than long sideburns. The effect was youthful in the extreme, and it was hard to believe that this man was dean of the Harvard University Medical School, professor of anatomy, renowned poet who had published a number of volumes to immediate critical success, and above all raconteur and wit.

It was a gray morning, high overcast, with a hope that the sun would shine through, but also the threat of rain, a typical August morning in the Housatonic valley, where the summer sun has trouble finding its way through mountain haze.

That morning Dr. Oliver Wendell Holmes was heading for the Pittsfield station of the New York, New Haven and Hartford Railroad. There he met Evert Duyckinck, publisher of the *Literary*

World, a New York City magazine, who had come up to the Berkshires for a week's vacation with Cornelius Mathews, one of his writers, at the invitation of Herman Melville, the young novelist whose *Typee* had created a literary vogue for tales of the South Seas four years earlier. Holmes knew young Melville. He knew the Melville family. Major Thomas Melville, a soldier in the Revolutionary War, had been Holmes's prototype for "The Last Leaf."

They were taking the train twelve miles to Stockbridge, to the house of Dudley Field. He was one of the well-to-do who had turned from Saratoga, the favorite watering hole of New York's famous of the period, to the quiet rural surroundings of the Berkshires. Field was of a literary turn of mind, and so he had planned this outing to bring together a number of prominent figures in the world of the pen, notable among them, Dr. Oliver Wendell Holmes.

The four men stood in the station smoking and chatting, with Dr. Holmes, as always, dominating the conversation with a flurry of puns. Then the train came puffing in. Dr. Holmes seized his new India-rubber bag containing a change of linen, and pumped his short legs to keep up with the others as they hurried to a coach. The engine snorted and the whistle blew, and with a screech of steel wheels on rails the train was off for Stockbridge.

In half an hour they were there, and waiting for them on the platform was a large, well-dressed gentleman, their host. He led them through the station to his carriage, and whisked them away to his rambling, white clapboard house on Stockbridge's Main Street, half a mile east of the Congregational Church.

At the house, Mrs. Field was preparing for this notable event, the capture by her husband of half the literary lions of the vicinity. Holmes and Melville had arrived. Still to come were Nathaniel Hawthorne, whose *The Scarlet Letter* had established him in the literary pantheon, and James T. Fields of Ticknor and Fields, Holmes's and Hawthorne's publisher, who also published Louisa May Alcott and many of the Boston and Concord literary figures.

Mrs. Field brought the arrivals from the train into the summer parlor, where they met the Fields' son and daughter. Champagne was brought to refresh them, and the talk began. There was nothing Holmes liked better than to sit in an armchair in a bower as he now did, looking out across the lawn at the trees, a glass of liquid refreshment in his hand, holding forth on the beauties of the Berkshire countryside in summer.

The others were late. Field suggested the early-comers might wish to see the view from Sacrifice Mount, named from a savage practice of the Indian tribe that inhabited that section of the valley two hundred years earlier. So they trouped off to the little knoll, the Field poodle dancing about their legs, and they admired the view from there.

When they returned to the house, the others had come. Nathaniel Hawthorne had driven over from his little red cottage halfway between Lenox and Stockbridge, and he had brought James T. Fields and his new wife. They had talked on the way about Hawthorne's new book, *The House of the Seven Gables*, which was just in the planning stage. Fields was exuberant; Hawthorne's *The Scarlet Letter* was still selling very well. On their arrival the talk became more general, and, as always, Holmes led it.

The one nonliterary guest in attendance was Henry Dwight Sedgwick, who observed wryly that he was the only one there who had not written a book. And that was true, if one counted their host's legal writings and ignored the women present. Sedgwick was the expert on local history and geography. His place in the party soon became apparent when Field produced several hampers filled with ice and Heidsieck champagne, and the whole party set out in three carriages, with Sedgwick riding along on horseback. They were heading for the foot of Monument Mountain, four miles south of town. There was much laughing in the carriages, for the effect of the Heidsieck had been salutary.

They had seen the mountain with its formidable ledges looming above them as they approached in the carriages. And from the base several of the men looked dubiously at their patent leather city shoes and city clothes. But their host and Sedgwick assured them that the way was quite gentle, and there was nothing to fear.

So with the servants carrying the hampers they headed upward along the well-trodden path, for Monument Mountain was a famous landmark of the Berkshires and visitors came from afar to ascend and look out over the valley.

Dr. Holmes sent one joke tumbling upon another as he ambled upward, stopping to make a pun for publisher Fields, and another for his host. Mathews later wrote an account of the adventure and referred to "puns flying off in every direction, like sparks among the bushes."

Duyckinck and Hawthorne led the way, talking animatedly about *The Scarlet Letter*.

Publisher Fields, a man of girth, chugged and puffed and wondered aloud what idiocy had persuaded him to make the ridiculous ascent.

But finally they reached the top, sixteen hundred feet above sea level, the rocky mountain summit above the carpet of pine and white birch, a mountaintop that Hawthorne likened to a "headless sphinx, wrapt in a rich Persian shawl."

There the hampers were opened. The corks began to pop and the party gained even more life. Melville climbed out to perch astride a jutting rock, far above the valley. Holmes watched in pretended horror as Melville pulled and hauled on mock lines, as though he were setting sail aboard a whaler. It almost made him seasick, the doctor said, "it was as bad as a dose of ipecac."

Now, the skies turned black, and a thunder shower moved in on Monument Mountain. As the rain began to pelt down and the ladies uttered small cries of distress, their host led them to a place of shelter just below the promontory. Dr. Holmes, the gallant, cut three pine branches to make "an umbrella," to the amusement of them all. He posed and gestured as David Dudley Field filled the silver mugs. The champagne flowed.

Cornelius Mathews, who fancied himself the most literary of them all and had a string of unsuccessful books behind him to prove it, read the poem "Monument Mountain," by the only other really important Housatonic writer, missing that day, William Cullen Bryant. The sad epic told of an Indian maiden who loved her cousin, but the tribe said their union would be incestuous, so she climbed Monument Mountain and threw herself from the rock to the ground far below.

The thunder crashed, the gales blew, the rain came down, and the champagne mugs were lifted high.

Coming down, they passed the cairn of stones that, tradition said, marked the spot where the Indian maiden in the poem had fallen from her peak. Then, a bit farther on, they were at the bottom, scarcely winded, and the carriages were waiting.

Back in the Field kitchen, the servants had been preparing the sort of feast dear to the hearts of nineteenth-century gentility. There were beef and chicken, turkey and duck, there were fish, and every sort of vegetable and fruit available in western Massachusetts, or whatever could be shipped by rail from New York.

Now Mrs. Field, on her husband's arm, led the way to the table, and he seated her at one end of the long board and moved to the other end himself. Hawthorne sat on the right hand of his hostess. Then came Eliza Fields, seated next to her husband in deference to their newly wedded state, and the others scattered about.

Dr. Holmes, on the right of his host, immediately took command of the conversation at that end of the table. They talked of sea serpents and poetry. Holmes had just spent many hours polishing "Astrea," writen for the Phi Beta Kappa of Yale University. The champagne was poured, and Dr. Holmes never once let there be a lag in the conversation.

The talk had begun with a claim that Englishmen were superior in intellect and constitution to all others. Melville took the bait and spoke hotly in favor of Americans. The little doctor smiled and pointed out that Americans were, after all, but displaced Englishmen, and then went on with a straight face (but that devilish twinkle) to say that his extensive studies of genealogy and genes had proved to him that Americans were growing stronger and larger than even their English ancestors (which was scientifically true) and that in twenty years or less men might be born who would grow to be sixteen feet tall (which was completely hyperbole). And, of course, they would have intellects in proportion. Giants indeed they would be, giants in poetry, giants in industry, giants in arts and letters.

Hawthorne, at the other end of the table, carried on brilliant literary conversation with his hostess, who was extremely well read, and did not get into the general argument Holmes had initiated about the superiority of Englishmen. But Melville was the one most worked up by the doctor's levity, for he was a passionate patriot, and was so bemused by this "attack" on America's fair name that not long afterward he wrote an almost jingoistic treatise on the virtues of American authors over all others.

But as Melville seethed, the conversation had switched and gone far beyond the comparison. After three hours their host announced that he had further exercise for them that afternoon. They would visit Ice Glen, a mysterious, dark-wooded canyon about a mile from the Field place, where boulders and huge trees had fallen helter-skelter, and where the sun seldom penetrated.

Once again the carriages were called out, and the party moved to the entrance of the glen. Hawthorne, with his dark intensity, observed that the glen looked as if it were the Devil's work. Melville was so much impressed that he later incorporated the place into *Moby Dick*. Hawthorne and Holmes went on ahead, engrossed in a discussion of poetry. Publisher Fields brought up the rear, perspiring with the unaccustomed effort and complaining that his two authors never waited for him. They should, he said, have more respect for his fat.

"Ah," rejoined Holmes. "Ten percent more to your authors and you'll have less fat to complain of."

The party continued on a high note, and if spirits were temporarily dampened by the eery quiet of the glen and the bearded Hawthorne's dire prediction, shouted in a sepulchral voice, that they were all heading for their doom, soon enough they were back out into the evening light.

It was nearly ten o'clock before the party broke up. Hawthorne and the Fieldses went back to his place by carriage. Holmes, Melville, Duyckinck, and Mathews were taken to the Stockbridge station to catch the late train. Before midnight, Holmes was home in his bed, relating his adventures to the long-suffering and dedicated Amelia.

CHAPTER

14

DR. HOLMES
AND THE HYPOCRISY
OF ABOLITION

PUBLIC LIFE CONSUMED NEARLY ALL OF HOLMES'S ENERGY AND WAK-
ing time, except during the summer months. Even then, while he
was at leisure from his Harvard duties and his lecturing, the professor, as he liked to be called at this stage of his career, was a busy
man. He lectured at the Berkshire Medical School in Pittsfield. He
wrote poems on request, particularly for such "occasions" as the
dedication of a statue, the Fourth of July, any number of centen-
nial celebrations, and, of course, the annual dinner of the Harvard
class of '29.

Berkshire days lasted until September, but the annual class dinner
was usually held in August, which had been the month of their
commencement in "the Yard." So, a few days after the Monument
Mountain outing, Holmes packed his satchel and took the train
to Boston. About half the class appeared at the Revere House for

the big dinner. As always, the wine flowed freely, and the conversation never died.

The professor then went back to Pittsfield and his family. Amelia, as usual, had stayed home with the children at Holmesdale. Nine-year-old Wendell, seven-year-old Amelia, and four-year-old Edward Jackson ("Ned") played in the barn, helped the hired men, and swam in the Housatonic River. When their father went walking to indulge his delight in the works of nature, sometimes little Wendell and the others trudged along, and he entertained and instructed them with bits of verse and stories about Indians and animals.

These occasions, however, were infrequent, for the professor was preoccupied with affairs of the mind. He often took the horse and carryall alone to make calls on his literary neighbors: Hawthorne, Melville, Catharine Sedgwick, Fanny Kemble, and Charles Sumner, who was just then turning to politics and was inclined to harangue his friends on the fugitive slave issue.

Holmes contended that the Union came first, and social causes second. He might lament the plight of the black slaves, but he would not stoop to take up a cudgel. Richard Henry Dana, Theodore Parker, Holmes's cousin Wendell Phillips, and many others had been at him, but he was immutable. He felt that the abolitionists were going too far, that they used "every form of language calculated to inflame," and he wanted no part of the quarrel.

So he kept his visits on a light plane, confined the conversations to stories and jokes and discussions of the beauties of nature and the representations of literature.

Nor would he take up a torch for the companion cause of Temperance. For the professor was of the old school of gentlemanly thought about the uses of alcohol. His father, the minister, had gone to Yale, sent there by his family with a trunk filled with all the sorts of spirits a young gentleman might need for entertaining in his rooms. Holmes had grown up with liquor and wine, and his three years in France had immunized him against the Calvinist linking of *spiritus frumenti* with the work of the Devil. The professor appreciated a glass of almost anything, and often more than one.

He was not above composing a poem (on request) as he had in the fall of 1842 for a Temperance dinner held by the New York

Mercantile Library Association—but that was largely because women were invited to this most unusual dinner, and the idea tickled his imagination.

But the warnings of his ministerial friends against alcohol left the little professor thirsty, if anything. To him only life was something important enough to be taken that seriously.

The professor, by 1850, was the undisputed literary lion of the Berkshires. It was he, no lesser figure would do, who was called upon to deliver a poem on September 9 at the dedication of the new Pittsfield cemetery.

Now there was a task for a literary man! To meld together a combination of pious respect for the undertaking, and yet refrain from the sepulchral; to bring together history and compassion and nature, accepting the preoccupation with the inevitability of death that so dogged his summer's fellow townspeople of the First Congregational Church he attended every Sunday. He had to carefully refrain from flippancy (which came so easily to him) and avoid the pit of banality. And he did it. It was not the sort of occasion that most appealed to the professor, but he had a deep sense of noblesse oblige, and he wrote a suitably lengthy verse for the occasion and delivered it himself in his pleasant voice.

The cemetery dedication more or less marked the end of his summer. Soon, he and Amelia packed up the children and closed up Holmesdale, house and barn, and gave the horse into the safe-keeping of neighbors. They took the train for Boston, to the house on Montgomery Place that had been a part of Amelia's dowry. The children were entered in schools, Amelia settled down to the winter life of a Boston housewife and mother, and the professor went back to the medical school on North Grove Street.

Holmes was publishing a good deal in this period, and consequently his renown as a writer was growing fast. The British edition of his *Poems* sold briskly. He delivered and published "Astrea," the poem for the Yale Phi Beta Kappa chapter.

Homeopathy and its Kindred Delusions and *Urania* were published by Ticknor and Fields, and in 1848 a new volume of poems was brought out by that publisher.

At the medical school that year, life was once more complicated by Harriot Kezia Hunt's reapplication for admission to the lecture courses. Holmes saw Miss Hunt once more. He agreed with her that there was no reason that she should not be allowed to study medicine just because she was a woman. He promised to take the matter up with the faculty again, and if the answer was favorable, to bring it before President Everett and the Board of Overseers.

He did so, too.

At the same time, Holmes was troubled by another problem, which brought his own emotions into direct conflict with his intellect; three black students applied for admission to Harvard Medical School.

All his life Holmes had been struggling against his own racism, engendered by that ancient tome, *The Negro Plot*. He accepted "the institution" of slavery. His father had lived in Georgia for several years, apparently among the most enlightened of slaveholders, and the Reverend Abiel Holmes had indicated the lot of blacks was not what some long-haired, wild-eyed abolitionists said it was. Holmes's own maternal grandfather had been a slaveholder in Pittsfield. Holmes had grown up in a Cambridge where blacks were excluded from the common on the holiday known as Artillery Day. He had always accepted the status quo, the common belief that blacks were inferior to whites.

But now three young black men came to Holmes: two were from Massachusetts, Daniel Laing, Jr., and Isaac Humphrey Snowden, and they came highly recommended by an associate of Holmes's from his Massachusetts General Hospital days. The Massachusetts Colonization Society was also behind these men because they wanted to study medicine before going to live in Liberia, the nation established by freed American slaves. To Holmes, that program made sense. Not even the most conservative Beacon Hill banker could object to such a purpose. William Lloyd Garrison and Wendell Phillips should embrace it, he believed.

The third black was Martin Robinson Delany, who came bearing equally hearty recommendations from several Pittsburgh doctors. He told a story of rejection by the University of Pennsylvania, Jefferson Medical College, and medical colleges at Albany and Geneva, New York.

Delany told him that just the day before he had been to Berkshire Medical School in Pittsfield. Dr. Henry Childs, the dean, had asked Delany if he intended to go to Africa. Berkshire had taken three students earlier, but only because they were sponsored by the African Colonization Society and were training to go to Liberia. Delany had said no; he was planning to stay in America. Dr. Childs had turned him down. Berkshire's trustees would not allow native blacks to study there.

Dr. Childs had sent him to Harvard for the express purpose of talking to Dr. Holmes, a man of goodwill. Holmes and Harvard were a "last chance."

Holmes read the young man's recommendations carefully. He considered the possible impact of bringing three blacks into a medical school of 113 white males.

It was anything but a good time for such a move. Holmes's cousin, Wendell Phillips, James Russell Lowell, Henry Ward Beecher, the Stowes, and the other abolitionists had created a dreadful stir that fall when an attempt was made to enforce the Fugitive Slave law. The slaves, William and Ellen Craft, had escaped via the Underground Railway to Boston. Agents of their owners learned of their presence and came after them. The abolitionists refused to let them be taken back to the South. The Crafts were aided in flight to England, but conservative Bostonians, including Holmes, lamented the shocking disregard for law and order.

By that time, however, spurred by Holmes, the medical faculty had already voted to admit Laing and Snowden. If the cases of those two and Delany were not the same, Dean Holmes chose to overlook that difference.

He turned and looked the young black man squarely in the face.

"The fee for the course of lectures is eighty dollars. Tickets for the dissecting room are five dollars, and there is a three-dollar fee for matriculation, payable to me."

It was as easy as that.

Delany found his wallet and paid the three dollars. He signed the student book and was registered at Harvard Medical School. Walking on a cloud, he went off to find Mr. Pettee, the bursar.

The three blacks entered the medical school building on North

Grove Street the next morning just before nine o'clock, and seated themselves in Dr. Jacob Bigelow's room to hear his lecture on the history of drugs and their medical uses (materia medica). The room fell silent as they came in. No other student spoke to them when the lecture ended. They walked together down the corridor to the next class. No one would sit near them. No one but the instructor and demonstrator would speak to them in the dissecting room, or in the library, where the students usually carried on a running general conversation.

Three afternoons a week, the students were taken to Massachusetts General Hospital to visit patients and see symptoms of disease —typhoid fever, tuberculosis, pneumonia. The three blacks were always a little enclave, alone together.

A month after lectures began, Harriot Kezia Hunt's application for admission to the lectures was approved by the Board of Overseers. Dean Holmes had sent it up with some careful annotations. Her admission was not inconsistent with the statutes of the University, he said. He would instruct Miss Hunt privately in anatomy, for he found it indelicate for her to be studying the human body in the presence of males. Further, he would arrange for her to have a separate place for dissection, for the same reason.

When the word came to the students in the first week of December that the imposition of three blacks at the school was to be followed by the unheard-of entry of a woman, the student body called an emergency session. The blacks were not invited. That night a majority of the Harvard medical students met to consider the new admissions program of their dean.

After much fiery talk that compensated in passion for what it lacked in Holmesian finesse, the students voted overwhelmingly to reject the presence of Miss Hunt. And then they passed a number of other resolutions against the blacks.

The admission of blacks would lower the reputation of Harvard Medical School and thus diminish the value of their own diplomas. Further, the admission of blacks would cause whites to boycott Harvard Medical School.

The white students said they could not consent to being "identified with the blacks." They would not walk with them in the street, or have them in their houses. Why should they be forced to sit in the same room with them?

Soon, if Dr. Holmes and the faculty let this course continue, there would be more blacks than whites in the school. Harvard would be ruined. If the faculty did not yield, the white students would quit.

Finally, after bringing forth all the economic and social justifications of racism that would be heard for nearly a hundred years after the Civil War, and threatening to destroy Harvard Medical School if it did not do their will, the student group had the arrogance to assume a high moral tone.

"Resolved That we have no objection to the education and evaluation of blacks but do decidedly remonstrate against their presence in College with us."

After this burst of hypocrisy the young Harvard racists adjourned and went home.

Holmes had the resolution the next morning. He also had on his desk another statement signed by twenty-six students who said they disagreed with all that had gone on in the student session, and advocated more education of blacks. A third resolution was signed by twenty-two students. They said they did not agree with either position, but wanted all students already enrolled to be left alone.

No one came to the defense of Miss Hunt.

The dispute threatened to disrupt the school internally more dreadfully than had the Parkman murder externally the year before.

That night Holmes called a meeting of the faculty at his house. Every professor had his say. At the end Holmes suggested a compromise: perhaps Miss Hunt could be persuaded to withdraw her application. In that way the faculty would yield something to the students. As for the blacks, Holmes stood firm. They had a "property right" in the winter lectures by virtue of having paid their fees, and if the white students would not honor human rights, perhaps they would honor property.

Holmes said he would see Miss Hunt. He went to her house next day and was at his most persuasive. She agreed to give up her new position—it was scarcely satisfactory anyhow if she was to be sequestered.

The professors sounded out some of the students during the day and found them, as before, divided. On the next night the faculty met again at the Montgomery Place house, and agreed to the Holmes proposal. But some faculty members insisted that the rebellion would crack the school, and Holmes could not sway them. In the end Holmes succumbed to racism. The blacks could finish the term, but they would be barred from future courses in the Harvard Medical School.

By the time this lame agreement was reached, the Harvard Medical School scandal had already reached the newspapers. One student sent a letter to the Boston *Journal*, protesting the admission of these people "of inferior mental ability." Again came the pious benediction: "Let blacks be educated but do not compel white men to be martyrs and to fraternize with them."

The conservatives of the Harvard community were shocked by the presence of the blacks. The radicals were shocked by the actions of both student body and faculty.

Dean Holmes had the distasteful job, then, of extricating the university from his attempted generosity. He informed the black students that they could not continue the following year. He wrote the Massachusetts Colonization Society to tell them that their experiment had failed. The result of mixing races was to anger the whites, he said, and this could do nothing but injure the school. Holmes did not believe what he said, but as with the Boston Medical Dispensary and puerperal fever, he was willing to advocate reform, but not to fight for it.

That year Snowden and Laing gained entrance to Dartmouth's medical school through Holmes's influence, and finished their education there. Delany would not yield. He stayed in Boston, the center of Abolition, waiting for the eruption that would certainly come when William Lloyd Garrison, Wendell Phillips, Charles Sumner, and Henry Ward Beecher became fully aware of the infamous treatment of black men in the cradle of liberty.

But no explosion came. Most of the abolitionist leadership of Boston were Harvard men, and where Harvard was concerned, well, things were different. The abolitionist newspaper, *The Liberator*, said nothing at all about the incident. Finally, in March, when the winter term of the medical school ended and it was too late to do anything, *The Liberator* ran a little note at the bottom of an inside page, offering a petition to the Board of Overseers of Harvard College that they open all classes in all schools to all persons without distinction of color. That was all that was ever done by the advocates of freedom to bring freedom to their own house.

Even the petition died an immediate death. It was obvious that William Lloyd Garrison and all the rest of the foam-flecked abolitionists were interested only in "the cause," the punishment of those God-defying Southerners who would not free their slaves. For its own sake, the welfare of black people did not matter.

Was it any wonder, then, that Oliver Wendell Holmes found it impossible to rid himself of distaste for these self-serving hypocrites?

15

THE LECTURER
FALLS AFOUL OF
HIS CHANGING WORLD

OLIVER WENDELL HOLMES WAS AT HIS BEST WHEN HE WAS TALKING. He had the sort of mind that responds immediately to the spoken word. His quick eye caught every gesture and expression, be it of a companion at the dinner table or in an audience of two hundred as he stood before them on the lecture platform. He could adjust. If sparkling wit was not apt for the occasion, he could turn, serious in a moment, to discussions of medical abuses or the glories of English poetry. His memory was astounding. Sometimes he used a prepared text, and sometimes he did not. He was most effective when he did not, playing to the audience the way an actor did on the stage, milking every phrase and every gesture.

In 1851, when Holmes made lecturing a major part of his life, particularly in the seasons when he was not teaching, he offered "History of Medicine," "Lectures and Lecturing," and "Love of Nature," which was by far his most popular. He received anywhere from forty to a hundred dollars per lecture, depending on the distance and the wealth of the group to which he spoke. He would go over to Nantucket for forty dollars to speak at the Athenaeum and stay at the Ocean House, but he would not go down to New York for less than a hundred dollars and expenses.

He hated to stay in other people's houses. He liked his privacy when he was not with his family. Traveling was torture for him, because he was a man of habit, and as he often said, he preferred to stay by the fireside of Boston. But the demands of those two houses were too heavy; he earned more in a few months on the lecture tour than he could at Harvard in a year of teaching.

The invitations were so many that he could arrange his schedule to suit himself. In December 1851, for example, Holmes delivered fifteen lectures, taught his courses at Harvard, and celebrated Christmas and New Year's Eve at home. Then he was off on New Year's Day to lecture in Salem.

In 1852 Holmes's literary credentials were strengthened when he was chosen to deliver a series of lectures to the Lowell Institute.

As Holmes had moved away from scientific subjects in the lectures of the previous year, for the Lowell lectures he chose to discuss "The English Poets." Having grown up with such classicists as Dryden and Pope, Holmes was not then actually as familiar with his modern English poets as he might have been. So in the summer of 1851 at Pittsfield, as he began preparations, he read all he could find on the moderns, and then he outlined a dozen lectures. He would begin with Samuel Rogers and Thomas Campbell. Lord Byron (whom he did not like) would be paired with Thomas Moore for comparison's sake, Sir Walter Scott with Macaulay, but Coleridge would have a lecture all his own and so would Keats, and Shelley, and Wordsworth.

The series opened on the evening of March 22, 1853. The hall was jammed with matrons from Beacon Hill and Cambridge and Commonwealth Avenue. There was scarcely any space left to stand against the wall. The past two or three years of Holmes's lecturing in the community had proved to all educated Boston that the hearers might be informed and they would certainly be amused.

Holmes began. His voice lacked a bit in resonance for a hall and audience so large, but he had the range, and he projected into the audience with eloquent gestures and merry eyes. He poked fun at Samuel Rogers' works, which were just then popular on both sides of the Atlantic. He ridiculed Campbell's poetry, and told his audience why. He was not posing as an expert, he said. He would state his opinions in the best manner possible, and that was all.

It was not quite all. His asides, his ripostes, his quick changes and puns, kept his audience attentive. They expected to be amused. They were. At the end, he closed with some verses of his own, and the crowd applauded the virtuoso performance.

So great was the approval that the first lecture had to be repeated the next afternoon to accommodate the ticket holders. All subsequent lectures were so oversubscribed they had to be given twice. It was the most successful season the Lowell series ever had. As the series progressed, and Holmes dealt with Southey and Landor and Tennyson and Browning, delivering his bright, witty opinions on their work, the audiences grew. Sometimes not even the ticket holders got their seats. The crowd would surge in and fill the hall an hour before the performance.

The Boston newspapers—at least the *Transcript* and the *Courier* and the *Globe*—loved Dr. Holmes. He had his detractors on the fringes of the Boston press and in the more jealous atmosphere of New York. Yet there was no doubt that the Lowell lecture series of 1853 established Holmes as a major "literary" figure. That did not mean that he was the best or most important writer. It did not mean that he was seen even by his friends as a major American author. It did mean that Holmes's aphorisms and jokes were on the lips of New England and that his stories and *mots justes* were repeated at dinner tables on Beacon Hill and far beyond, into the American hinterland.

Holmes's lectures became ever more "popular," more designed to please his public. When he found that some pun or riposte or literary reference did not go over in Woonsocket, as it had in Dorchester, he deleted that remark and substituted another calculated to give the impression he sought. He attempted to range human emotions, to satirize his world, then to make his audience move with him from nostalgia to sadness to happy laughter.

Whatever motives had stirred him in the beginning of his public lecturing, as he went on he became ever more the performer whose purpose was to amuse for money. He knew it, and he told Emerson and other intellectual acquaintances to stay away from his lectures. He recognized that these talks were little more than a form of entertainment. In a later era he might have been a nightclub performer, as was the pianist and songster Tom Lehrer, also a Harvard teacher.

Holmes kept changing his repertoire, as a performer does. He would not go to upstate New York and the farther reaches with lectures on the English poets. He devised a lecture called "The Americanized European," which discussed differences between the American and European societies, based on his theory that climate controlled human activity. He revised that one and tried it again later on. "The Heart's Own Secret," "Lyrical Passion," and "Our Second Selves" were all literary steps downward, designed to please rural populations.

For more sophisticated audiences he added "Literary Tribunals," which was a discussion of the important characteristics and personalities of authors, critics, lecturers, and editors. It was a sly and witty study; with tongue in cheek he finally placed lecturers on a pedestal above editors and mere authors.

He lectured almost every free day, with only a few weeks off in August and September to rest at the summer place in Pittsfield. He went as far afield as Cincinnati.

And the strain began to tell on him.

Lecturing outside Boston meant traveling by train, and in the middle of the nineteenth century railroad cars were either overheated or not heated at all. If one wanted air, one opened the windows. After a long, jolting train ride, then came a drive to the inn, which turned out to be either run-down or operated by an overenthusiastic landlord who heaped unwanted courtesies upon the tired traveler. There was always a preliminary meeting with "the committee" that had arranged for the lecture. This called for tact and good humor, even though Holmes might be wheezing with an asthmatic attack and want nothing more than an hour's rest before his performance. If there was time, he took tea with the com-

mittee, and ruined his stomach with bad tea and indigestible
pastries. Then, after the lecture, almost invariably someone wanted
to entertain the doctor at supper, which meant more dreadful
food. Or, if they did not, and he was escorted back to his inn and
paid his fee by the committee, then either the kitchen would be
closed or the late meal cold and inedible.

Lecturing in the towns was bad. Lecturing in the country villages
was worse. New Hampshire farmers dragged from their hearths by
their wives would brave the snow and wind in carts and shays to
catch a glimpse of the celebrity. Since he was a "city feller," although famous, he was naturally under suspicion, and as many of
his sallies sailed a foot above their heads, the atmosphere tended
to worsen by the moment.

Except for the schoolteacher and the minister, there was little
use in talking Wordsworth to those people. Even when he stepped
down to "Lyrical Passion" and "Our Second Selves," the farmers sat
stolid in their chairs and never cracked a wink. Holmes was seldom
party to their after-lecture discussions, but he could imagine what
they were like. What the wives really wanted was an evening away
from the moos and cackles of the livestock, and all that would stir
those granite farmers would be a diatribe from Theodore Parker
or a blast from Wendell Phillips. The country committees both
near and far had heard of Dr. Holmes, but after they heard him in
the flesh, they were not so sure they wanted him.

So by the winter of 1855 Holmes was thoroughly sick of lecturing.
But over his head hung the house on Montgomery Place and the
farm in Pittsfield. Oliver Wendell Holmes, Jr., was fourteen years
old that winter. Little Amelia was twelve, and Neddie was nine.
That meant it would not be long before the costs of college were
added to Holmes's worries, and already there were dancing lessons
and the piano.

In the middle of the 1850s another concern was taking shape for
Holmes. The American Medical Association kept pressing for the
improvement of medical schools, which would mean a longer lecture program. Such purely clinical schools as Tremont, said the
AMA, should be integrated into the university schools. Holmes
could see in 1855 that it was a losing struggle, and it would not be

long before Tremont went out of existence and Harvard took over. As the direct result of his medical activities and his lecturing, Dr. Holmes, the man who hated unpleasantness and controversy, found both hanging about his head.

For years, the medical practitioners who held that a doctor could do no wrong had been sniping at Holmes's treatise on puerperal fever. In 1852 his friend Elisha Bartlett had called to Holmes's attention a series of such attacks by Dr. Hugh L. Hodge of Philadelphia. Hodge went about lecturing on "The *Non*-Contagiousness of Puerperal Fever," and so aroused Bartlett that he wrote Holmes for a copy of the puerperal fever paper to refute the "shallow and dangerous" statements.

Holmes was growing very short of copies of the puerperal fever treatise. Over the years since 1843 his supply had been steadily diminished by similar requests. So in 1854 he prepared a new publication, with a comprehensive introduction that took note of his critics and their claims. He was so aroused by the abuses that he referred to "two widely known and highly esteemed practitioners, professors in two of the largest medical schools of the Union, teaching the branch of art which includes the Diseases of Women, and therefore speaking with authority," who, "addressing in their lectures and printed publications large numbers of young men, many of them in the tenderest immaturity of knowledge, have recently taken ground in a formal way against the doctrine maintained in this paper. . . ."

And then, in a move that was unconventional, to say the least, among the careful brethren of medicine, Holmes named the two: Dr. Hodge of the University of Pennsylvania School of Medicine and Dr. Charles D. Meigs, who taught obstetrics and gynecology at Jefferson Medical College in the same city. Thus Holmes immortalized two of the most wrongheaded doctors of all time, who had been the cause of the deaths of thousands of women. Meigs lived to have a further distinction: he went down in history as the American doctor who, during his lifetime, opposed virtually every new and sane development in medicine and did untold harm by teaching wrong instead of right methods.

It was the murderous results of puerperal fever that aroused

Holmes to unusual passion. He warned his whole profession of the coming wrath of the people: ". . . if there is any voluntary blindness, any interested oversight, any culpable negligence, even, in such a matter and the facts shall reach the public ear; the pestilence carrier of the lying-in chamber must look to God for pardon, for man will never forgive him."

He had in this charge indicated the culpability of his two enemies, and when the new work was published in 1855, they rose in fury.

Holmes's work, said Meigs, was like "the jejeune and fizzenless dreamings of sophomore writers."

But the American Medical Association took a different stance, and so did many important medical journals. They had independent evidence and backing for Holmes. In 1846, far off in Budapest, Dr. Ignaz Semmelweiss had come to the same conclusions that Holmes had reached. Semmelweiss brought into practice in his hospital wards the same sort of cleanliness that Holmes advocated, and in Budapest, the puerperal fever death rate dropped.

In 1847 Semmelweiss had published his findings. He, too, accused doctors of action barely short of mass murder. Those accusations aroused the same sort of vicious attack everywhere in Europe. The self-serving could not bear the criticism.

Little by little, the body of evidence and the number of believers grew. Dr. Channing, who had told the Boston Society for Medical Improvement that puerperal fever was noncontagious, reversed himself with a realism and generosity rare among doctors. Such approval became general, and in a year the Holmes-Semmelweiss theory was generally accepted in American medical circles. The move to clean up the hospitals and clinics was under way. Dr. Meigs suffered the final indignity when reviewers of his medical textbook corrected the author's error and cited their authority: Dr. Oliver Wendell Holmes.

But that medical controversy was overshadowed in Holmes's life in 1855 by another, which stemmed from changing social attitudes.

The fire-eating abolitionists of New England had been gaining ground steadily in the years since Lowell had attacked Holmes for refusing to join the cause. Holmes continued to object to their didacticism as much as he had objected even as a boy to the same quality in the orthodox Calvinist ministers.

In his poetry for dinners and meetings, and on the lecture platform, Holmes satirized and sometimes attacked the extremists. When Daniel Webster made a major address, calling on all Americans to support the Union at any cost, Holmes congratulated him. When Holmes's classmate, Isaac Morse, a Louisiana congressman, refused to come to any more class reunions in Boston because of the attitude of the abolitionists, Holmes wrote him sympathetically. From time to time he expressed in conversation and on the podium the hope that above all the Union would be saved.

Privately, Holmes spoke to his cousin Wendell Phillips about his distaste for the excesses of the abolitionists. Since Phillips was one of them, the conversation strained family bonds as well as national.

Deep beneath his conservatism was Holmes's own gentle racism. He thought of himself as a privileged person who carried a heavy weight of responsibility for his inferiors. The Reverend Abiel Holmes had instilled in him that philosophy in boyhood. Among those inferiors there was no doubt in his mind that the blacks led all.

He had nothing against blacks. In virgin territory he believed they should be free. But he also believed that in a society such as that of the South, where blacks outnumbered whites, it was essential for the whites to maintain control; the specter of the slave plot again.

Holmes had been misused, insulted, and offended by many of Boston's self-proclaimed saviors. Years earlier when he had given that serious medical lecture on nutrition, "The Natural Diet of Man"—prompted by a vegetarian craze that ran through New England—he had been attacked viciously by vegetarians.

Holmes had often spoken of the delights of the brimming glass. For this he was denounced from podium and pulpit by the prohibitionists who masked themselves as Temperance advocates. Holmes believed in Temperance. He loathed prohibitionists. Now, he was too often harried by abolitionists to see them in anything but the same light. Indeed, most abolitionists were also prohibitionists, and some even vegetarians and homeopathic enthusiasts. Holmes had observed that such extremists flocked well together. He called them all "moral bullies."

Holmes carried this contempt with him on his lecture rounds, and aired it when the occasion offered. One day in December 1855, when he addressed the New England Society in New York City, he discussed social change, and let fly in one breath at Boston's abolitionists and a new Maine law prohibiting the sale and consumption of alcoholic beverages.

Holmes thus infuriated Horace Greeley, editor of the powerful New York *Tribune,* a man of violent passions, who had recently abandoned the commune theory of Fourierism for Abolition and Prohibition. Which came first in the fiery editor's heart? Which evoked his most trenchant editorializing? It would be hard to say, but in a sentence Oliver Wendell Holmes had managed to attack both of Greeley's most cherished concepts. To Horace Greeley criticism of his ideas was a declaration of war.

The *Tribune* attacked Holmes, and the attack was picked up by every abolitionist journal in the land. He was called most un-Christian names from Christian pulpits. His character was blackened as darkly as the skin of any Carolina Gullah. His sincerity was questioned. His motives were impugned. He became in the winter of 1855–56 the favorite whipping boy of the abolitionist press, and even old friends seemed to turn against him. The Boston newspapers, most of which had previously said nothing but good about Dr. Holmes, now lamented his wrongs. Wendell Phillips criticized him publicly.

Holmes was lampooned, caricatured, and blasted all across the land. He became, in fact, the embodiment of the abolitionists' greatest concern. He was the man of goodwill, who would not pervert his heritage to join the cause. And the abolitionists, true to their puritan roots, despised no one more than an unbeliever. The spirit that had impelled their fathers to hang Quakers and force Roger Williams from the Massachusetts Colony drove the abolitionists to try and destroy Dr. Holmes.

Publicly, Holmes temporized and tried to answer wrathful criticism with reasoned argument. Privately, he was appalled by the hatred heaped upon him, and by his sudden emergence as a symbol in a struggle that he had never wished to enter.

Now began the lowest period of Holmes's career. In 1856 he retaliated against his newspaper critics in a new lecture, "Critics and Criticism," which was largely directed at the unfairness of the press. The newspapers used their ultimate weapon: they ignored him. That year a Massachusetts doctor left Harvard University a bequest of fifty thousand dollars to establish a chair of anatomy and physiology, but only on condition that the teacher be forbidden to lecture to the Lowell Institute, Lyceums, or indulge in other ventures "amusing the public." There could be only one target for that attack, and although Harvard refused the legacy because of the strings on it, Holmes was cut by the viciousness of a hatred that extended even beyond the grave.

That year Holmes decided to pull in his horns. He would not lecture anymore outside his immediate home grounds. There would be no more trains or drafty inns. Holmes was tired. He was bruised, and he felt his world closing in on him. As if to emphasize it, in the summer of 1856 he decided he could no longer maintain the Pittsfield property, with his growing expenses and diminished income. He put it up for sale, the great pine tree he had watched grow for seven years, the elms he loved so well, and the broad fields that nestled against the sparkling waters of the Housatonic. In a matter of months the place was sold, and Holmes's whole way of life was changed. It would never be quite so pleasant or so carefree as it had been during those seven years.

16

MR. LOWELL,
IN A NEW BOAT,
OFFERS DR. HOLMES
A LIFELINE

BOSTON IN THE EARLY 1850S WAS ALIVE WITH LITERARY ACHIEVEMENT. In the winter of 1851 Hawthorne was working on *The House of the Seven Gables,* for which publisher Fields waited anxiously in his offices above the Old Corner Bookstore.

Holmes dropped in there frequently, as did Lowell, Sumner, Longfellow, and Edwin Percy Whipple, the critic, who was a fellow lecturer with Holmes and Emerson on the Lyceum circuit. They would stop by for a minute and stay an hour.

Holmes was not really a member of the literary elite, but he was following the New England tradition. Literature in America had always been a pastime of men of substance. Edward Everett was an educator and for a time editor of the *North American Review.* George Bancroft was a Harvard professor, a poet, a contributor to the *Review*. John Greenleaf Whittier was a newspaperman who wrote poems on the side. Longfellow was a teacher. One had to make a living. As Judge Story, Holmes's old law teacher, said: "Few of our ablest men have leisure to devote exclusively to literature or the fine arts." There were professional authors in America, but they were considered by the elite as hacks.

In the 1830s, while Holmes was eschewing literature and studying medicine in Boston and in France, transcendentalism descended on New England and overpowered the literary community. *The Dial* was the organ of the new literary movement. Its apostle was Frederic Henry Hedge and its disciples were Margaret Fuller, Emerson, Bronson Alcott, John Sullivan Dwight, and W. H. Channing. Its core was the Symposium Club or the Transcendental Club. Again, transcendentalism was partly a Cambridge-Harvard product, although its root was in Concord; even Thoreau spent some time at the university. Margaret Fuller edited *The Dial*; she was that fearsome schoolmate of Holmes's youth who would arise at five in the morning, walk until six, practice the piano until seven, read a literary work in French until eight, study philosophy until nine-thirty, go to Greek lessons until twelve, and then practice piano again until dinner at one. She would then spend two hours reading Italian, go riding for exercise, then play again until supper. She would read some more, play some more, sing a little, and then at eleven go upstairs in the house in Cambridge to write in her diary for an hour. She had always frightened Holmes half to death.

She, Dr. Hedge, and Emerson kept *The Dial* very tightly in their hands, and even had Holmes been the sort of thinker who could have melded into their environment, quite probably he would never have forced his way into the heart of the transcendental movement. To be sure, Holmes was turned another way to scientific medicine; but had he chosen letters, Fuller and Hedge would have been too complex for him.

Hedge, who had brought the transcendental ideas to his American friends from Germany, believed that literature could derive only from suffering: ". . . We have our orators, our statesmen; but the American poet, the American thinker, is yet to come."

Hedge wrote those words in 1840, the year that Holmes and

Amelia Jackson had married and Holmes was dividing his time between Tremont Medical School and Dartmouth, so busy teaching that he could not even spare the time for reunions of the Harvard class of '29.

"He who would write an epic," said Dr. Hedge, with the unction of authority, "must make his life an epic. This touches our infirmity. We have no practical poets—no epic lives. Let us but have sincere livers, earnest, whole-hearted, heroic men, and we shall not want for writers and for literary fame. Then we shall see springing up, in every part of these Republics, a literature such as the ages have not known—a literature commensurate with our idea, vast as our destiny, and varied as our theme."

The Dial died; Emerson published his first volume of poems and went to Europe, and on his return he joined the antislavery movement. He and Longfellow and Lowell met occasionally in Boston, but usually by chance. They talked sometimes about a club: object, to dine and talk.

Sometimes on a Saturday, Emerson would leave his woodpile and his study in Concord and head for Boston, either to see his publishers about some detail or to stop by the Athenaeum to pick up a book. Usually he dropped in at the Old Corner Bookstore on Washington and School streets, if for no other reason than to find a luncheon companion. There he met Horatio Woodman, a lawyer who was fascinated by literary people and who introduced himself as a man who knew Emerson's transcendentalist confrere, Bronson Alcott. Woodman listened when Emerson spoke wistfully of the difficulties of literary people in finding outlets and opportunities for discussions. Out of that conversation came a series of dinners given by Woodman for various literary men, and Woodman began to have hopes that he could insert himself into the glittering literary society. This desire coincided in a way with the yearnings of Francis H. Underwood, a young abolitionist who wanted to start a magazine.

The two outsiders, Underwood and Woodman, attempted to attract the attention of the insiders.

In 1853 Underwood's hopes were raised when he approached the publishing house of J. P. Jewett with the idea of an antislavery literary magazine. Underwood wrote any number of literary figures in New England, asking that they become contributors.

Underwood did not seek out Holmes, because as far as he knew Holmes was really not producing any material of particular literary value. This was true enough at the time; Holmes's efforts were devoted to the Harvard and Tremont medical schools and to his lecturing. His occasional poems did not count.

Francis Parkman, the historian, did not consider Holmes to be a serious author. Among the literati, only perhaps Lowell took Holmes seriously, and that largely on the basis of a personal friendship that had flourished.

By November Underwood was almost ready to publish. He expected to have the first issue out in January, and it would include writings by Theodore Parker, Henry Thoreau, Edmund Quincy, Lowell, and Thomas Wentworth Higginson, an increasingly popular critic. All these men were abolitionists tried and true. Underwood also had high hopes of getting Mrs. Stowe and John Greenleaf Whittier in the second issue.

But in less than a month all his hopes were dashed by the bankruptcy of Jewett. So the idea got no further than the chairs of the Corner Bookstore and the luncheon tables of the inn around the corner.

Three years later Underwood finally found a publisher who was interested in bringing out a new magazine and had the capital to support it. The publisher was Moses Dresser Phillips, president of Sampson & Company of Boston.

Late in 1856 Underwood was able to begin serious negotiation with most of the writers he had earlier asked to contribute to the new publication.

Just at the time, Holmes's fortunes and prospects seemed dimmer than ever before. The administrative work at the medical school had become so burdensome that he gave up the deanship and its small stipend, rather than continue to be bogged down, although he needed the money.

Motley criticized Holmes for riding so many horses simultaneously and thus never getting anywhere. Holmes, said Motley chidingly, could become great, but only if he would follow two rules: "One, devotion of your faculties and your time to one great object—the other, cotton wooling of your ears absolutely to all handclappings and greasy mob applause of mercantile lecture rooms."

Had Holmes decided to abandon literature and the podium for medical research and scholarship, he would have been cheered on by Amelia. She hated the abolitionist controversy and the pain it brought her husband.

When Underwood approached the serious New England writers, he knew just what he wanted. He wanted Lowell as editor, because Lowell had a reputation for brilliance acquired as editor of the short-lived *Pioneer* magazine in 1843. Lowell was a poet and essayist, and politically an abolitionist. So, too, would be most of the contributors.

The theme of the magazine would be antislavery, if Underwood had his way. Underwood's major claim to fame was his connection with the publication of *Uncle Tom's Cabin*, which he had supervised in the production stages four years earlier. Ever since he had believed there was a market for an abolitionist magazine, and he had Harriet Beecher Stowe's encouragement.

But Lowell had doubts about the direction of the enterprise. Having failed with a magazine of opinion, he recognized the need for variety. And that is how Oliver Wendell Holmes's name came into the picture. Holmes represented Harvard, Cambridge, and conservative, nonpolitical Boston. Lowell wanted Holmes above all others to write for the magazine, and he knew what he wanted Holmes to write. He recalled the two essays, "The Autocrat of the Breakfast Table," that Holmes had done for the ill-fated *New England Magazine* years before. That sort of humor, sophisticated and gentle, was to be a balance to the heady tracts on slavery that Underwood so dearly loved. And so Lowell accepted Underwood's invitation to edit the new publication, but on the condition that they get writers like Holmes to participate.

After all the preliminaries, Moses Dresser Phillips held a dinner party at the Parker House for a number of persons who had shown tentative interest in contributing to the magazine. Dresser explained his project and Underwood amplified, and the guests who sat down at three o'clock in a room at the Parker House first listened and then began a lively discussion of what a magazine ought to be and do. There were Ralph Waldo Emerson, Henry Wadsworth Longfellow, James Russell Lowell, John Lothrop Motley, J. Elliot Cabot, and Oliver Wendell Holmes.

The decision was made final that day. There would be a magazine and the literary leaders of New England would be the flesh and blood of it. Lowell would be their editor.

They stayed at the table for five hours talking. When Holmes slowed for a moment, Lowell or Emerson picked up. Publisher Phillips, who in the early formation period had cast a suspicious eye on the undertaking, was as enthralled as only the hardheaded businessman can be by literary men. He went home to say it was "the richest intellectual day" in his life.

And the next evening it was repeated. The contributors returned the favor to the publishers, and gave a dinner at the same establishment. This time Dr. Holmes came up with a name for the magazine. It should be called *The Atlantic Monthly*, he said.

And so it was. One of the brightest publishing ventures of America was launched.

In the beginning, it was agreed that all prose and poems would appear anonymously, but that plan went awry. "The Autocrat of the Breakfast Table" contained so many allusions and so many phrases familiar to those who had heard Dr. Holmes lecture that he was immediately given away, even if he had seriously wanted secrecy. And if there were any doubt at all, the Autocrat's contribution ended with a poem, a practice that had become Holmes's trademark on the lecture circuit. He had done far more than rehash the old article from *New England Magazine*; he had used the format and very little else. In the pages of *The Atlantic*, the Autocrat, sitting at his breakfast table, surrounded by others of the boardinghouse, bubbled on, interrupted here and there with observations on every aspect of life that interested him, from the mutual admiration society of cultured men, to the way of a maid in spit curls. He spoke of Dr. Johnson, and his Boswell, and Burke, and Goldsmith as if they were at the next table. Dr. Johnson was Holmes's ideal; Holmes had been born a hundred years after Dr. Johnson, and he considered himself that literary lion's equal in another century. He was forever comparing the course of his own career to that of England's great talker.

Holmes did not say so much in his writings, but "The Autocrat" healed his bruised ego, and far more. As Emerson said later, the literary Holmes was like an old pear tree that seemed to grow dormant, bore nothing for ten years, and then suddenly began to produce remarkable fruit.

For the first time the literary Holmes was taken seriously by the figures who had worked with single-minded purpose in those years when he had flitted between medicine, poetry, and the lecture hall. They welcomed his success. It was almost impossible not to like the slender, smiling, friendly doctor, even though he did sometimes annoy with his cocky usurpation of the table conversation. But all knew that Holmes was a gentle man, and a gentleman of Boston. He was undeniably amazing. His abilities as a medical teacher also gave Holmes a mystique among literary men. They were not long on scientific knowledge, but they respected its growing influence in the world.

The Atlantic Monthly was an instant success, too. It was as if America were waiting for just such a magazine. And above all stood the Autocrat. In the South, the magazine was pilloried for its "African features," but even there the educated planters liked Dr. Holmes's Autocrat. In Georgia, in Pennsylvania, in New York, and across the Atlantic Ocean, *The Atlantic Monthly* surged, and left behind it a bubbling wake.

England had been waiting for some sign of literary maturity in America, and along Pall Mall *The Atlantic* was adjudged to be the vehicle of that growth. Some English readers knew Longfellow. Some knew Motley's history of the Dutch Republic. Some knew Mrs. Stowe. At first a few knew Dr. Holmes from that slender volume of verse that had been published nearly a decade before in London. After the first issue of *The Atlantic*, thousands joined them. Thackeray, that current rage of London, praised Holmes inordinately—as was his fashion with his enthusiasms. The Autocrat series, he said, was literature. Soon that enthusiasm spread on both sides of the Atlantic.

For what the Autocrat did was relate in easy conversational style the manners and concerns of educated Americans. The insights were many, the prose was witty, the whole was irresistible to the educated classes.

And so, Holmes came to a literary prominence with "The Autocrat of the Breakfast Table" that he had not before enjoyed.

Yet it was not as easy as all that for Holmes. It now seems apparent that Underwood, the effective publisher of the magazine, did not like Holmes. One day when Thomas Wentworth Higginson praised the Autocrat articles, Underwood observed sourly that he was pleased Higginson liked them because he had gotten a lot of complaints from people who considered Dr. Holmes to be a tiresome little bore. Those people, of course, might have been numbered among Underwood's radical abolitionist friends, but they represented a faction that wrote frequently to the editors of *The Atlantic Monthly*.

Perhaps there were more complaints about Holmes's writings than others': it was the way of extremists then as now to be voluble, and Holmes had angered nearly all of them. After his New York speech, which virtually accused them of treason to the Union, he repeated the charge in his "Ode for Washington's Birthday," before the Boston Mercantile Library Association.

But as even Underwood came to understand, Holmes was an essential part of the new magazine. Lowell had himself, Mrs. Stowe, and a dozen others to write fiery abolitionist notes. Whittier could contribute lyricism, Longfellow would be the rhapsodist, Emerson would think his deep and murky thoughts and transfer them to the page. Hawthorne would tell his tales. Louis Agassiz, the naturalist, would write about the processes of life. Motley would lend the solidity of a historical approach, and Holmes sliced away with his literary scalpel. He poked fun, and a little ridicule, but so gently that even the object of the humor sometimes found himself laughing with the others.

In the Autocrat articles, Holmes, the dilettante, was at his most enjoyable. He would begin with a few paragraphs about the values of conversation and switch to the dullness of sermons, jump to a brief consideration of the thought processes, and then talk about fast horses. Did anyone in his reading audience wonder why Britain led the world in racehorse production, while America was first in trotting horses? Holmes had a ready answer: Republican America's trotting horses were useful—Republican; aristocratic England's racing horses were otherwise useless—aristocratic. And then from horses he was on into the vocabulary of racing, and from there soaring in a discussion of the literary life.

If he went to visit friends, he wrote about them. He visited Governor Swain on Naushon Island, and (without naming names) wrote all his impressions of the trip. Then, in the second of the Autocrat papers, he was off on a poetic flight: "Sun and Shadow," followed by a discussion of private theatricals (to which he consigned his own Lyceum lectures). A poem, "This Is It," described the raptures of the amateur stage, and he slipped in a few digs at the Temperance-teetotaler crowd in a hilarious tale.

The Autocrat had been asked by a certain rural committee to submit a poem for a celebration. Believing the occasion to be "festive and convivial," the Autocrat had written accordingly. From the president of the committee he had received a note of approval, except for some "slight changes" that had been made by the local clergyman, "to remove all objection and keep the valuable portions."

ORIGINAL AUTOCRAT POEM
AS CHANGED BY PROHIBITIONIST MINISTER

Come! Fill a fresh bumper—for why should we go
      logwood
While the ~~nectar~~ still reddens our cups as they flow!
      decoction
Pour out the ~~rich juices~~, still bright with the sun,
          dye-stuff
Till o'er the brimmed crystal the ~~rubies~~ shall run.
    half-ripened apples
The ~~purple-globed clusters~~ their life-dews have bled;
        taste   *sugar of lead*
How sweet is the ~~breath~~ of the ~~fragrance they shed!~~
      rank poisons   *wines!!!*
For summer's ~~last roses~~ lie hid in the ~~wines~~

stable-boys, smoking long nines.
That were garnered by ~~maidens~~ ~~who~~ ~~laughed~~ ~~through~~ ~~the~~ ~~vines.~~
scowl   howl   scoff   sneer
Then a ~~smile,~~ and a ~~glass,~~ and a ~~toast,~~ and a ~~cheer,~~
strychnine and whiskey, and ratsbane and beer
For all ~~the good wine, and we've some of it here.~~
In cellar, in pantry, in attic, in hall,
Down, down with the tyrant that masters us all!
~~Long live the gay servant that laughs for us all!~~

Well, what did the breakfast table think?

The Autocrat's friends said he ought to charge the committee double his usual rate. He had, he said, but he didn't get paid *at all.*

And that, said the Autocrat, was why thereafter he always demanded a "fourth-proof rectified impression" of all his verses. That last was pure Holmes. Since the day that Park Benjamin had rewritten a *single word* of one of his poems, no other editor had dared interfere with author Holmes—and, of course, all who knew him knew that. So to his editors and friends, Holmes added an inside joke. He ended that Autocrat paper with a good New England quip: "Put not your trust in money, but put your money in trust."

There was the master dilettante at work.

He also presented here one of what the critics S. I. Hayakawa and Howard Mumford Jones called his "familiar verse"; a poem called "The Old Man Dreams":

O for one hour of youthful joy!
Give back my twentieth spring!
I'd rather laugh a bright-haired boy
Than reign a gray-beard king. . . .

Then he was off discussing novels and why they were written, followed in short order by a discourse on the lowly marigold.

More nonsense, more sampling of the rills and pools of American life, more excursions into the corners of American thought; and then—suddenly—Holmes switched gears, and there before the reader was:

THE CHAMBERED NAUTILUS

This is the ship of pearl, which, poets feign,
Sails the unshadowed main—
The venturous bark that flings
On the sweet summer wind its purpled wings
In gulfs enchanted, where the siren sings,
And coral reefs lie bare,
Where the cold sea-maids rise to sun their streaming hair.

Its webs of living gauze no more unfurl;
Wrecked is the ship of pearl!
And every chambered cell,
Where its dim dreaming life was wont to dwell,
As the frail tenant shaped his growing shell,
Before thee lies revealed—
Its irised ceiling rent, its sunless crypt unsealed!

Year after year behold the silent toil
That spread his lustrous coil;
Still, as the spiral grew,
He left the past year's dwelling for the new,
Stole with soft step its shining archway through,
Built up its idle door,
Stretched in his last found home, and knew the old no more.

Thanks for the heavenly message brought by thee,
Child of the wandering sea.
Cast from her lap forlorn!
From thy dead lips a clearer note is born
Than ever Triton blew from wreathed horn!
While on mine ear it rings,
Through the deep caves of thought I hear a voice that sings:—

Build thee more stately mansions, O my soul,
As the swift seasons roll!

Leave thy low-vaulted past!
Let each new temple, nobler than the last,
Shut thee from heaven with a dome more vast,
Till thou at length art free,
Leaving thine outgrown shell by life's unresting sea!

There, nestled amid the bustling prose of Holmes's third Autocrat paper, was what literary authorities regard as his finest poem, in a class quite by itself among his works. Poe might have praised "The Last Leaf" inordinately, but Poe was dead, and his taste did not rule.

"The Chambered Nautilus" was a masterpiece of American poetry; Holmes knew it was among the very best things he had written. He said he felt an exaltation while writing it. That emotion must have come because "The Chambered Nautilus" summarized his own humanist, almost deist, philosophy. But there it was, a pearl in the heart of the lotus he fed his readers.

There would be much, much more in the Autocrat series in the same vein of sly humor and immense erudition that had attracted Thackeray, and caused that English savant to say, when he went back after his Boston visit, that Holmes's Lowell Institute lectures were the highlight of his American trip.

The Autocrat's pages in *The Atlantic Monthly* were always bouncing with life. The same high-browed abolitionist preacher who would smart and rant at the Bowdlerized version of the winebibber's poem, would write down "The Chambered Nautilus" and quote it in his sermons. The serious scholar who would jib at Holmes's thrusts at scholarly dullness would laugh at his jokes on himself: "Extract from My Private Journal (*To be Burned Unread*)."

Holmes was a master of timeless fun—the essence of that joke would be revived by cartoonist Walt Kelly a hundred years later in a *Pogo* adventure ("Burn Before Reading"). Some of the Holmes references would wither with age, but the kernel of Holmes's humor would not.

And for those who were not satisfied with the swift convolutions of his prose, Holmes always had an original poem or two. "The Deacon's Masterpiece, or, The Wonderful One-Hoss Shay" appeared in the eleventh of the Autocrat papers.

THE DEACON'S MASTERPIECE,
OR, THE WONDERFUL ONE-HOSS SHAY
A LOGICAL STORY

Have you heard of the wonderful one-hoss shay,
That was built in such a logical way,
It ran a hundred yards to a day,
And then, of a sudden, it—ah, but stay,
I'll tell you what happened without delay,
Scaring the parson into fits,
Frightening people out of their wits—
Have you ever heard of that, I say?

Seventeen hundred and fifty five,
Georgius Secundus was then alive,—
Snuffy old drone from the German hive.
That was the year when Lisbon-town
Saw the earth open and gulp her down,
And Braddock's army was done so brown,
Left without a scalp to its crown.
It was on the terrible Earthquake-day
That the Deacon finished the one-hoss shay.

Now in building of chaises, I tell you what,
There is always somewhere a weakest spot,—
In hub, tire, felloe, in spring or thill,
In panel, or crossbar, or floor, or sill,
In screw, bolt, thoroughbrace,—lurking still,
Find it somewhere you must and will,—
Above or below, or within or without,—
And that's the reason, beyond a doubt,
That a chaise *breaks down*, but doesn't *wear out*.

But the Deacon swore (as Deacons do,
With an "I dew vum," or an "I tell *yeou*")
He would build one shay to beat the taown
'N' the keounty 'n' all the kentry raoun';
It should be so built that it *couldn'* break daown:
"Fur," said the Deacon, " 't's mighty plain
Thut the weakes' place mus' stan' the strain;
'N' the way t' fix it, uz I maintain,
Is only jest t' make that place uz strong uz the rest."

So the Deacon inquired of the village folk
Where he could find the strongest oak,
That couldn't be split nor bent nor broke—
That was for spokes and floor and sills;
He sent for lancewood to make the thills;
The crossbars were ash, from the straightest trees,
The panels of white-wood, that cuts like cheese,
But lasts like iron for things like these;
The hubs of logs from the "Settler's ellum,"—
Last of its timber,—they couldn't sell 'em,
Never an axe had seen their chips,
And the wedges flew from between their lips,
Their blunt ends frizzled like celery-tips;
Step and prop-iron, bolt and screw,
Spring, tire, axle, and linchpin too,
Steel of the finest, bright and blue;
Thoroughbrace, bison-skin, thick and wide;
Boot, top, dasher, from tough old hide
Found in the pit when the tanner died.
That was the way he "put her through."
"There!" said the Deacon, "naow she'll dew!"

Do! I tell you, I rather guess
She was a wonder, and nothing less!
Colts grew horses, beards turned gray,
Deacon and deaconess dropped away,
Children and grandchildren—where were they?

But there stood the stout old one-hoss shay
As fresh as on Lisbon-earthquake-day!

EIGHTEEN HUNDRED; it came and found
The Deacon's masterpiece strong and sound.
Eighteen hundred increased by ten;—
"Hahnsum kerridge" they called it then.
Eighteen hundred and twenty came;—
Running as usual; much the same.
Thirty and forty at last arrive,
And then came fifty, and FIFTY-FIVE.

Little of all we value here
Wakes on the morn of its hundredth year
Without both feeling and looking queer.
In fact, there's nothing that keeps its youth,
So far as I know, but a tree and truth.
(This is a moral, that runs at large;
Take it.—You're welcome.—No extra charge.)

FIRST OF NOVEMBER. —The Earthquake-day,—
There are traces of age in the one-hoss shay,
A general flavor of mild decay,
But nothing local, as one may say.
There couldn't be,—for the Deacon's art
Had made it so like in every part
That there wasn't a chance for one to start.
For the wheels were just as strong as the thills,
And the floor was just as strong as the sills,
And the panels just as strong as the floor,
And the whipple-tree neither less nor more,
And the back-crossbar as strong as the fore,
And spring and axle and hub *encore*.
And yet, *as a whole*, it is past a doubt
In another hour it will be *worn out*!

First of November, 'Fifty-five!
This morning the parson takes a drive.

Now, small boys, get out of the way!
Here comes the wonderful one-hoss shay,
Drawn by a rat-tailed, ewe-necked bay.
"Huddup!" said the parson.—Off went they.
The parson was working his Sunday's text,—
Had got to *fifthly*, and stopped perplexed
At what the—Moses—was coming next.
All at once the horse stood still,
Close by the meet'n'-house on the hill.
First a shiver, and then a thrill,
Then something decidedly like a spill,—
And the parson was sitting upon a rock,
At half past nine by the meet'n'-house clock,—
Just the hour of the Earthquake shock!

What do you think the parson found,
When he got up and stared around?
The poor old chaise in a heap or mound,
As if it had been to the mill and ground!
You see, of course, if you're not a dunce,
How it went to pieces all at once,—
All at once, and nothing first,—
Just as bubbles do when they burst.

End of the wonderful one-hoss shay.
Logic is logic. That's all I say.

With only a two-em dash, and no extra paragraphing, the poem was followed by another observation on an entirely different matter—the problems of slang.

The wide-ranging Autocrat spoke on any subject, as Holmes the lecturer was wont to do, as Holmes the dinner-table conversationalist could scarcely be restrained from doing. The Autocrat papers were not signed, but long before the twelfth and last of them was published, anyone who knew Holmes knew their writer. There was simply no one else in all the world who could have written them, but the inestimable dilettante himself.

17

THE LITERARY FIGURE

IT WAS A MEASURE OF HOLMES'S LITERARY POSITION BEFORE *The Atlantic* era began in 1856 that he was not among the organizers of the new literary club that sprang up that year.

Boston, taking its cue from London, was becoming a city of clubs. The Radical Club was one of the foremost. There Holmes's cousin Wendell Phillips met with William Lloyd Garrison, Theodore Parker, James Freeman Clarke, and equally ardent souls, to outdo one another in fulminations against the social evils of slavery. Holmes would never have been asked to join that club, and would not have been interested had he been invited.

But when the Saturday Club was formed that year, Holmes was upset because he was not considered for inclusion among its distinguished members. For the Saturday Club membership consisted of the men Holmes most admired in New England. He knew them all: Richard Henry Dana, a successful lawyer; Emerson; Motley; Lowell; Whipple, the critic; Agassiz; John Sullivan Dwight, poet and transcendentalist; Ebenezer Rockwood Hoar, another lawyer; Benjamin Peirce, the educator; Samuel Gray Ward; Thomas Appleton; and Horatio Woodman, the lawyer who was the moving figure in the club's organization.

Holmes was so upset by this snub that when he sat down to write the Autocrat papers in their stream-of-consciousness style, the very first matter that came to mind was the Saturday Club. Holmes unburdened himself to his readers, obviously addressing his friends of "the club," although, observing the delicacies of the day, he did not mention names.

The Autocrat contrived to have asked of him by an outrageously didactic young divinity student at the "breakfast table" if he belonged to a "Society of Mutual Admiration."

No, said the Autocrat, a little sadly. Once he had belonged to such an organization, Le Société Médicale d'Observation, "a body of scientific young men in a great foreign city who admired their teacher, and to some extent each other." But no more . . .

Lowell, of course, saw this plaint as he read copy on the article for the first issue of *The Atlantic*. He invited Holmes to a meeting of the Saturday Club, and Holmes obviously comported himself with unusual restraint—he did not attempt to dominate the conversation. At that same meeting, Longfellow also appeared as a guest. Both men were asked to join the club.

The Saturday Club was named because it met on the last Saturday of each month. There were no bylaws, no officers, no rules except the unwritten one that a single blackball was enough to deny membership.

The members assembled at the Parker House at three o'clock for a dinner that began with sherry and soup, went on to fish, and included five more courses with two kinds of wine. On occasion a member decided some event demanded champagne.

Up on the wall at the end of the room hung the oil portrait of Harvey D. Parker, founder of the hostelry. Usually Longfellow went to that end of the table and Agassiz went to the other end. These, then, became the loci of two conversations.

Emerson usually sat on Longfellow's left, and Holmes sat across from him, with his back to the windows. He liked to see the faces of his listeners when he talked. Dana sat next to Emerson. The crowd might number from three to twenty.

When Lowell was there, he and Holmes were usually engaged in amiable argument. The topic could be anything, for the various members of the club were forever coming and going around the country or to Europe, and the varied nature of their occupations gave rise to dozens of subjects. Holmes seemed to be at ease in any of them; his mind was like a pack rat's nest, filled with glittering metaphors and odd bits of information.

Motley might be at the table, talking learnedly of *The Rise of the Dutch Republic,* the book that had established his international reputation as a historian. Holmes could carry the conversation right along. Lowell had returned from Germany and Italy, where he had spent a year preparing for his Harvard professorship. Holmes could talk animatedly of the Rhine and the works of art in Italy's museums.

The only trouble with Holmes and Lowell was that when they sat together, hardly anyone else at that end of the table got a word in edgewise.

Down at the other end, Louis Agassiz's big, booming laugh would break in from time to time. But the "talker" at that end was Tom Appleton, rich man, philanthropist, Longfellow's brother-in-law, who, his friends said, was "the second best talker in Boston," Holmes being the champion. Holmes was not above a sly joke at a fellow member's expense, either. One day Holmes met Appleton in the street and Appleton told him a fine story. After Holmes had stopped laughing and they had each gone his own way, with mutual salutations and reminders of the Saturday Club meeting coming up, Holmes thought about the story. He was willing to bet that Appleton would tell that story at dinner; it would be his *pièce de résistance.*

So when the club met, Holmes burst out—over the soup—with Appleton's tale. It created all the sensation he had hoped, and when he glanced down at the other end of the table, there was Appleton, his lower lip stuck out. The poor fellow didn't have anything to say for the rest of the afternoon.

It really did not matter what the subject was, the idea was to begin talking. Holmes said talking stimulated his thinking juices; at the Saturday Club they must have been flowing all the time. One day, Motley offered a proposition, knowing full well that Holmes and Lowell would take opposite sides of it. And they did. Holmes disagreed with Motley, and Lowell disagreed with Holmes, and they were soon all talking at once. A stranger would have been quite dismayed with the speed of retorts and apparent order of even so frenetic a discussion. Edwin Whipple, who observed one of these contests, judged that Motley was two-sixteenths of a second faster in retort than Holmes, and nine-sixteenths of a second ahead of Lowell.

One day someone brought Dr. Calvin Stowe, the minister, one of the most orthodox moralists of Calvinism, and Harriet Beecher Stowe, his writer wife. Mrs. Stowe still basked in the success of *Uncle Tom's Cabin*. Lowell was at the far end of the table that day. He made a point of telling author Stowe elaborately that the greatest novel in the English language was *Tom Jones*. Holmes was in his usual place, demonstrating loftily to Dr. Stowe that the profane swearing they all lamented among the lower classes really originated in the pulpit. The Stowes left the Saturday Club that evening with intellects reeling.

Sometimes Holmes would bring his brother John to the meetings. John became a favorite with a number of the members because he had all Holmes's wit and almost none of his ego. *Frère de mon frère*, he once signed an autograph. He wrote poems—never published them. He studied the law—and gave up its practice. He lived a long life as a Brahmin bachelor gentleman, going everywhere in Cambridge and Boston society, producing nothing in a material sense. John had remained at home in Cambridge with his mother, writing many letters to friends when they were abroad. He was the literary gentleman personified.

From their friends' viewpoint, John had one great attribute, the product of family intimacy: he could bring Holmes up short. One day, when Holmes was talking loftily about music and began the tale of how he had learned to play the violin, John broke in.

"I can testify to it; he has often fiddled me out of the house as Orpheus did Eurydice out of the infernal regions. . . ."

Everybody laughed. They liked to see the little doctor given a taste of his own medicine. But one of Holmes's virtues was that he, unlike Appleton, could laugh as loudly (almost) as the rest at jokes on himself.

Sometimes Holmes came to the club with James T. Fields, his publisher, whose patriarchal beard was menaced by his feeding habits. After dinner, a group might then adjourn to Fields's house for a convivial glass and more conversation. Fields had moved into a house on Charles Street, a few doors down from Holmes, and because of it, their association grew closer than the usual author-publisher relationship. They both lived on the Charles River then; the Charles in those days meandered about an extensive estuary that reached into Holmes's backyard. Just offshore he kept his little fleet, and on a fine morning he would go out early for an hour's rowing before coming back to prepare his lecture for the medical school.

The separate life of the Autocrat was soon-enough known at the school on Grove Street, too. Holmes's growing literary fame did nothing to hurt attendance at his medical classes. A young man received a thorough course in anatomy and something in the literary way as well. Professor of monotony, one clod once wrote on a paper addressed to Holmes. But it was not true. The laughter, the applause, the foot stomping that emerged from the amphitheater when Holmes was lecturing told another story. A Holmes lecture might be anything else, but it would never be monotonous.

One day, in the course of illustrating a point in physiology, he looked down at the cadaver. That poor dead clay was but a shadow of the human being, he said.

"After all, it is a good deal like inspecting what remains of the fireworks on the fifth of July."

When talking about the action of the vasomotor nerves on the arterioles in the regulation of the circulation of the skin, he described how the nerves "suddenly relax and fill the surface capillaries with blood."

He stopped, looked up and around the benches, and smiled a leprechaun smile. "You know . . . that pleasing phenomenon that some of you may witness on the cheek of that young person whom you expect to visit this evening."

No, never before had an anatomy course been taught like a

literary course. The professor was all the more effective for that. Talking of the aging process, he said, "You have no doubt noticed the extraordinary way in which elderly people will suddenly shut up their faces like an accordion?"

Students did not forget Dr. Holmes's simile.

But the world very quickly forgot most of the talk that went on around the Saturday Club table. It was evanescent, dealing as it did with the affairs of the day, and depending in such large part for effect on the *bon mot* and mien of the talker. Nor was very much of the Saturday Club conversation ever recorded anywhere.

The talk was much too timely, for one reason. When Andrew P. Peabody had served for so long as president pro tempore of Harvard that it seemed obvious he would be confirmed in the job, and then in a surprise meeting the overseers elected another, someone mentioned it at the Saturday Club table.

Holmes piped up in Latin: *Sic vos non vobis nidificatis apes.* He was funning with two lines from Virgil: *Sic vos non vobis melli-ficatis apes* (Not for yourselves, O Bees, you honey make) and *Sic vos non vobis nidificatis aves* (Nor for yourselves, birds, do you build nests). And the translation of Holmes's Latin Bowdlerization: "Not for yourself, A. P., do you build the nest."

All those scholars at the table who had studied Latin declensions until "de teeth clenched" understood immediately. Here, in the presence of their peers (almost all the Saturday Club members were Harvard men), they could lord it up a bit. Such jokes lost their punch to non-Latin scholars, and even in the writing down. The world of the twentieth century being filled with a preponderance of non-Latin scholars, most of Holmes's best lines would hardly be appreciated if they had been saved.

The joke was passed around in Cambridge and Brahmin Boston and regarded as another *bon mot* of the irrepressible little doctor. His reputation was such that most of the aphorisms heard in polite society were attributed to him. Lowell came in second in this department, and Tom Appleton third.

Holmes's reputation spread so fast in literary circles that a young man from California sent him a sample of poetry with the request that the doctor tell the writer honestly if it was worthwhile for him to keep on with his efforts. Holmes had dozens of such requests. He glanced at nearly everything and then Amelia prepared letters of rejection. But this young man's work had an appeal of its own—a style. Holmes wrote back to him, and told him by all means to keep on writing.

Years later a man called on Dr. Holmes in Boston and was invited to the Saturday Club. There he told that tale of his poetic beginnings. Did Dr. Holmes remember?

"Yes," said Dr. Holmes. "I do remember."

The guest at the Saturday Club that day was Bret Harte.

CHAPTER

18

THE PERFECT DILETTANTE
WRITES—A NOVEL?

The Atlantic WAS LIKE A NEW SUN BRIGHTENING UP THE ANGLO-American intellectual scene, and it was not long before Holmes was as well known in London as in the United States. He had a claque working for him in Dickens, Thackeray, and Motley, who had gone to London to oversee publication of his new literary work on the United Netherlands.

Further, Holmes's articles were so erudite, with their classical allusions and their Latin and French asides, that the work of this writer who had attended Andover and Harvard impressed readers who had attended Eton and Oxford.

The success of "The Autocrat of the Breakfast Table" caused Holmes to undertake a new series in 1859. He called it "The Professor at the Breakfast Table."

In the interim Holmes had become more aggressive toward some old enemies. In his first paper, the Professor attacked the orthodox Calvinists, *and* the homeopaths, *and* the spiritualists. For that purpose he invented Little Boston, a character filled with patriotic zeal and homely philosophy, a perfect foil to the Professor's erudition.

From the beginning the Professor series called down far more wrath upon the head of its author and *The Atlantic*'s editors than had the Autocrat series. But Holmes was prepared for it. Conservative he might have been in his political beliefs, but he was no reactionary, and he made that plain enough. In the face of the prohibitionists, he wrote in praise of wine. He cast many an aspersion at the type of New England matron who put on dark gray dresses, with a countenance and spirit to match. He laughed at puffed-up society folk and their claim that his Professor was inconsistent with the Autocrat. "Don't be consistent, but be simply *true*."

Holmes was then and later decried as a provincial sort of person. He would not ever have quarreled with that characterization, in the sense of his being a person whose life was bound up in Boston and New England. He would have quarreled with the pejorative view that to be thus provincial was to be somehow less than knowledgeable. To him Boston was everything desirable. Little Boston said it best—Boston was "the hub of the Universe."

There was, however, a major difference between the Autocrat papers and the Professor papers: the first were lively and superficial. The second were dull and perhaps more profound. At least they were intellectual, and very much concerned with theological problems. One reason for this was the eruption of the simmering resentment Holmes had nurtured for years against the orthodox community of divines. Since the days when Holmes and his father had traveled about Massachusetts on Sundays in the prototype of the "wonderful one-hoss shay," he had questioned the conventional puritan belief in earth, heaven, and hell and the preachers' mapping of the various roads that led from the first place to the other two. In 1858, still lecturing on the Lyceum circuit (although only around home), he felt impelled to enter the theological lists with a talk, "The Chief End of Man."

From the Lyceum's standpoint, the lecture was an immediate disaster. Holmes's contention that the chief end of man might be found in his works on earth was taken as a direct challenge by the Calvinists, who attacked Holmes and the groups who asked him to speak. Holmes's chosen Unitarians were liberal enough in their theology to applaud the Holmes concept, but not the Congregationalists. The fury of the Congregationalists led the Unitarians to make Holmes their principal speaker at their Massachusetts festival —and this infuriated the Calvinists more. Holmes was already under grave suspicion, because he refused to accept Abolition as the next goal of America; he had poked fun at Temperance and quite properly speared most of those advocates as outright prohibitionists. Now, he challenged the very tenets of his father's faith, and this was too much. The powerful religious organ, *The Congregationalist,* suggested that Holmes should be proscribed from the lists of Lyceum lecturers.

So the battle was joined, and Holmes used the Professor to smite his enemies. In so doing, he may have cost himself the attention of some readers who were outside the lists. Years later, to a casual eye, the Professor makes much harder reading than the Autocrat. In another sense, of course, this difference is an indication of the provinciality and journalistic quality of much of Holmes's writing; he was more concerned with "here and now" than with the great truth that would stand the test of time. But what more was to be expected? Holmes was, after all, writing for a contemporary audience, much more so than in his best poems, which *have* stood the test of time. *The Atlantic* was a magazine, not a stone tablet; and if what Holmes produced was journalism, as editor Ogden Reid once said in claiming Holmes as his own, then journalism was what sold magazines in the 1850s.

One special aspect of the Professor papers did last—the "hub of the Universe" idea. In the May issue of *The Atlantic,* Holmes claimed Boston was the "thinking center of the continent, and therefore of the planet." Later he said that "the heart of the world beats just under the three hills of Boston."

It was true just then. No other city in America could hold a candle to Boston as a civilized center. And even a hundred years later, long after Boston had lost all right to make any special claims, Bostonians secretly believed their city was still "the hub."

Except for this excursion, the Professor was not half the man the Autocrat had been; he was less literary, more didactic, more quarrelsome, more given to reaching into Dr. Holmes's old rucksack for subject matter (religion, medicine, quackery). Even outside the religious community there was a considerable dissatisfaction with the Professor's performance. He became incontrovertibly controversial.

The reason for the fading luster of the Professor's papers in *The Atlantic* became clear soon enough. Holmes was not putting so very much of his thought into these papers in 1859. His mind had turned toward a novel. It began to appear in *The Atlantic* in December 1859, just after the end of "The Professor at the Breakfast Table," under the title "The Professor's Story." Later it was published as a book under the title *Elsie Venner*.

As a novel, *Elsie Venner* is not first class. Holmes was not really a novelist, at least not in the school of Hawthorne and Melville, who concerned themselves with human character. Holmes was interested in human beings in another way—a far more medical way. *Elsie Venner* is the story of a neurotic young woman in the grip of forces she could neither understand nor control. Her mother was bitten by a rattlesnake before her birth, and the result (quite believable in 1859 society) was a girl whose personality was half woman, half snake.

The combination was bound to lead to disaster, and of course it did in Holmes's book. After a romance the young woman died a tragic death. Holmes's purpose was to suggest the control of hereditary factors over the body. But many a reader remained unmoved by Elsie. One real result of the snake bite was that Elsie never came to life. The author's "medicated" approach showed through. *Elsie Venner* was a fictional case study of a psychological problem, and the characters could not overcome it.

Elsie Venner came under attack from many sides, most of them wrongheaded. Much of the criticism reflected Holmes's continuing battle with the forces of orthodoxy in old-fashioned religion and old-fashioned medicine. After all, he was still fighting phrenologists, homeopaths, the medical quacks, and above all, purveyors of puerperal fever in childbirth.

The objection of the Calvinists to *Elsie Venner* was based on Holmes's contention that Elsie did not need the services of a minister of the gospel to save her, but the services of a physician. This caused some of Holmes's friends in Boston to charge that he was "going Mohammedan." But his purpose in *Elsie Venner* was stated clearly enough in the preface he affixed to the book when it was published by Ticknor and Fields in 1860: "Through all the disguise of fiction a grave scientific doctrine may be detected lying beneath some of the delineations of character."

He was considering "good and evil" in terms of human personalities, studying, in his own way, what would later be called the tenets of psychiatry. No true novelist ever suggests that "in the disguise of fiction" he has pursued some other end.

Critic Leon Edel dismissed Holmes as a force in American literature. Hayakawa and Jones suggested that *Elsie Venner* could not be taken seriously as a novel, although if viewed as an essay, it was excellent. Further, they credited Holmes with considerable virtue as a skillful historian of the manners, speech, and scenery of New England in his time. Finally, they said he did contribute here to the development of the "novel of purpose" in America.

The nature of the attacks against *Elsie Venner*, and the nature of the defenses, are signs of what Holmes was going through. He was trying to be a literary man. In that, he was encouraged in his efforts by his friends, Emerson, Lowell, and Motley. But he was not heeding Motley's caution that he must stop spending himself so recklessly. While *Elsie Venner* was being written, chapter by chapter for *The Atlantic Monthly*, Holmes was also refining a thought he had chanced to state in one of his Professor papers—the idea that homeopathy was to medicine what spiritualism was to religion. Spiritualism was coursing the land, in homeopathy's company. Down in New York, Commodore Vanderbilt, whose reading was confined to the financial pages and who hardly believed in anything but a stock certificate, suddenly took to putting salt cellars under his bedposts and consulting those two curvy seers, Tennessee Claflin and Victoria Woodhull, who were functioning as stockbrokers when they were not reading palms or feeling heads. And the commodore suffered no more than a mild case of this hysteria, compared to thousands of others. Ouija boards, crystal balls, and seance parlors boomed.

The moralist in Holmes objected to this "foofaraw" as much as to homeopathy. He prepared a strident lecture for the meeting of the Massachusetts Medical Society, "Currents and Counter-Currents in Medical Science."

He gave the lecture on May 26, 1860 (*Elsie Venner* was then running in *The Atlantic*), and it created all the stir that he could have hoped for. But the stir was of a most unpleasant sort. Holmes raked the medical unbelievers across hot coals. He castigated "heroic dosers" as poisoners. He said that those who placed their faith in drugs alone were as wild and superstitious as phony seers. He criticized his medical brethren for not studying disease, and suggested that almost all of the medicines they used should be thrown into the sea—even if that would murder the fish. His contemporaries, Holmes indicated, were hardly worth being called doctors of medicine.

When the speech was over, the audience sat, stunned. It was not until the following day that the conservative doctors pulled themselves together. Then, in their fury, they met and passed a vote of censure against Holmes. Later, that vote was overturned by the Massachusetts Medical Society as a whole, but at the moment it was a fine scandal: the eminent Dr. Holmes in open quarrel with the whole medical profession. That was how it seemed, particularly to the Congregationalists who took this new quarrel as proof that Holmes was deranged, if not in the hands of the Devil.

Combined with the mixed reviews his *Elsie Venner* received (adulation from the Boston *Transcript*, scorn from Christian publications), the medical society quarrel did much to give Holmes a difficult year. It was obvious, however, that in 1859 when he wrote *Elsie Venner*, Holmes was still very much the medical educator concerned with theories of medicine.

Elsie Venner had another attribute. In the opening pages of the novel, Holmes undertook to establish the social atmosphere of which he would speak. It was the same atmosphere in which Holmes had grown up, and the people in the novel were Holmes's sort of people. They belonged to an aristocracy that he held had a greater permanence than mere money, for money could be dissipated by inheritance in a single generation. The aristocracy of Holmes's creation had grown to be a caste. By "repetition of the same influences, generation after generation, it has acquired a distinct organization and physiognomy."

Holmes described a youth of the sort he meant:

> . . . Commonly slender,—his face is smooth and apt to be pallid,—his features are regular and of a certain delicacy,—his eye is bright and quick,—his lips play over the thought he utters as a pianist's fingers dance over their music—and his whole air, though it may be timid, and even awkward, has nothing clowning.

Here the mature Holmes might have been describing the young medical student who set out for Paris in 1833.

What characterized this youth as different from others, say New Yorkers?

> He comes of the *Brahmin caste of New England*. This is the harmless, inoffensive, untitled aristocracy. . . . There are races of scholars among us, in which aptitude for learning, and all these marks of it I have spoken of, are congenital and hereditary; their names are always on some college catalogue or other. They break out every generation or two in some learned labor which calls them up after they seem to have died out. . . .

There was the enunciation of an intellectual snobbery that was to be a major factor in the history of New England from Holmes's time to the present. The distinction made by the Massachusetts intelligentsia had existed for many years. No one had put a name to it before Holmes—his statement gave to the inchoate feeling of many Bostonians a title they were to embrace and foster in the years to come. Even today, a Harvard man knows there is something special about his position; and if he comes from Boston, he is certain that he is privileged above all other men except those peers whose lineage and education equal or surpass his own. This snobbery began to break down in the second half of the twentieth century with the emergence in California of universities in direct challenge to the Ivy League, the movement of population to more salubrious places in the West, and the transfer of many of the sons of the Brahmins to such distant climes. But nearly one hundred twenty years after Holmes coined the phrase, the caste of which he was such a proud member continued to believe in its own existence.

CHAPTER

19

DR. HOLMES DECLARES
WAR ON THE CONFEDERACY

IN THE LAST MONTHS OF 1859 *The Atlantic Monthly* FELL INTO economic difficulties. The cause was the death of Moses Phillips. Times were hard and Phillips' Sampson & Company had many debts, but the awesome presence of Moses Phillips had been better than cash in the bank in this financial crisis. When he died in August, the creditors panicked, and the publishing firm was bankrupt. The company fell into the hands of receivers who wanted to sell off the valuable parts. *The Atlantic* was profitable in a small way, however, and while James T. Fields was traveling in England, one of the receivers went to his partner, William D. Ticknor, and persuaded Ticknor to make an offer of ten thousand dollars for the publication. Meanwhile, the creditors tried to sell the magazine elsewhere. It was offered to Lowell, but he and Holmes and their friends did not want to become publishers. When Fields came back from Europe, he discovered that he had just bought a magazine.

Having bought it, Fields decided with his usual confidence that he would run it. He was competent enough, this big, shaggy figure. Before he was a publisher he had been a poet. Had his life been guided in a slightly different direction, he might have become a literary figure of some importance. He kept Lowell on as editor for just one year, and then took over the editor's chair himself. Part of that reason was financial; part of it was that Fields wanted a less literary and more popular publication that contained more fiction and more life. He worried that the magazine might become "dreary," as some said it threatened to do under Lowell.

The change of editor created a crisis for Holmes. Would Fields want as much from him as Lowell had? With the Autocrat series, the Professor series, and then *Elsie Venner,* he had contributed more to the magazine than any other person but Lowell himself. So if Lowell was out, would he be too?

Holmes needed to have no fears. Fields had considered the Autocrat series as "among the great literary 'strikes' of our time." He wanted much more from Holmes. It was a part of his plan to liven up the magazine by increasing the popular writing of just the sort that Holmes did.

The Atlantic's circulation rose to four hundred thousand copies. Holmes had helped make all this success and *The Atlantic* had helped make him a national and international literary figure. Two slim volumes of Holmes's poems had appeared in England before 1857, but the Autocrat articles created a Holmes cult in England. Some critics called him the greatest American writer since Washington Irving. Furthermore, Holmes had made a considerable amount of money out of the magazine. Moses Phillips had paid him ten dollars a page, and Fields continued to do so.

In 1858, with the publication of *The Autocrat of the Breakfast Table* in book form, Holmes suddenly realized how famous he was; *The Autocrat* sold ten thousand copies in three days, and another ten thousand in the next few weeks.

On the heels of that triumph, and because of it, Holmes had a letter from a lawyer named W. O. Bartlett, in New York, who represented Robert Bonner, the publisher of the weekly *Ledger.* Bonner was a shrewd businessman, and he knew a success when he saw one. He offered Holmes a thousand dollars a year for a half-column a week. But the catch was that Holmes would have to write exclusively for the *Ledger*.

Holmes took the offer to Lowell, with whom he could deal on "literary" terms, since Moses Phillips paid out the money. Lowell advised Phillips to give Holmes a raise, and it was done. Yet, even that was not enough for a successful author who had Holmes's expenses.

Young Wendell was a student at Harvard College. Holmes was forced to buy a piece of property next to the Charles Street house to prevent disturbances. Literary fame brought new expenses. He was deluged with letters that had to be answered, and requests to speak and write that demanded decisions. He really needed a full-time secretary, but he did not feel he could afford one. Amelia helped him enormously. She sorted out the correspondence and invented his rejection letters, and took care of matters that did not insist on his personal attention. But it all took time, and it all cost money.

So by the spring of 1861, before the Confederates struck Fort Sumter, Holmes complained again to Lowell, who was just then winding up his affairs as editor of *The Atlantic*. He had not gotten nearly so much for "Asylum for Decayed Punsters" as he thought he ought to have gotten. He had other offers, he suggested mysteriously, and he might be inclined to move on.

Lowell hastened to inform Fields and suggest that Fields smooth Holmes's feathers. "An essay from him is as good as a chapter," was the departing editor's assessment of Holmes's value to *The Atlantic*. Fields concurred. Never again did Holmes have reason to complain about the payment he received from *The Atlantic* for his work. For the rest of his life he published very little elsewhere.

The difficulties of making a living had caused Holmes to leave the raising of the children to Amelia. They had gone to "dame school" and then to a school conducted in the basement of the Park Street Congregational Church.

Wendell went to the Private Latin School on Boylston Place, conducted by E. S. Dixwell, a pedagogue who had the finest qualifications. Dixwell ran a Harvard grind machine—the purpose of it to mold the minds of young men for delivery across the Charles to Harvard College when the time came.

The Holmes children played with their cousins (Wendell's best friend was John T. Morse, Jr., whose mother was Amelia Holmes's sister). They went to school with their cousins and their cousins twice removed. They went to church with their uncles and their cousins' cousins.

Within the Holmes family, all these relations were growing somewhat tenuous as the children began to mature and think for themselves. As Dr. Holmes had grown to detest the cant of his father's church, young Wendell came to dislike the far less stern strictures of his family. Church came every Sunday, and young Holmes did not like Sundays because of it. Wendell and Neddie, his younger brother, were already thoroughly sick of being known as "Dr. Holmes's sons." They shied from his poetry. They flinched at his jokes at the breakfast table (that was the single meal at which they could usually be found all together). The generation gap was real, so clearly seen by the doctor that on one occasion he asked Henry James, Sr., if his sons did not detest him—with the clear implication that the younger Holmeses had no use for their father.

Probably it was the normal Oedipal relationship of all children, enhanced by the doctor's failure to be a guiding father. He was too busy, in the first place, and from his own inheritance there was no memory of days of fishing or tramping through the woods with his father. When Holmes and Abiel Holmes went traveling, it had been on the business of the Lord.

Holmes found his entertainment outside the home. He was forever going to some dinner or other, honoring the commonwealth's agriculturists, hearing a paper on some half-forgotten incident of Massachusetts history, gossiping with his cronies at the Saturday Club, dining with doctors at the medical society. Occasionally, Holmes took the boys down to the Charles to row. But sculling, like all that Holmes did, was solitary work. He taught them to row their own boats. His intimate conversations with his sons were almost entirely admonitory: occasional lectures on morality and the need for personal discipline, which both Holmes boys called "twaddle."

Poor Holmes could not help the lectures; he once said he had "the iron of Calvinism in his soul" and could not get it out.

And so the children grew with little regard for their male parent's occupations or abilities. They did not read his books. They were moderns, of a new age.

They were, however, a lively enough crew, and not at one another's throats. As the children came to maturity, they showed bright and inquiring minds, and Holmes had more difficulty in maintaining order at his own breakfast table than the Autocrat ever did in his boardinghouse.

Big Amelia would appear first, and then the doctor, and the children—one by one; and they would sit down and start talking. Soon they were all talking at once and no one was listening to any other. To outsiders, it was exhilarating, if somewhat confusing. "A nest of wrens," one of Amelia's friends called them.

After Wendell, Jr., moved to Harvard in the fall of 1857, he boarded with a family in Cambridge. Even though the horse railroad had been extended to Cambridge, the trip was too long to be made twice a day. Father and son must both have been relieved at the escape offered so gracefully.

Young Holmes's Harvard career was not particularly distinguished, but he was in less trouble than his father. His whole class of '61 was less belligerent than the notorious class of '29, at least until near the end.

Wendell had been growing more excited all winter. For several years he had been listening to his cousin Wendell Phillips' call for abolition of the curse of slavery. His emotions had risen high by December 1860. Boston tempers had reached such heat that when Cousin Wendell was scheduled to make a fiery address to the annual meeting of the Massachusetts Anti-Slavery Society at Tremont Temple, he was threatened with violence by the anti-abolitionists in the community. Young Wendell vowed that he would join a bodyguard to see that Cousin Wendell came to no harm. James Freeman Clarke, Edmund Quincy, and Emerson were also going to speak—all of them friends of Dr. Holmes, all of them in direct opposition to the doctor's views.

Wendell went to the meeting. Cousin Wendell was there, and so were the other speakers, surrounded by men armed with guns. The floor and the platform were filled with friends of Abolition. The balcony and the halls were filled with "ruffians full of whiskey and blasphemy."

As Phillips rose to speak, the balcony jeered and the floor cheered. The noise was so great that hardly anyone in the auditorium could hear what he said. The same was true of the speeches of the others. The meeting broke up without violence, but also without shedding light: the abolitionists were still fiery for Abolition; the antis were still cursing the destroyers of the Union.

But the next day the mayor feared violence would indeed come, and so the Tremont Temple was closed to the further deliberations of the society. Wendell Phillips and his friends had to meet in private to conduct their business. It was not at all what they wanted to do.

That winter was too cold for Dr. Holmes to be out rowing on the Charles; he'd be dodging drifting ice if he did and chancing a cold that would make his asthma kick up. Militiamen marched along Commonwealth Avenue, and he saw them as he walked for exercise. Holmes wondered, as did every other thinking man in Boston, just what the new President would be able to do to turn back the clock and prevent the Southern states from actually withdrawing. For although the Southerners were leaving Washington, preparing to establish their government in Richmond, Boston just could not believe the Union had been rent asunder this way—not after all these years.

The secession of South Carolina hit young Holmes and his friends even harder than it did the doctor. Six other Southern states declared their decision to follow South Carolina, forts began to fall, and the Union garrison in Charleston fled to Ford Sumter in the middle of Charleston Harbor. Each bit of news sent the young Harvard men into further spasms. In April, when Fort Sumter fell, Oliver Wendell Holmes, Jr., and several other seniors got together for a stormy and liquid bull session. It ended with their breaking the windows in a freshman's dormitory room opposite theirs.

President Felton and the faculty could have thrown them out of college. But because of the tremulous nature of the times, they satisfied the needs of discipline by exacting apologies and ten-dollar fines.

President Felton also wrote Dr. Holmes a letter of complaint. The immediate matter was window breaking. But there was more. Young Holmes had been rude to Professor Francis Bowen, the most orthodox of religionists, and had written blasphemously in the Harvard magazine that a philosophical man might eschew religion altogether. What had gotten into the Holmes boy?

Dr. Holmes might not approve of his son's behavior, and often did not. But the blood of the Holmeses ran thick, and he did not like Bowen anyhow—they usually quarreled at meetings of the American Academy of Arts and Letters. Dr. Holmes conferred with Wendell, who said it did not matter; he was going to enlist.

Three days later, Boston was further shocked. The President called for seventy-five thousand volunteers, militiamen from the loyal states, to help him put down the insurrection in the South.

Massachusetts had the militia ready. The new governor of the commonwealth, John Andrew, answered the call and asked Lincoln how he wanted the troops dispatched. The answer was to send them by rail, and a few days later the Massachusetts men reached Baltimore, where they were stoned and fired upon as they crossed the town. Four men were killed and more than forty wounded. The word reached back to Boston; and if there had been any lingering sentiment there for the Southern states, the death of Massachusetts men at the hands of slavery sympathizers was enough to quell it.

Dr. Oliver Wendell Holmes was convinced that the situation of the Union had passed beyond the ability of mere words to rectify. He agreed with Wendell, Jr., when on April 25, he enlisted as a private in the 4th Battalion of infantry. His father came down to the armory to see the boys off to Fort Independence and was as proud as he could be of his son in his light-blue Zouave trousers tucked into gaiters, with the dark-blue tunic and red cap.

That very day Dr. Holmes set out to deal with the letter of complaint from President Felton. He called on the president and informed him that Wendell had enlisted.

So had a number of other Harvard seniors and Felton was not pleased with the behavior of these young Turks, defying all tradition to leave college two months before graduation. Harvard College was Harvard College. What right did a mere war have to interfere with the orderly processes of education? What were these young men going to do about commencement? Dr. Holmes did not know. Dr. Felton informed Dr. Holmes that it seemed apparent that Wendell was no longer a candidate for the bachelor's degree.

Dr. Holmes withdrew. Young Holmes and his other Harvard friends who had rushed to enlist would have accepted Felton's judgment. They expected to be sent south to fight the war as soon as their training was complete. But that was not the view of the authorities. The 4th Battalion finished its training, and then its members were returned to Boston and Cambridge and told they would have no further duties at the moment except to drill when called upon.

Private Wendell Holmes had expected to be in battle. Instead, he found himself back at home wondering what he was going to do to get into the fight. He went to see his cousin, Colonel Henry Lee, to apply for a commission. Then, having nothing better to do, he went back to finish the academic year at Harvard.

On the morning of June 21, the class of '61 assembled in front of Holworthy Hall and marched to the First Church, the church of Abiel Holmes until the quarrel with the congregation had taken it from him. The class day exercises reeked with tradition and Brahminism. Holmes the father had been poet of the class of '29, and so Holmes the son was poet of the class of '61. The faculty was not pleased with young Mr. Holmes, however. As editor of the Harvard magazine he had made "rude and unbecoming allusions to members of the faculty." By joining the army, he sacrificed his position as a class leader. Only the leaders of the class took part in the commencement exercises, the greatest accolade Harvard could bestow. Wendell, Jr., was now denied, cast into the bottom of the pit. He was given no commencement role.

Commencement came on July 21. That young Holmes did not have a part in it pained his father far more than Wendell. Young Wendell's interest was in that commission. He did not even attend commencement.

Dr. Holmes did all he could to help his boy get what he wanted, and because he was Oliver Wendell Holmes, Boston Brahmin, he succeeded. When Colonel Lee said it was going to be difficult because he had so many applications, Dr. Holmes went to see Colonel William Greene, who was organizing another regiment. He pulled strings. He went to see Governor Andrew. Andrew was a Free-

Soiler, one of those who "bled for Kansas." Most Brahmins detested Andrew as a common politician, and not one of the anointed of the Somerset Club; but Holmes liked him well enough that he wanted to put the governor up for the Saturday Club.

The governor spoke to his secretary, and Colonel Lee received a letter. Private Oliver Wendell Holmes of the 4th Massachusetts became Lieutenant Holmes of the 20th. Lieutenant Holmes found it was not so hard when your father was a literary lion.

For years the lion had refused to consider what might happen if the wedge were driven between the states. Now it had happened, and his whole concern was that the Union triumph and the country be made whole again. If this had to be done by the sword, then he had furnished one of the sword-bearers. He would do what he could to further the Union cause.

The doctor had also gone to war. Once the fatal shot was fired at Fort Sumter, he did not hesitate a moment. His weapons would be the pen and the podium. For four years he would encourage the soldiers, praise the home-front workers, shame the slackers, and lift up the hearts of the weary.

"Whatever miseries this war brings us," he wrote for *The Atlantic*'s September issue, "it is making us wiser, and we trust, better. Wiser, for we are learning our weaknesses, our narrowness, our selfishness, our ignorance, in lessons of sorrow and shame. Better, because all this is noble in men and women and is demanded by the time; and our people are rising to the standard the time calls for. . . ."

These were brave words. The first battle of Bull Run had been fought before they became type. The Union troops attacked, faltered under counterattack, panicked, broke, and ran.

The words were finding full meaning in Holmes's own life, too. No one could say that Dr. Oliver Wendell Holmes was doing less than his duty to family, commonwealth, country, and to God. He could not be in the front lines in 1861—he was fifty-two years old—but he regarded himself as a soldier every bit as much as the lieutenant in blue who was heading on a circuitous route to a little place on the Virginia bank of the muddy Potomac, called Ball's Bluff.

20

THE FIRST LEAF FALLS
FROM DR. HOLMES'S BOUGH

WITH THE DEPARTURE OF HIS SON ON THE ARDUOUS TRAIL OF WAR, Holmes threw himself with a new ardor into his teaching. Ever since the Reverend Abiel had given him a magnifying glass when he was a boy, Holmes had been interested in optics. He had invented a hand stereopticon; with it, Neddie could put a photograph of the old gambrel-roofed house in Cambridge in each side of the slide carrier, look through the lenses, and the photo popped out, with the bushes standing out in front and the line of poplars quite visible *behind* the house.

Holmes could have patented the hand stereopticon and made a considerable amount of money from it, but he did not. He was a Brahmin, not a merchant. He gave the idea away.

Most of Holmes's work with lenses involved microscopes for the laboratory and dissecting room. He had brought home with him from Paris a Raspail microscope. Over the years he had sent for better ones from Paris and then from Germany. He bought one of the celebrated Oberhaeusers. He enlisted the assistance of Professor

Agassiz in the preparation of slides. He adapted the microscope for his students' use in the classroom, to show his young men ovum of toad, trachea of silkworm, blood of frog, tail of tadpole, and skin of human. He had been offering a course in microscopy since 1855. He was, in other words, teaching histology as well as anatomy, at no extra charge.

With the outbreak of the war, for the first time in her life Amelia Holmes also moved into the public eye. She insisted on doing something to help in the war effort. She joined the Massachusetts Sanitary Commission, whose members rolled bandages and prepared medicines. Soon the governor made her head of the commission in Boston.

In October 1861, as Amelia left morning after morning for the Sanitary Commission, Holmes was busy preparing a coming series of lectures. His first lecture would be "Border Lines in Medical Knowledge," in which he intended to show the incoming students how wide were the fields of medical ignorance, how vast was the unplowed ground for them to conquer. He was particularly concerned with the interaction of brain and body function. *Elsie Venner* had indicated what was in his mind. It was an unknown field he called "anthropology" (which is now a misnomer), but what he was talking about was *psychology* and *psychiatry*.

Holmes was still preparing on October 21, a little more than two weeks before the introductory lecture was scheduled, when his friend James Freeman Clarke came to the house on Charles Street with a message: word had been received that the 20th Massachusetts had engaged the enemy at Ball's Bluff, on the Potomac. Colonel Lee had been captured. Of twenty-two officers in the regiment, only eight had been unhurt. Clarke was sorry to tell them that Wendell was listed among the seriously wounded.

Had it been possible, the doctor would have leaped aboard a train and rushed to treat his son. But he did not even know where Wendell was. A telegram allayed their worst fears—Wendell was still alive. Then came a letter the lieutenant had written October 23, in which he described what he had seen of the battle and how he had been wounded.

The lieutenant's letter was followed by others. When Oliver Wendell Holmes, Jr.'s, name became known, he had all the attention anyone could hope for. General Nathaniel Banks stopped by to talk to him. Lieutenant Colonel Francis Palfrey, who had taken over the regiment after Colonel Lee's capture, wrote Dr. Holmes that Wendell was doing remarkably well: "Today I found him smoking and deriving much satisfaction from the contemplation of the photographs of certain young ladies . . ."

When a writer for *Harper's Weekly* discovered that Oliver Wendell Holmes, Jr., was in the hospital, he wrote that young Holmes had been "wounded in the breast; not in the back; no, not in the back." The Massachusetts men comported themselves well in the battle, unlike the troops at Bull Run, unlike two regiments around them who had fired and fled. It seemed important to make that clear, to show that all Yankees did not turn tail and run, as the Confederates said sneeringly. And so the 20th had its share of publicity—not more than its share. Even the "Seceshes" were saying Massachusetts would have suffered fewer casualties if the troops had not refused to surrender.

Within the week, Lieutenant Holmes was moved to the Hallowell house in Philadelphia, where the Quaker family of a college friend made sure he had the finest medical attention.

Holmes managed to get down from Boston. He found Wendell "fat and in good spirits," he who on the first night in the field had been certain he was going to die.

With his usual energy, Dr. Holmes took charge. He engaged rooms at the Fifth Avenue Hotel in New York, and wrote Amelia in Boston that he and Wendell were coming and the hero should have his sister's room, which was lighter and airier than his own. He engaged a whole section of six seats on the coach, and had a mattress thrown across them for the lieutenant.

After the hero arrived at 21 Charles Street, that first day there were three callers, two young women and his cousin, John T. Morse, Jr., "Fatty" of the old days. On the second day Dr. Henry Jacob Bigelow, Holmes's long-time associate, came and probed the wound, while Dr. Holmes assisted with the ether. He pronounced it clear, and thereafter the doctors let the wound alone to heal.

Admiring young ladies came from all the Brahmin haunts of

Boston to comfort the stricken warrior. He told the tale of Ball's Bluff so often that it came out like a recitation. Holmes's friends came, too: Professor Agassiz and President Felton, to whom the war had become a reality almost matching Harvard College, with the shedding of so much Harvard blood. British novelist Anthony Trollope dropped by, a big, beefy, red-faced Englishman wearing spectacles, and cracking jokes in a great loud voice. With a tinge of envy, the doctor noted that "the young hero" received visits *"en grand seigneur."* For the first time, Holmes was not the center of attention in his own house. By December, young Holmes was walking. A week later he accompanied his father to breakfast at the Fieldses' down the street. Publisher Fields was entertaining Charles F. Browne, who wrote as "Artemus Ward" and was as famous as Holmes.

The lieutenant was at home for several months. When he was able to move about he was called back to duty, but it was recruiting duty. It was March 1862 before he returned to his regiment to be promoted to captain.

All Holmes's conservatism was behind him. He carried on a continual correspondence with Motley, who had been appointed minister to Vienna. He wrote Motley about the "shoddy" manufacturers who would cheat the men at the front for monetary profit, delivering rotten food and faulty military supplies and equipment.

"You know better than I do the contrivances of that detested horde of mercenary partisans who would in a moment accept Jeff Davis, the slave trade, and a southern garrison in New England . . ."

He wrote poems for dozens of occasions, fiery patriotic poems, such as "The Voyage of the Good Ship Union":

> Tis midnight; through my troubled dream
> Loud wails the tempest's cry;
> Before the gale, with tattered sail
> A ship goes plunging by.
> What name? Where bound?—The rocks around
> Repeat the loud halloo,
> —The good ship Union, Southward bound:
> God help her and her crew! . . .

Holmes was called to register for the draft, but Governor Andrew gave him a certificate of release. The doctor was deemed too valuable in what he was doing in Boston to go and pry bullets out of soldiers and saw off shattered arms and legs.

His relaxation was the Saturday Club. Holmes almost never missed a meeting of the Saturday Club that year. When Anthony Trollope came, of course nothing would do but that he must be brought to the club to meet the literati. He came to Holmes's end of the table. He talked so loud and laughed so hard that Lowell, who was sitting on Trollope's right, thought he might be deafened by this "cerberus." Lowell was also taken aback by Trollope's vivid description of his working habits: he would arise at five and write before breakfast, writing just so many pages each day, "just like a shoemaker on a shoe, only taking care to make honest stitches."

Holmes listened to all this, smiling. Trollope mentioned Madeira. Holmes leaped into the conversation.

"You don't know what Madeira is in England."

That was a typical Holmesian ploy, guaranteed to start an argument.

"I'm not so sure it's worth knowing."

"Connoisseurship is with us a fine art. There are men who will tell you a dozen kinds, as Dr. Waagen would know a Carlo Dulci from a Guido."

"They might be better employed."

"What is worth doing is worth doing well."

"Ay, but that's begging the whole question. I don't admit it's worth doing at all. If they earn their bread by it, it may be *worse* doing . . ."

Here Trollope erupted in such loud laughter at his own joke that he nearly deafened Lowell.

Holmes was pained.

"But you may be assured . . ."

"No, but I mayn't be asshored. I won't be asshored, I don't intend to be *ass*hored . . ."

Lowell could scarcely hear anything now.

And so it went. No matter what Holmes said, Trollope cut him down, and then defended himself with such furious laughter that no one could hear the doctor's ripostes.

Meanwhile Emerson and Lowell, turning away from the fray, had a good talk about the latest literary fad. But finally Trollope turned to Lowell, too, and roared out that England was the only country in the world where such a thing as a peach was really understood.

Lowell appealed to Hawthorne for aid.

Hawthorne just sat there, looking at them from behind his beard. Then Hawthorne spoke.

"I asked an Englishman once who was praising their peaches to describe to me what he meant by a peach, and he described something very much like a cucumber . . ."

That put Trollope down. The friends of the Saturday Club liked to see Dr. Holmes humbled now and again, but when it came right down to it, the club was not only for admiration, but it was also a mutual protection society.

If 1861 was a hard and uncertain year, 1862 turned out to be even more so. That summer, Sarah Wendell Holmes died in the gambrel-roofed house in Cambridge, where she had lived all those years since Abiel's death with Holmes's younger brother, John.

And then, on September 17, came another of those dreaded telegrams.

Wendell had been wounded at the battle of Antietam. This time he had been shot in the neck. He was discovered lying in a farmhouse by William LeDuc, an officer of General Dana's staff. The surgeon shook his head.

"It's my duty to try and save those who have a chance of recovery. This officer has none."

All the doctor would tell LeDuc was that he might wash off the blood, plug up the wound with lint, and give the officer a pill of opium. Then let the officer keep quiet—and die.

LeDuc did what he was told to do, then sent the telegram to Dr. Holmes in Boston.

The wound was much less serious than it appeared. Captain Holmes recovered enough in three days to be on his feet, and he went to Hagerstown, again en route to Philadelphia. In Hagerstown he was taken in by Mrs. Howard Kennedy, who did her part for the Union by nursing wounded soldiers. At her house Wendell met an attractive young woman. He wrote his father not to bother coming to meet him. He would be home in a few days. He was an adult now, he indicated, and expected to be treated as one.

But Dr. Holmes had started off on the morning of the eighteenth to search for Wendell.

He wanted, of course, to be sure that his son was getting the best treatment. But how much was the precipitate rush southward due to the father's own insistence on being involved in the war and seeing some of it for himself? Dr. Holmes moved south, stopping to talk to people along his way, and savoring the sights and sounds of the danger zone.

On September 25, he encountered Captain Holmes on the Hagerstown-Philadelphia train.

"How are you, boy?"

"How are you, Dad?"

The captain was obviously not overjoyed to see his father.

Again, the Holmes prominence smoothed their way back to Boston. The president of the Philadelphia, Wilmington, and Baltimore Railroad was Harvard President C. C. Felton's brother. He arranged for a special couch to be put aboard a car destined for New York. Holmes and Captain Holmes traveled in style. They stayed at the Fifth Avenue Hotel again, and the doctor left his son for a while to go out about the city and absorb the atmosphere.

All this, as the captain observed sourly to himself, was obvious preparation for an article. When they returned to Boston, Holmes wrote "My Search After the Captain," which appeared in the December issue of *The Atlantic Monthly*.

It was a matter that hung between father and embarrassed son for years thereafter.

Captain Holmes was soon well and with his regiment, but he was wounded in the heel in May 1863, and again back in the airy room of the house that overlooked the Charles River.

Dr. Holmes watched over him, and assumed he kept Wendell's spirits up with jokes: Dr. Bigelow had fashioned a plug of carrot to keep the heel wound open and draining properly. Dr. Holmes came into the sickroom and pinched Wendell's heel to test the feeling in it.

"What vegetable have I turned your carrot into?"

"I don't know."

"Why into a Pa'snip."

No laughter.

Dr. Holmes's jokes needed a larger audience; that was the trouble: Wendell knew his father would use the story just that way.

But if the doctor was not totally appreciated in the bosom of his family, he was stoutly defended by his friends of the Saturday Club. When Emerson read "My Search After the Captain," he was impelled to write in his journal:

> What a convivial talent is that of Wendell Holmes! He is still at his Club, when he travels in search of his wounded son; has the same delight in his perceptions, in his wit, in its effect which he watches as a belle the effect of her beauty; would still hold each companion fast by his sprightly, sparkling, widely allusive talk, as at the Club table; tastes all his own talent, calculates every stroke, and yet the fountain is unfailing, the wit excellent, the *savoir vivre* and *savoir parler* admirable.

The reaction of Oliver Wendell Holmes, Jr., to "My Search After the Captain" was never recorded.

In 1862 and 1863 such poetical writing as Holmes undertook had strongly patriotic overtones. For the Phi Beta Kappa dinner he composed a song about old graduates, but it was really about youth of the new generation giving their lives for their country. After the second battle of Bull Run, he wrote "Never or Now," to help the faltering recruiting drive.

> Listen young heroes; your Country is calling,
> Time strikes the hour for the brave and the true!
> Now, while the foremost are fighting and falling,
> Fill up the ranks that have opened for you! . . .

Nobody ever measured the effectiveness of Holmes's poetry, but such patriotic fervor did have its influence. He was worried lest it not be strong enough; he had brought himself to such an emotional state about the war that he attacked those who did not share it. Victims of "spiritual anemia" he called them.

Holmes's war effort consisted of his writing for *The Atlantic* and a return to the lecture platform with "The Inevitable Trial," which he delivered as the Fourth of July oration in the city of Boston's celebration of 1863.

Holmes addressed himself to the major questions before the Union: could the war succeed?—there was doubt about it in 1863 in Boston. Did not the open sympathy of Europe for the South make separation inevitable? Should not the Union seek a negotiated peace?

No, answered Holmes. "We are fighting for our existence." He spoke of the Constitution, the Declaration of Independence; he termed the war a holy war, and he called upon citizens of Boston to renew themselves for the effort that lay ahead.

It was a stirring speech, coming from a favorite character of the city, not a politician, but a patriot, and it moved his audience.

Speeches, poems, hymns, all were dedicated to the cause that year. Governor Andrew spoke of Holmes's value to the commonwealth. The Saturday Club members said he had "come to the rescue" after the second battle of Bull Run.

The Saturday Club never faltered, though Motley and others were off on the nation's business. A dozen members attended every meeting. In 1864 they celebrated the three-hundredth anniversary of Shakespeare's birth, and of course the tercentenary poem was written and recited by Holmes.

Hawthorne did not come to Boston often in those days, but once, Holmes encountered him at Fields's during breakfast, and they began to talk.

"By the way, I would write a new novel if you were not in the field, Mr. Hawthorne."

"I am not. And I wish you would do it."

"I wish you would come to the club oftener."

"I should like to, but I can't drink."

"Neither can I."

"Well, but I can't eat."

"Nevertheless we should like to see you."

"But I can't talk either."

"You can listen, though, and I wish you would come."

At the end of March 1864, Hawthorne came from the country and stopped off a few days to see publisher Fields. Hawthorne's family was worried about him and wanted Holmes to have a look at him. Holmes found Hawthorne a sick, shrunken man, nearly deaf, heading south to see if a warmer climate would restore his health. The doctor could see the shadow of death on his friend's pale brow.

On May 19 Hawthorne died in New Hampshire, and five days later Holmes and the other old friends went to Concord to bury him. Longfellow was there, and Emerson, Channing and Judge Hoar, Agassiz and Lowell, publisher Fields. It was as if the Saturday Club—the *Atlantic* group, the literati of New England—had all gathered at once in that one place, Hawthorne's Sleepy Hollow, with Franklin Pierce, a former President of the United States, to honor this giant.

New England's spring did its best for them that day; the sun was bright and the day warm with a gentle breeze. The dark green of the pines and the light green of the burgeoning maples intertwined. The church was festooned with delicate white blossoms and Holmes remarked that it seemed more a happy meeting than a funeral.

The Reverend James Freeman Clarke read the service in church and at the grave, where the apple blossoms wafted above the naked earth.

The clods dropped. And then they all came home, Holmes, Emerson, Longfellow; silent together. The first of them had gone. The light of literary Boston was dimmed a little.

CHAPTER

21

THE SUCCESSFUL FAILURE
OF *THE GUARDIAN ANGEL*

HOLMES'S WRITINGS FOR *The Atlantic* COMPRISED WHAT FIELDS called the best war articles in the magazine. In the spring of 1864 Fields was after him for another serial novel about life in America, but Holmes refused to write it, even though Fields tempted him with money and excellent publishing terms.

Holmes said he was turning down the offer for two reasons: first, he wanted to devote all possible time to his professorship. Second, Holmes said, "I have no particular need for money . . . and am willing to wait until the stimulus is a little stronger. . . ."

Wendell was off at the front, drawing his captain's pay. The demands on the Holmes purse were not great. But would Hawthorne have said the same, or Emerson, or Longfellow, that they would not write because they did not need money? There was something modern in Holmes's attitude, more like a twentieth-century "professional" or a performer than a major literary figure.

In this sense, a poem Holmes wrote six years before described his attitude:

CONTENTMENT

"Man wants but little here below"

Little I ask; my wants are few;
I only wish a hut of stone.
(A *very plain* brown stone will do.)
That I may call my own;
And close at hand is such a one,
In yonder street that fronts the sun.

Plain food is quite enough for me;
Three courses are as good as ten;
If Nature can subsist on three,
Thank Heaven for three. Amen!
I always thought cold victual nice;
My *choice* would be vanilla ice . . .

In the words of another era, Holmes said he did not want to be a rich man, he just wanted to live like one. Or, in the idiom of the Saturday Club—stolen from Motley—if life would provide him with the luxuries, he would be glad to dispense with the necessities.

He was called upon for literary advice by aspiring young writers, many of whom came bearing letters from mutual friends. T. B. Aldrich submitted a number of poems and asked the doctor what he thought of them.

Aldrich and all young poets ran the same dangers, Holmes said. "The first is being spoiled by the praise of women, the second being disgusted by the praise or blame—it matters little difference which —of the cheap critics. You may have noticed that our poets do not commonly ripen well, they are larks in the morning, sparrows at noon, and owls before evening. . . ."

Holmes dealt with it all, assisted by Amelia. He was unfailingly jolly, friendly, and helpful.

He would often call on publisher Fields in his offices at the Corner Bookstore and pass a few minutes of light conversation. One day he came in, carrying a small book under his arm, and behaved mysteriously. It was, he said, the most marvelous book, the most valuable book, a unique book, the richest book he had ever opened. And he carried on thus until Fields and his companion were dying for the name of this work. Then, as Holmes dropped off his manuscript and was closing the door behind him, he twinkled at them. The book? Oh, yes, it was Nat Upshur's checkbook—Nat Upshur being the richest miser in all Boston.

Holmes got on well with his publisher, and Fields liked to show the doctor off as the most glittering jewel of his writing collection. Two or three times a week Fields would arrange those literary breakfasts at his house, and Holmes almost always came down the street to join in. Most of the literary figures of America came to Fields's one time or another; Mrs. Fields * suggested later that the only one who did not was Edgar Allan Poe. Since Poe died in 1849, he, then, could be forgiven. Sometimes Lowell would be there, and he and Holmes would always talk, talk, talk.

"I like your lyrics, you know, Holmes."

"Well . . . but there is something hopping about them. To tell the truth, nothing has injured my reputation so much as the too great praise that has been bestowed upon my 'windfalls.' After all the value of a poet to the world is not so much his reputation as a writer of this or that poem, as the fact that the poet is known to be one who is rapt out of himself at times, and carried away into the region of the divine; it is known that the spirit has descended upon him, and taught him what he should speak."

That casual breakfast comment was as shrewd an analysis of Holmes's own work as was ever made. Holmes sensed that he would go down in history as a minor poet—if at all.

Holmes knew that his literary talent was slender. Oddly enough, the charmed circle of Boston and Concord seemed to favor Holmes's work more than that of any other. Lowell, for example, could not bear Walt Whitman; Emerson criticized Longfellow and Longfellow criticized Hawthorne, who criticized Emerson; but few of them found it in their hearts to be critical of Holmes. Perhaps because

* This was Annie Fields, the publisher's second wife. Eliza, his first wife, had died tragically a few months after their marriage.

his bright spirit buoyed them up, the others forgave him everything.

There was a good deal of back scratching in the Boston literary community in those days. Holmes often asked Fields to get notices and reviews of the works of friends into *The Atlantic*. Holmes introduced Lowell's "Biglow Papers" in the magazine. And the literati were always advising one another on future courses. Harriet Beecher Stowe, with whom Holmes had become quite friendly during the war years, wanted him to do a book on religion. Fields wanted that novel that Holmes had spoken to Hawthorne about writing, and shortly after the war ended he began pressing Holmes to get down to it.

Holmes had been moved from mild irritation to outright anger by some of the criticism of *Elsie Venner*. The quarrel went back even further; in the Autocrat papers Holmes had deplored the Calvinist methods of teaching children religion. In "The Chief End of Man," his 1858 lecture, he criticized the catechism of the Congregationalists. Many groups objected to that lecture. The Winchester Library Association asked him for a lecture and stipulated that it be any but "The Chief End of Man."

"No," said the doctor briskly, "it will be that or none."

"None."

So it was none. The Library Association retreated angrily. Holmes stood his ground belligerently.

His religious philosophy, which Mrs. Stowe wanted him to expand in a book, was akin to Ibsenism. It was a demand for individualism and a plea that each person be allowed to follow the moral dictates of his own conscience. This attitude frightened and infuriated the conservative Protestant religious leaders.

Holmes was accused of "religious parricide" in his literary treatment of his father. He was called a pagan. One divine suggested that Harriet Beecher Stowe was in bad company when she associated with the likes of Holmes in the pages of *The Atlantic Monthly*. *The Atlantic* was supposed to be a "family paper," said one preacher, and, as such, was no place for such irreligious outrage.

The attacks were so annoying to Holmes that he let himself be tempted to reply in the fifth installment of *The Professor at the*

Breakfast Table, entitled "The Professor Finds a Fly in His Tea-cup."

That answer brought about wrathful frothings from the religionists. The Boston *Recorder* (as virulent as any publication in its castigation of Dr. Holmes) said his writings were the product of a sick brain. The *Recorder* also attacked *The Atlantic* for publishing Holmes. The New York *Courier and Enquirer* accused Holmes of "poisoning the minds of the people."

The uproar grew to be so great that some friends of *The Atlantic* predicted mournfully that unless Lowell and Fields took Holmes out of the magazine, the whole venture was headed for the ash can.

All concerned weathered the diatribes, but Holmes did not forget them. No one in his household did either, because he talked endlessly about his troubles.

Thus when Fields pressed Holmes for the new novel, the extremists of Protestantism were much on Holmes's mind. Amelia had borne more criticism of her husband than she cared to do. She was torn in the growing quarrel between Holmes and her older son, the captain, who had taken exception to Holmes's use of him as a sort of guinea pig.

For years Holmes's writings had made sidelong references to his homelife. But Oliver Wendell Holmes, Jr., was a grown man. He had been three times wounded in the war, and suffered through many campaigns. He came home because that was what one did if one were from Harvard and Boston in 1865. At home he recuperated from wounds and illness in the last year of the war. When he was well enough, he decided to study the law. Or, rather, his father helped him decide. He was, the younger Holmes said, "kicked into the law" by his father. There was ample reason for it: Holmes's brother John had been a lawyer practicing in Boston briefly before he retired to be a Cambridge gentleman and the strong arm of their mother. Holmes's father-in-law, Justice Charles Jackson, had been an important figure, a judge of the Massachusetts Supreme Court.

There was a certain tension in the household in 1865. Wendell was living at home, largely because of the high expense of living away from home. Ned was a sophomore at Harvard, and Little

Amelia was a gregarious social butterfly on the Boston scene. They were all, every one of the five of them, highly opinionated, and except for Wendell, vivacious people. The older son of the doctor was inclined more to introspection.

The blush of remembrance of "My Search . . ." was still with him. And Dr. Holmes did not help matters on the home front at the Harvard commemoration day on July 21, 1865, when the whole family went to Cambridge and he presented a lyric poem in celebration of peace, a sort of antidote to Lowell's heavier ode.

> Tell us, O father, as thine arms enfold
> Thy belted first-born in their fast embrace,
> Murmuring the prayer the patriarch breathed of old,—
> "Now let me die, for I have seen thy face!"
>
> Tell us, O mother,—nay, thou canst not speak,
> But thy fond eyes shall answer, brimmed with joy,—
> Press thy mute lips against the sunbrowned cheek,
> Is this a phantom,—thy returning boy?

Oliver Wendell Holmes, Jr., late a captain, brevet colonel of the Union army, sat there in his uniform, squirming. There was his father again, exposing the whole family's emotions.

The other members of the Holmes family were all very private persons, perhaps because Holmes was so much a public person. The antics of husband and father embarrassed them too. Amelia was a woman of strong character—she had to be to live with Oliver Wendell Holmes.

Holmes gave an indication of her spark in a scene after the Fieldses gave the family a fine new barometer to celebrate the housewarming at 21 Charles Street.

The barometer had been delivered. Holmes said it should hang in his study, "where I can look at it at least once an hour every day of my life."

Amelia said the barometer should go in the parlor, where the rest of the family could enjoy it.

"Why no, my dear; the study is the place."

"I'm sure it should go in the parlor. It's too handsome for your old den."

"I shall keep it in the study."

"I don't think that's fair."

"I'm sorry. Can't help it."

"It's too, too, bad."

Holmes began humming "Mid pleasures and palaces . . ."

But Amelia would not listen.

"I will have it, you horrid . . ."

The irrepressible doctor put all that scene into a letter which he sent the Fieldses to tell them just how much the Holmeses enjoyed the gift barometer.

Living in that atmosphere, Amelia and the others became even more private, she as much to protect the children from Holmes's literary exploitation as for any other reason.

Thus, while James T. Fields was pressing Holmes exuberantly for a new novel, Amelia was using all her powers of persuasion to keep him away from the literary lists. But "money," Holmes said, "is an argument of great weight to all those who . . . are surrounded by numerous family."

And surrounded Holmes was in the beginning of 1866: there were his two sons' clothing, books and fees, cash for Ned's board, and spending money for all three. Little Amelia needed a decent wardrobe, as she was expected to conduct her share of entertainments for the young women who waited in Brahmin style to be carried off by knights in Boston broadcloth. Big Amelia had to have a cook and maid to run the house and help her to attend to her duties as a matron of society, and Holmes had his club and his various societies and his never-ending spending on exhibits for his medical lectures, for which the university showed much intellectual enthusiasm but considerably less financial support.

So, in spite of Amelia's distaste, Holmes succumbed to Fields's arguments and began work on the new novel.

By the end of the summer Holmes had completed a part of the book. Since he had sold the Pittsfield house, and particularly since the death of his mother, he and the family often went to Cambridge to visit his brother John, and stay in the gambrel-roofed house.

Holmes had taken over his father's old study and did some of his writing there; in the summer it was far more pleasant to be in Cambridge than in Boston. But by mid-September he was working on the book in the Charles Street house, and had finished the outline and enough of it that he was willing to show it nervously to Fields. The publisher came to the Holmes house one evening and went into Holmes's study.

What he read was the tale of a young girl, Myrtle Hazard, fifteen years old, but proportioned more like a woman than a young girl, who, as the book opened, had disappeared. Her guardian, Miss Silence Withers, had placed an advertisement in the *State Banner* and *Delphian Oracle* (Holmes did love to have fun with his newspaper names). In Oxbow Village tongues were wagging, even as officers dragged the pond.

"They needn't drag the pond," said Miss Cynthia Badlam, thirty-five, second cousin of Miss Silence Withers. "They needn't go beating the woods as if they were hunting a partridge—although for that matter Myrtle Hazard was always more like a partridge than she was like a pullet. Nothing ever took hold of that girl—not catechizing nor advising, nor punishing. It's that dreadful will of hers never was broke. I've always been afraid that she would turn out a child of wrath . . ." Miss Badlam wept.

Miss Silence Withers, with whom Miss Cynthia Badlam dwelt, "was forty years old, a shadowy, pinched, sallow, dispirited, bloodless woman with the habitual look of the people in the funeral carriage which follows next to the hearse. . . ."

She agreed that their trial would not be so great if they only knew that Myrtle was dead. Myrtle was very much alive.

Earlier, in order to whip Myrtle into shape, Miss Silence had set out to teach her obedience. When Myrtle would not eat brown bread and went up to bed supperless, next morning, there was the untasted supper. When Myrtle would not touch it, she was carried to the garret and chained there.

"An awful place, festooned with cobwebs . . . worms gnawing day and night . . . old hairy spiders . . ."

Eighteen hours the child was kept in the garret, but remained unsubdued until rescued by the maid, Kitty Fagan, and carried off to her house and stuffed with goodies.

When Myrtle was ten she was wandering about the garret one day and came upon Uncle Malachi, who had done away with himself. "That was a shock."

Now, a returned fifteen-year-old Myrtle had visions. Myrtle had fever. Myrtle was unconscious and the doctor came. He left. The Reverend Mr. Stoker came. He wanted to "establish intimate spiritual relations with her."

Soon they were taking long walks, and one evening in the beeches he asked her to sit down by him.

"No," she answered, with something that chilled him in her voice. "We will not stay here any longer. It is time to go home."

Myrtle had a mysterious dream. The Reverend Mr. Stoker had made an assignation with her in his study, making sure no one else was about, but in the nick of time, the night before, came the dream. In the dream she saw—her guardian angel showed her—the true reptilian nature of the Reverend Mr. Stoker. His wicked designs on her body became clear to her. Myrtle sent him a note. She would not come.

"The Reverend Mr. Stoker uttered a cry of rage . . ."

In the end, Myrtle found love and happiness. As for the Reverend Mr. Stoker, the church fell on him and flattened him like a pancake.

Fields spent two hours in the Holmes study, and emerged "perfectly enchanted." "The perfect fruit of life," he called it. And should not James T. Fields know? He had raved over Hawthorne's *The Scarlet Letter*, and it had made that author. He had whipped Whittier's work into shape, not afraid to force changes in words and rhymes. He had published Edward Everett Hale's *The Man Without a Country*, as poignant a bit of patriotic fluff as ever captured the imagination of an entire country.

Fields agreed to pay Holmes $250 apiece for twelve installments of *The Guardian Angel*! Holmes told Amelia triumphantly.

"I wish you wouldn't publish it, Mr. Fields. I wish Wendell would not publish anything more. It will only call down the newspaper criticism and where is the use?"

"Well, Amelia, I have written something now which the critics won't complain of. You see, it's better than anything I have ever done."

"Oh, that's what you always say, Wendell, but I wish you'd let it alone."

The two men brushed Amelia Holmes aside, and settled the details of publication. It would be the lead matter in *The Atlantic* for an entire year, and then it would be brought out in book form.

The first installment was published in January. The Calvinist community took one look and began to scream. By May the attackers were virtually running amok in the literary world.

Holmes was not prepared for the fury of the religionists; neither was Fields. But what hurt most was an attack in the new New York magazine, *The Nation*.

The Nation was edited by E. L. Godkin, who was as fine an editor in his own way as Fields. But like many a new publication, *The Nation* needed to acquire a firm circulation foundation. One way to stimulate interest was to attack "the biggest kid in town"—and the biggest magazine in American intellectual circles was undoubtedly *The Atlantic*. So when *The Nation* was founded, Godkin shrewdly turned the magnifying glass on *The Atlantic*, searching for weaknesses where his stiletto would draw blood and attract readers.

The searching was done by a *Nation* columnist named John R. Dennett. He picked through *The Atlantic* and did not like much that he saw there. He did not like *The Guardian Angel*. He charged that Holmes's work was reeking with sexuality, and compared it most unfavorably to Henry James's *Poor Richard*, which was running in *The Atlantic* at the same time.

Dennett was joined by hundreds of Calvinist preachers who aimed their fire at *The Atlantic*. Holmes was trying to do for his generation what Sinclair Lewis did much more skillfully in *Elmer Gantry* a half century later: scathe the erring preacher. Although when parishioners found *The Guardian Angel* distasteful and canceled subscriptions by the hundreds, Fields never backed away. The book was brought out in the fall of 1867, and the adverse critics had a new chance to throw bricks. Critic Dennett again took on the distinguished author:

When he had written "The Autocrat of the Breakfast Table," Dr. Holmes would have done well, as it has since appeared, if he had ceased from satire. That series of papers gave him a brilliant reputation, which from that time forward he has gone on damaging, diminishing it by each new book, diminishing the brilliance of it at any rate, though it may well be that he has extended it among more people. He has never stopped hammering at the same nail which he hit on the head when he first struck. "The Professor" took away something of the estimation in which we had been holding "The Autocrat"; "Elsie Venner" took away a little more; and "The Guardian Angel" takes away a larger portion than was removed by either of the others.

Under such brutal dissection and the thunder from fire-and-brimstone pulpits across the land, it might have been expected that book publication of *The Guardian Angel* would have been a failure. It went to twenty-three editions. So while Holmes and Fields had to suffer many slings and arrows, and some of Holmes's dearest friends tactfully reminded him of the genius he had shown in *The Autocrat*, both Fields and Holmes could commiserate, even cry, as they carried their earnings to the bank.

CHAPTER

22

THOSE PLEASANT EVENINGS
AT THE SATURDAY CLUB

ONE EVENING JUST BEFORE THE WAR, HOLMES, LOWELL, AND FIELDS
dined with a young man from the West—Ohio, to be exact. His
name was William Dean Howells. The twenty-three-year-old Howells had come to Boston in the certainty that there was "the hub
of the Universe," as Holmes had said, to ask for the job of assistant
editor of *The Atlantic Monthly*. Fields was just then in the process
of taking over the editorship from Lowell in order to save money,
and this was no time to be adding staff, so Howells did not get the
post. But he did strike Holmes and Lowell (and Fields) as an up-
and-coming young man, and the four hours of talk at the dinner
table in the Parker House put the seal on that opinion.

The young man was able to hold up his end of the talk, even
contribute bits from his western experience, so different from that
of Boston.

Here, at the height of the prestige of the Boston Brahmins,
Holmes recognized in Howells the presence of the "uncombed

youth who goes to college and startles the hereditary class leaders by striding past them all." The doctor had been thinking of some farm boy from Vermont or New Hampshire when he wrote those lines, but here was the creature in the flesh.

Holmes encouraged young Howells as best he could, and when the evening ended he turned to Lowell.

"Well, James, this is something like the Apostolic succession. This is the laying on of hands."

Lowell agreed. The youth would become *somebody*.

Holmes brought the young man from the West to his house. Howells became a friend of the family, and when he returned to Ohio he wrote frequently to Wendell, Jr. He also wrote to Fields, but the years went by and he did not get the *Atlantic* job.

In 1865 Howells secured a job as assistant to editor Godkin of *The Nation* in New York. Then Fields did offer Howells a job. Howells was quick to take it, and moved to what was undeniably the cultural capital of the nation.

In the days of Holmes's father Boston had been called the Athens of America. In 1855 the Reverend Theodore Parker had observed shrewdly that it was more like Dublin—full of Irishmen. Dr. Holmes would have called it the "Paris of the West," had he not been so imbued with Boston's importance in its own right.

And that was a part of the exasperating charm of the Boston Brahmins. In Providence they said, "Boston folks are full of no-tions." In New York they claimed that all Bostonians were born with spectacles so they could immediately assume the nearsighted "Boston look," which meant that one was examining with care every facet of the perplexing world. Some New Yorkers said that when you went to Boston you had to pass an entrance examination, and when you left, if they liked you, they gave you a sort of degree —"passed Boston."

Boston was already changing into the "Proper Bostonian" society dissected much later by Cleveland Amory. The merchant and banker were moving to the forefront as the whole United States built and prospered, prospered and built, in the two furious dec-ades that followed the Civil War. Businessmen were beginning to buy up the old houses on Beacon Hill and to mingle with Social

Boston and Financial Boston. They were even beginning to knock at the doors of the Saturday Club.

Publisher Fields brought all manner of people from all corners of the world to dine there. One evening Lowell would be telling tales about an educated parrot. Dana would have a funny story about an undertaker who married his assistant "because she was so handy in the business." Lowell would chide Longfellow for printing private verses that had been invented as tribute to Agassiz, who was on his way abroad. When Holmes was there, which was almost always unless he was sick with an asthmatic attack, he would discourse on homeopathy and call them all ignoramuses, with a little laugh that took away the sting, then he would say that if it were Longfellow talking about Dante, he, Holmes, would be the ignoramus.

Together this stellar company sent every guest away from the table with the feeling that he had been touched by some force.

That was the conceit and the glory of the Saturday Club. The members knew they were important, that words passed around the table would be repeated at a hundred Boston tables in the month that would intervene before their next meeting, and then travel to New York and Washington and even California. They came armed with their best manners and their best stories. The club had a reputation to uphold, and the members worked hard at keeping it up.

Many were invited, but few were chosen to join the distinguished ranks. Sometimes there was dissension, as when Charles Eliot Norton blew up after *all* the members he had proposed in one season were blackballed. Norton threatened to form a new club, and for a time Lowell seemed ready to join him. Holmes was not sympathetic. He believed in exclusivity. He also could be waspish, with a blackball or with a word. Once Lowell kept interrupting him when he talked, so Holmes stopped and turned petulantly to his friend, "Now James, let me talk and don't interrupt me."

But if one did not ever interrupt Dr. Holmes, there would be nothing but a monologue at his end of the table, and generally he recognized this fact. On one occasion, after a distinguished visitor had appeared and Holmes had hogged the conversation all evening so that the others did not get a word in, he got up from the table, apologizing. "I came to listen," he said, "and then I talked too much again. . . ."

When Bret Harte came to the club, he talked of having seen a rattlesnake, owl, and squirrel all living in the same hole in the ground. Not to be outdone, Dr. Holmes recalled how quickly a rattler's poison killed—he had seen a dog bitten by a rattlesnake (part of his research for *Elsie Venner*); the wound was treated immediately, but within thirty minutes the dog died.

Holmes then tried to turn the talk to one of his favorite subjects: homeopathy. Longfellow had been going to the homeopaths again. Longfellow exasperated Holmes as much as did his brother John Holmes sometimes, because after so many years Longfellow still had a lingering belief in homeopathy that Holmes had not been able to erase, despite many hours of argument across the dinner table. Longfellow simply sat, encased in that huge beard, and smiled at him benignly. Let his little friend rave on, the poet would continue on his way.

Bret Harte then raised the point—interesting to the crowd—that homeopathy seemed static, while medical science seemed dynamic, and having wrested the conversation back from Holmes, Bret Harte told more stories about the West.

When Agassiz was in town and at the club, he often dominated the meetings with his brilliant displays and an odd idea: at the time he suggested that if he could secure an elephant fetus, he would have the form of the mastodon. If he could find a tapir fetus, he would give them the megatherium. These were days in which the world was becoming conscious of the evolutionary processes, and discoveries of the petrified remains of prehistoric animals sent the Sunday supplements into hysteria. In all sincerity, one member asked Agassiz one evening if the dodo would have been good to eat. "Oh yes," said Agassiz, and then launched into long dissertation.

As the club's reputation spread, the newspaper reporters tried to get inside the Parker House. But publicity was sternly disallowed. One evening a reporter captured Dr. Holmes at the door as the club was assembling, and asked him how the club ran, how they proceeded at their meetings.

"Oh, we do nothing but tell our old stories."

Old stories, new stories, old stories with new endings, they told them all over the years. Holmes leaned on the club more as he grew older, and particularly as he came under serious criticism from outside. He was a shy man in many ways, although his ebullience masked it.

In these later years Holmes often referred back to his childhood. When Longfellow's translation of the *Divine Comedy* was published, he held readings; and Holmes went to most of them. He said it reminded him of *Pilgrim's Progress*, a book he held should never have been put in the hands of children, with its City of Destruction, and black-horned Apollyon, and Giant Despair.

Sometimes Holmes went afield to lecture, drawn by a generous fee. In the fall of 1867 he went to Montreal, where he came down with an attack of asthma.

One reason that Holmes was sacrificing himself once more to lecturing was his growing expenses. That year Wendell had his *Wanderjahr*, his chance at the grand tour that Holmes had managed to wring for himself with much difficulty from his reluctant family more than thirty years earlier. The doctor, who believed in traveling first class, would not suffer his son to do less. So he took on additional chores to find the money.

In the late 1860s Holmes played a very important role in the publication of *The Atlantic*—indeed, in much of all Fields published. Fields seemed to feel that Holmes was a good barometer of popular opinion.

Fields's health was beginning to fail, and he turned over ever more duties to others. Howells became all but editor of *The Atlantic* in 1868. All the control Fields retained was final say on what went into each issue. Howells selected, Howells edited, Howells was in touch with the authors.

In 1869 Fields took his wife Annie on a trip to Europe, and left the magazine in Howells' hands, but with the proviso that Howells would consult with James R. Osgood, his new partner, Lowell, and above all, Holmes.

Following the vendetta against Holmes over *The Guardian Angel*, there had been other disasters for *The Atlantic*, occasioned by the frantic outbursts of a beleaguered Calvinism. The British novelist Charles Reade had published *Griffith Gaunt*, a far more sensational sexual novel than anything brought out in America. Fields knew he was taking a chance by publishing it, but risked it, and brought down the wrath of the churchmen once more. The case brought more attention and more canceled *Atlantic* subscriptions.

Fields was prepared to accept that course again if need be, but in his absence he wanted the wiser, older heads to consult with Howells, so that if they got in trouble it would not be inadvertent.

Fields had scarcely left Boston when the trouble struck. It came in the form of an insistence by Harriet Beecher Stowe that she was going to expose Lord Byron to the world as a dreadful person who had committed incest with his half sister and deserted his innocent young wife for a succession of mistresses and a life of wickedness.

This was strong medicine for 1869, even though it concerned a figure who had died more than forty years earlier. Mrs. Stowe had burned for years with the heat of the secret entrusted to her by Lady Byron in 1857: that Byron's incest was the reason for the failure of her marriage. But Lady Byron had sworn Mrs. Stowe to secrecy until after her death, and although Lady Byron died several years earlier it had not seemed appropriate to disturb public memory with the sordid story.

But in 1869 the Countess Guiccioli published her memoirs. She had been Byron's mistress in his last years and she claimed that Byron had been driven to other women by his frigid wife.

This charge set Mrs. Stowe's blood aboiling.

Mrs. Stowe turned to *The Atlantic*, where she had been publishing regularly for years. In the absence of Fields, she asked Dr. Holmes's literary counsel. She was not asking, she said, whether she should publish the article; that was a foregone conclusion. But would he help her? She wanted his "delicacy and insight" to guide her.

Holmes and Mrs. Stowe had been friends since that day when the Stowes had been gently taken over the coals at the Saturday Club. Of course he would help her. So in time along came the manuscript. Howells read it and approved of the whole, although like everyone he found the concept shocking. Holmes read it, found her approach "chaotic," and suggested a number of changes, which he made for the most part, with Mrs. Stowe's approval.

He wrote Motley in London, warning him confidentially to expect a literary bombshell to drop in the middle of August when the September issue of *The Atlantic* came out. There was no question in his mind about the veracity of it—he accepted Mrs. Stowe's reportage. On the whole, he seemed to relish the scandal.

Lowell read it and thought it was dreadful, and did what he could to stop the whole process. But Holmes told him he could not stop it, only Mrs. Stowe could, and if *The Atlantic* did not publish it she was prepared to take it elsewhere.

When the September *Atlantic* came off the press with "The True Story of Lady Byron's Life," the explosion was immediate.

One of the difficulties might have been the heavy editing of Mrs. Stowe's article by her well-meaning friends. In the fashion of the day, the article did not call a spade a spade; Mrs. Stowe never declared flatly: Byron committed incest with his half sister Augusta Leigh. She was not even named, but any good Victorian could certainly draw conclusions from what *was* said: "He fell into the depths of a secret adulterous intrigue with a blood relation, so near in consanguinity that discovery must have been utter ruin and expulsion from civilized society . . ."

That was enough. Newspapers and periodicals on both sides of the Atlantic Ocean attacked the article, and then began on the author. The difficulty was that whatever the truth of the charge against Lord Byron and his half sister—nearly all the other "facts" in the article were incorrect. Mrs. Stowe said the marriage had lasted two years; in fact it had lasted only shortly over a year, and so on.

English critics suggested that Mrs. Stowe had been bedazzled by shoulder rubbing with a member of the British nobility. Americans, said these critics, were notoriously romantic about titles. In Mrs. Stowe's case it was true; she had been overwhelmed by her intimacy with Lady Byron on a trip to England, and for years dropped names outrageously.

The bad press stunned Mrs. Stowe. It was almost as bad for publisher Fields, who was in England when the dam burst. His friend

Dickens wrote him sadly, "Wish you had nothing to do with the Byron matter. Wish Mrs. Stowe was in the pillory."

Harder to take than the outright attacks were the malicious cartoons and jibes that appeared in the papers. Mrs. Stowe was depicted as a harpy and a keyhole snooper. If the Holmes uproar and the Reade affair had hurt *The Atlantic* sorely, the Lord Byron scandal was a disaster. It lost *The Atlantic* fifteen thousand subscribers, and although Howells succeeded to the editorship of *The Atlantic* that year and was to serve for ten years in the post, throughout his editorship the magazine never regained that circulation.

Mrs. Stowe was so upset she undertook a book to enlarge on the article. Fields, Osgood & Co. would publish it; they had to for their own sakes as well as that of their author. Holmes tried to be helpful. He wrote consoling letters to Mrs. Stowe encouraging the book because "I think we all perceive now that the battle is not to be fought here, but in England." He told her that he had been taking her side, and that on one occasion so had Henry James, Sr.

In it all, Holmes's sympathy was increased by his own Calvinist disapproval of Lord Byron. He assured Mrs. Stowe that she had done the right thing, ". . . that the true character of a man, who has diabolicized the literature of his century and hung his pure and injured wife in chains to dangle before all the unborn ribalds of coming generations, ought to be known. . . ."

At the September meeting of the Saturday Club the talk flew thick and fast. Tom Appleton, now "a portly medieval gentleman," was just back from London, with all the gossip about Byron and Mrs. Stowe from that side. The older members outdid themselves in their recollections. And down in New York, Jay Gould and Jim Fisk had just failed to corner the gold market, foiled in the end by the action of a President Grant who was not as beguiled as the conspirators had expected.

Holmes and his friends must have talked about it for hours.

23

JUST WHAT HAPPENED
TO THE POET?

AFTER THE BAD REVIEWS OF *The Guardian Angel* IN 1867 GAVE
Amelia every right to say "I told you so," the doctor had not written much. He produced little more than an occasional poem, a
lecture here and there, and the season's medical lectures for the
Harvard Medical School.

In the summer of 1869 the ever-optimistic publisher Fields asked
him for a third novel. Holmes replied vaguely: many other matters
had been on his mind and he had laid down the pen.

Personal, medical, and public matters were uppermost in
Holmes's mind. All three of his children were in the courting stage.
Ned was engaged to Henrietta Wigglesworth, whose family met the
Holmes's approval. It was true: Holmes was sixty years old and he
still had no grandchildren. That was because the strictures of
Brahminism produced a late-blooming race. Little Amelia was
twenty-six, and as yet unmarried. Wendell, Jr., was twenty-eight,
still living at home. He had just passed the bar examination and was
seeking appointment as a law lecturer at Harvard.

The medical school had been thrown into intellectual turmoil with the coming of Charles William Eliot as the new president of Harvard.

Most bothersome of all these matters was the messing about with his city by a government that seemed to have gone mad over "development." Dr. Holmes was having a great deal of trouble with the city fathers, who insisted that progress must bring some major changes in the flow of the Charles River that ran behind the Holmes house. For as long as anyone could remember the Charles had ambled comfortably down to the sea, its estuary growing wider and more circuitous from Cambridge onward. Holmes had bought the Charles Street house because it backed onto the tidal basin. He kept his boats literally in his backyard. The children had grown up "river rats," as had those of all the families along Charles Street.

Now in the middle of 1869 the commonwealth and the city proposed to fill in a large portion of the tidal basin of the Charles at the rear of Beacon Street. An association of property owners was formed, Dr. Holmes became one of its leaders, and they began to bombard the newspapers with letters.

But the government moved majestically onward in its superior purpose of crowding Boston in the same successful manner that the city fathers of Manhattan were doing "down south." One could not quarrel with success, could one? New York was growing bigger, richer, and more important all the time. Could Boston do less?

The matter came to a head in November with a public hearing in the Green Room of the statehouse on Beacon Hill. The eminent Dr. Holmes was the first witness called.

Identifying himself as a "moderate property owner" on Charles Street, Holmes launched into a recitation of the evils that would be brought by following the city plan. In his role as a concerned citizen, he reminded the fathers of the principle of good faith, under which people had brought property expecting it to remain untrammeled and unchanged. The city fathers did not bat an eye, it was not their problem.

He appealed to their pecuniary sensibilities: everyone concerned would lose money by the change. The city fathers were unmoved; it was not their money.

He changed roles, became the medical authority. The Charles tidal basin served as a cooler for the city. The flow of the westerly and southerly winds purified the hot, sticky air that came into Boston. If the authorities meddled with nature, the suppression of this ventilating area would have an adverse effect on the city's children. The city fathers let these warnings pass over their heads.

The medical Holmes spoke of erysipelas and hospital gangrene. He described the evils of cataracts. The city fathers were not moved.

Holmes saw himself failing and became the lecturer.

The project would be rash. Rash financially, dangerous to the harbor, threatening to the public health, ruinous to the beauty of the capital, unjust to the city, and dishonorable to the commonwealth. A city father looked at his watch.

Holmes the poet came forth. He talked softly of the mothers and children he saw walking out over the west Boston bridge for a breath of pure, clean air. The city fathers yawned.

Was he finished? they asked.

Holmes signified that he was.

Next witness.

Sadly, Holmes prepared to move his family from the house that had been so pleasant a home to them for a dozen years. He built a brick house at 296 Beacon Street. His library and the parlor and the dining room all faced the back, overlooking the river. The front was a narrow-windowed brownstone with a long flight of stone steps. Down below, the developers filled in his estuary and created Back Bay Boston.

If Dr. Holmes at sixty did not have much influence with the city government, still he was respected and virtually lifted to a pedestal in the Harvard community. His course in anatomy was as popular as ever, and if the sexagenarian was not quite as spry as he had been ten years earlier, the jokes had been refined, and the humor mellowed by experience. No one complained about Holmes as a teacher; no one would ever complain. But change came in quite another direction.

The same forces that had destroyed the Charles River estuary were at work to build a bigger and better Harvard. In the case of the medical school, it meant responding to the cries of the American Medical Association to lengthen the period of study for the medical profession.

Holmes had no objection to that course. He recalled M. Louis' long apprenticeship and advice to his students to accept a similar regimen. But the Louis method indicated more emphasis on clinical teaching. President Eliot and the Board of Overseers wanted to extend the lecture courses and add more of the new specialities of science.

Holmes called this ridiculous. "Just as certainly as we spin out and multiply our academic predilections we shall work in more and more stuffing, more and more rubbish, more and more irrelevant, useless detail which the student will get rid of just as soon as he leaves us."

"Do as I say," Holmes also warned, "not as I do." Back in 1865 Holmes had counseled a young correspondent who had written for advice on a medical career. The youth said that he, like Dr. Holmes, also felt the stirrings of the muse from time to time. What should he do?

"The country does not take to literary doctors," Holmes warned. The young man might be much better off to go into business if he felt he had literary substance in his soul. His own sons, he said, were going to devote themselves to the law. He hoped wholeheartedly.

For as Holmes grew older he accepted the judgments of his friends Dana and Motley that he had spread his seed too thin. Even in medicine it was becoming a danger, as the advocates of "pure science" gained influence. Holmes fought what he saw as an over-extension of the Harvard Medical School. The medical school, he said, ought to be designed to meet the needs of the general practitioner, and the rest should be left to the doctor himself.

The young reformers of the medical school had President Eliot's ear, however. Eliot, being "a new broom," was not hard to persuade into making major changes.

Holmes saw all this coming. He was amused in a way. When he had spoken about the possibility of bringing women into the medical profession, these reformers had been the first to object.

So much for "liberalism."

Since Holmes's Paris years, the center of scientific medicine had moved to Vienna and Berlin. The Germanic mind had organized medical education to a fine degree: it took five years of medical school and strict examination to make a Viennese doctor, as compared to the American system of three years, a total of twelve months of classes and perfunctory oral examinations.

Holmes was really above the battle. In the struggle the conservatives were led by Holmes's old friend Dr. Bigelow. Reform won the day—Emerson was a member of the Board of Overseers who sanctioned the revolution.

Holmes was not overly sad: his own situation was much bettered by the administrative changes that ended the fee system and gave him the highest salary of any medical professor. In fact, after Emerson had taken up the idea at the Saturday Club and Holmes got used to it, he was one of the most ardent and effective supporters of the change.

Holmes was, as usual, ahead of his time. He made the Phi Beta Kappa address for 1870 on the subject "Mechanism in Thought and Morals." He was carrying out psychological experiments in his laboratory many months before Harvard Medical School hired its first professor of psychology and medicine.

In the big house on Beacon Hill, Holmes was even more nearly deified than he was at the medical school. The fame of *The Autocrat* had submerged the criticisms of *The Professor* and the two novels that angered the Calvinist community. Time and gray hair had sanctified even the Autocrat's faults.

For many years, when notables came to Boston, Dr. Holmes was one of the treasures the community trotted out for inspection and admiration. When Chih Ta-jin, most exalted royal ambassador of the Middle Flowery Kingdom from far-off Peking came to "the hub," Mayor Nathaniel B. Shurtleff presided over the festivities. Anson Burlingame, the United States minister to China, was there, along with Senator Charles Sumner, General Irvin McDowell, Commodore John Rodgers, Emerson, President Hill of Harvard, the Reverend George Putnam, Whipple, and Dr. Holmes.

In 1871 the Grand Duke Alexis of Russia came. There was the usual state dinner, with Holmes, Boston's poet laureate, providing the verse. There was a grand ball, and Holmes donned white tie and tails and brought Amelia in her fine gown. The Duke gave a dinner for a handful of Boston's leaders, including Longfellow, Lowell, and Holmes.

This sort of attention was a fair barometer of Holmes's place in Boston at the height of its glory.

That year, Fields was virtually in retirement, but he continued to ask Holmes for something important for *The Atlantic*. Howells and Osgood were asking too, but Holmes felt more at home with his old friend. In the summer of 1870 he persuaded Fields to come to the Beacon Street house for an evening of talk, so that he might try out some of these literary ideas.

After that, he began work on "The Poet at the Breakfast Table."

Holmes's own breakfast table was a lively place, a training table for the Saturday Club, one might say. The doctor sometimes found the going rough, for little Amelia could talk even faster than her father—her friends said she could talk faster than the Reverend Phillips Brooks, and he held the championship as the fastest talker in Boston.

Wendell, Jr., was so bemused by the law (he brought his briefcase to the table with him) that he made no attempt to conquer through speed, but through force of argument. Wendell had learned to end his sentences with "but," which let him interrupt his father without being accused of rudeness.

Ned, the younger boy, was like his Uncle John; he cheerfully accepted a seat in the background and occasionally convulsed the table with an aside directed at the talker of the moment.

"The Poet at the Breakfast Table" was the mature Holmes. It was written nearly fifteen years after *The Autocrat*, and the differences showed.

These differences reflected much of what had happened in American life since 1857. One need not look so far to see the change, one need only travel by the new cars to Cambridge. The old, yellow, gambrel-roofed house was going up for sale to the Harvard Corporation. For years the pressure to sell had been intense, and by 1870 there seemed no sense in keeping the house any longer. Taxes were increasing. The house needed repairs. John Holmes was rattling around in it, and Holmes's thought that he might divide his time between Cambridge and Boston had not materialized. He seldom used the library he had taken over from his father. When one was sixty, he found, the need to move around was not so great. Harvard wanted the house, to tear it down and build a monolith to join the others. The brothers consulted: let the college have the house.

Right there in Boston the changes had been enormous. Boston Public Garden had a new equestrian statue of George Washington that reminded Holmes of Christian Rauch's statue of Frederick the Great in Berlin. Boston had built a huge coliseum for the Peace Jubilee of 1869. President Eliot was turning all Harvard University over "like a flapjack" beneath Holmes's gaze. Agassiz, the scientific naturalist, had ushered in a wave of specializing, and now the scientific scene was subdivided into specialists. But no more so than the medical world: Holmes said he would not be surprised if "the surgeon who deals with dislocations of the right shoulder declines to meddle with a displacement on the other side . . ."

Old buildings were torn down, new buildings put up. Tracks and noise were to come to Commonwealth Avenue. Steamboats smoked up the harbor where a tall forest of masts had once brought visions of ghosts to a child.

Holmes's first Poet paper was an exercise in nostalgia. He wrote about the gambrel-roofed house, its history (which he had traced back to 1707), and people (mostly clergymen) who had visited the house in the days of his youth.

He admitted in the opening paragraph that he talked half the time to find out his own thoughts, "as a schoolboy turns his pockets inside out to see what is in them."

Here, for the first time Holmes admitted that *The Negro Plot*, which he had found in his father's library, had given him that feeling about blacks "which it took Mr. Garrison a good many years to root out."

But most of the Poet was less self-revealing, and certainly less interesting to those who had hoped the scintillating wit of the Autocrat would be turned again on the world around them in 1872.

In the second Poet paper, Holmes had some fun with a character whom he thought to be an entomologist, but who decried the title.

He was *not* an entomologist, the science of insect study was too vast. He was, perhaps, ventured the Poet, a coleopterist (an expert on beetles).

Still too vast. Scarabeeist was more like it.

So the Poet had him captured at last—an expert who devoted an academic life to one small family of beetles, no more, no less. To Holmes, the scarabeeist was the epitome of the new sort of specialist that was ravaging the country.

He poked fun at his own medical profession with all its new "Ophthalmoscopes and Rhinoscopes and Otoscopes and Laryngoscopes and Stethoscopes, Thermometers, Spirometers, Dynamometers, Sphygmomanometers and Pleximeters and Probes and Probangs . . . apparatus for doing everything but turn you inside out."

There was talk of Keats and Coleridge and Charles Lamb. One of the characters around the breakfast table this time was the astronomer, who opened the whole cosmos to Holmes. There was discussion of theological questions, but in so composed a vein, so philosophical, so low keyed, that not even the radical Calvinists complained.

"We have studied anthropology through theology; we have now begun to study theology through anthropology."

Such a statement might have called down the wrath of the religionists before the Civil War. But the war and the triumph over slavery, if it was that, had blunted the arrows of the radicals. What was William Lloyd Garrison to do for an encore? They were tired; much of a war-weary, increasingly materialistic public found them tiresome. Calvinism was on its last legs in New England, and Holmes had no trouble on the theosophical score.

He could, and did, repeat some of his old charges, but the words echoed as in an empty room. There were no attacks from the pulpit.

And Holmes was much more mellow. "As people grow older," he said, with the prescience of an older man, "they come at length to live so much in memory that they often think with a kind of pleasure of losing their dearest possessions. Nothing can be so perfect while we possess it as it will seem when remembered. . . ."

Holmes knew that as a scientist, doctor, essayist, novelist, and serious poet, his world had come to an end. He was the most honored among the literary men of Boston, and the honors doubled every year. But somewhere back there in the thick of the fray had come the high point. Holmes ended the Poet series feeling that all the future was anticlimax. The pure poet, if he had ever existed inside that skin, had died a natural death, and his requiem had been "The Chambered Nautilus." Nothing Holmes had written since could touch its literary qualities.

24

MARK TWAIN'S FATEFUL
NIGHT AT THE ATLANTIC CLUB

HOLMES KNEW THAT "THE POET AT THE BREAKFAST TABLE" WAS A
drastic change in the Holmes style. He called it a "resurrection." At
the end of the series he stepped out of character to become himself
for a paragraph, and to offer fealty to the long-suffering Amelia,
who had borne with him through all his literary miseries of the
middle years.

"To you Beloved," he said in dedication, "who have never failed
to cut the leaves which hold my record, who have never nodded over
its pages, who have never hesitated in your allegiance, who have
greeted me with unfailing smiles . . ."

Amelia had never complained at the long evenings spent at the
Saturday Club, at Fields's entertainments for visiting authors, at
dinners—almost all of them for men only—which her husband attended several nights a week, year after year. But there was a more
poignant reason for Holmes's dedication. His wife of nearly four
decades was no longer the same woman. Her memory was gone, and

it would not be long before she was unable to cope with the outside world at all. She seldom went out, and never alone. Soon Holmes would employ a full-time companion to look after her. The change in her was remarkable and rapid. But all Holmes's world was changing far too fast to suit him, even the Saturday Club.

New faces joined the table every year, new names to learn, men of literature and letters, science, the elite society of Boston intellectual achievement. Membership was a sign that a man had arrived. Howells was editor of *The Atlantic* for four years before he was taken into the club. It was not a question of dislike or of distrust; the Saturday Club took its time about bestowing the accolade. The acceptance of Howells meant a major change, for here was the shaggy young man from the West, who had, as Holmes observed wryly, "cheated some native Esau out of his birthright." Speaking as the Brahmin—it should have been a Bostonian to succeed to the editorship of *The Atlantic* in the best of all possible worlds.

In 1875 the club took in E. L. Godkin, editor of *The Nation*, who had to travel up to Boston from New York for the meetings. There were a few such men of letters from far-off places, but still the club continued to be a Boston stronghold, with mostly Boston members and mostly talk of literary affairs that developed in Boston.

In the 1870s Nahant was a popular summer resort, and the Holmeses went there several times. In the summer of 1873 Longfellow was there, too. So was his brother-in-law, Tom Appleton, and many other famous Bostonians. George Peabody, the wealthy banker who had earned a fortune in England and established what later became the House of Morgan, was in Nahant, and Holmes dined with him, along with Longfellow, Charles Sumner, and Tom Appleton. Cabot Lodge had a dinner for the same group. Henry James had a party for Holmes, Longfellow, and Sumner. It was almost like the Saturday Club, all summer long.

This Boston literary society of which Holmes was the linchpin had grown inward over the years, no matter what the evidence to the contrary given by the acceptance of a Godkin or a Howells. The names were too often the same as those of the Cambridge and Boston Harvard crowd, those of Back Bay and Beacon Street and Commonwealth Avenue.

Holmes wrote a few poems and a review here and there. He revised some of his medical lectures and put a more popular tone to them for local organizations. As his fame spread, he was burdened by more correspondence; everyone who ever wrote anything, it seemed, bethought himself of the kindly Autocrat as one who could be sought out for criticism and help. He could not do it, he would not do it, and he became a little waspish about the demands that forced him to hire outside secretarial assistance to fend off the assaults on his time.

Holmes's duties at the medical school grew more onerous as progress brought change. He still was the consummate lecturer and demonstrator of anatomy. But in the old days he had used his own judgment in the examination of students for the medical degree. Sometimes he was rigorous; sometimes, if he knew the student well, he might be so casual as to seem careless. When William James, son of his old friend, came to him for examination, the doctor asked him to describe a major nerve in the cranium. James did so.

"If you know that, you know everything. Now tell me about your dear old father."

End of examination.

Under Harvard's modernized system, examinations were standardized, and Holmes had to read and evaluate some two hundred papers a year written by the young men who crowded his lecture room.

In the changing times, the grand affairs, such as the celebration of the Chinese ambassador's visit and the grand duke's triumphant tour, were replaced by less pretentious entertainments. Boston did not often give those big banquets anymore, and if it would give them, Holmes would demur. He did not like the crowds; he objected to "those horrible cold dinners washed-down with interminable spouting."

But as a literary leader he still had to make his appearances, and as the wives of merchants and lawyers and bankers took over the social reins, Holmes found himself the constant recipient of invitations to dine. His fame was such that he was the first on many a hostess's list. If she could get Dr. Holmes, her dinner party would be a success. He tried to please, although often at these affairs he felt like "an electric eel . . . that couldn't be touched without giving a shock."

The house was unusually quiet those days. Little Amelia married Turner Sargent and went off to live with him. Ned married Henrietta Wigglesworth, and Wendell married Fanny Dixwell, whom he had known for donkey's years but had virtually ignored in his pursuit of the law. Only Wendell and Fanny remained "in the nest." They took over the third floor of the big house. Wendell could not afford to maintain a household of his own on his meager legal earnings.

Holmes's routine had slowed considerably. He no longer went out rain or shine onto the Charles in one of his boats. He was most likely to be found, in mornings and those afternoons that he did not teach, in his library, its bay windows overlooking the Charles, the Memorial Tower of Cambridge looming in the distance.

It was a bright room. Two more circular windows threw light on the alcoves between the bookcases and the microscope that stood beside his desk. Three of the walls were lined with his books. He was forever being sent books—medical books, poetry, essays, novels, *belles lettres*. But few of these graced his shelves. The books he kept were those he had bought for the most part: medical books, treasures of the past, his collection from the days in France and all that he had added to it, and the medical and literary works that had been written by his friends and by those whose abilities he particularly respected.

The writing desk stood in the center of the library. Over it a drop-light hung from the ceiling. Several easy chairs were scattered around the room. A large mirror hung over the fireplace. The little available wall space was hung with pictures, one a Copley portrait of the Reverend Mr. Cooper, a New England minister his ancestors had known. The drawing room, whose walls were decorated by Fields's barometer and a number of reproductions of famous paintings, was just across the hall from the library.

Holmes was growing a little deaf. That meant that when he went to the Saturday Club or to a dinner, he talked even more than usual, because he did not hear half of what was said to him.

In the early 1870s a number of deaths delivered a series of small shocks to Holmes. Phineas Barnes, his Andover schoolmate and friend, died in 1871. Mary Benjamin Motley, the girl Holmes had courted and his friend had married, died in 1874; so did Charles Sumner. Agassiz died in 1874, too. The list of the old members of the Saturday Club was growing shorter, so short that Longfellow said he did not like to come to the club unless he could be sure that Emerson or Holmes would be there. Lowell was abroad and the new people made Longfellow nervous.

By 1877 those four figures, Lowell, Longfellow, Emerson, and Holmes, had been raised onto such high pedestals in the Saturday Club, and all of literary Boston, that the presence of any one of them was enough to mark an occasion as "important." They needed not speak—their arrival was enough to bless the occasion.

It had become the custom of *The Atlantic Monthly* to honor its important contributors with a promotional dinner, the first of which was staged in 1874. If Henry James came to town, for example, Howells arranged a dinner for him. So when John Greenleaf Whittier reached the age of seventy, Howells and the publisher planned a dinner. Such an occasion promised to draw Longfellow, Emerson, and Holmes all together. It would be a night to remember, another triumph for *The Atlantic.*

As Howells was in charge of the occasion, he searched for the finest literary speaker. He approached Mark Twain, whose fame as an after-dinner speaker had drifted up from New York and Hartford. Howells had brought Mark Twain into *The Atlantic Monthy*'s stable of writers. He suggested to publisher H. O. Houghton, who had taken over *The Atlantic*, that Twain's name would guarantee the success of the program. Houghton agreed. Twain had already spoken once or twice in Boston. His open western style had kept the audience in stitches.

Twain realized that this Whittier dinner was important to his publishers. He also knew from Howells that Emerson, Longfellow, and Holmes would be there. As well as any other American, Mark Twain understood the importance of these figures to the literary "hub of the Universe."

Having racked his mind for a new idea, Mark Twain came to what seemed a perfect solution to the problem. Whittier must be honored, but Emerson, Longfellow, and Holmes must not be slighted. He would use Emerson, Longfellow, and Holmes as figures in the speech itself, thus emphasizing his respect for them, paying obeisance before all those assembled at the Brunswick Hotel, one of Boston's more pretentious dining rooms.

On the evening of December 17 the group of fifty diners in formal dress assembled around the U-shaped table at the Brunswick. The guest list might have been called the *Who's Who* of literary Boston. The dinner was the finest that could be put together, the wines superb: Chablis, Claret, Mumm's Dry, and Roederer Imperial. The conversation, at least around Holmes, Emerson, Longfellow, and the guest of honor, grew ever more scintillating as the bottles were passed.

The dinner progressed. As dessert came, toastmaster Howells got on with the business in hand. Flowers and messages for Whittier were delivered to the table. They came from all over America.

Eyes moved from the figure of Whittier, to Emerson, to Longfellow, to Holmes. Whittier's face was shining with the joy of the occasion. Emerson seemed even graver than usual; he sat unsmiling, the transcendentalist oblivious to the noise of the busy talkers around him. Beneath his white mane Longfellow beamed benignly at his table companions.

Holmes was himself, flashing his swift smile, gesturing, posing, turning to one companion and then another, never stopping the flow of his talk.

Howells said a few words, and then got on with the speakers. William Winter read a poem he had written for the occasion. And then, with a touch of pride, Howells introduced the major speaker of the evening, Mark Twain.

Here, said Howells, was one of his most important contributors, and one of his dearest personal friends, Samuel G. Clemens, Mark Twain, "a humorist who never left you hanging your head for having enjoyed his joke."

Mark Twain arose.

He had studied the art of after-dinner speaking so well that he was as good at it in his way as Dr. Holmes was at making bright conversation. Mark Twain's talks always appeared to be impromptu. They were anything but; Twain said the best speech was not the off-the-cuff talk, but the counterfeit of it. He had spent weeks standing in his library speaking to chairs and a bust, preparing the speech for the Whittier dinner. A little indifferent grammar here, a humorous allusion there, a false start—they were all in the performance.

Now, resplendent in white tie and tails, his handsome mane of hair and moustache bristling, standing in the light above the crowd of glittering celebrities, Mark Twain began to speak.

He would tell them a story, he said, of a remarkable experience that had befallen him in his California days. It had been in 1864. One day at dusk he found himself near a mining camp in the high Sierra without lodging. He came upon a lonely miner's cabin. He asked for shelter. The suspicious miner asked him to identify himself.

"I'm Mark Twain."

He was the fourth literary man who had been there in twenty-four hours, the miner said coldly. "Consarn the lot. I'm going to move. I ain't suited to a littery atmosphere."

Twain said he had asked the miner to explain that strange remark.

The miner said that the night before three tramps had descended on him. They had eaten all his food, drunk all his whiskey, and played euchre, cheating most of the night. They had identified themselves as Henry Wadsworth Longfellow, Ralph Waldo Emerson, and Dr. Oliver Wendell Holmes.

When he identified the tramps as Emerson, Longfellow, and Holmes, the audience was supposed to laugh. No one laughed.

They had recited bits of verse from their poems. Mark Twain began to satirize some of their verses. . . .

As he went on, Twain felt his audience stiffen. The expressions on the faces "turned to a sort of black frost."

Someone coughed. A shudder passed around the head table.

"Mr. Emerson was a seedy little bit of a chap, red-headed. Mr. Holmes was as fat as a balloon, he weighed as much as three hundred, and had double chins all the way down to his stomach. Mr. Longfellow was built like a prize fighter. His head was cropped and bristly, like as if he had a wig made of hairbrushes. His nose lay straight down on his face, like a finger with the end joint tilted up. . . ."

Someone at the end of the table laughed and choked it off. But as for the rest: a heavy silence "weighing nearly tons to the square inch, descended on the room."

Emerson did not bat an eye. Longfellow sat with a benign smile on his face, as if waiting—or was that smile freezing there? Dr. Holmes's eyes were on his program. He was writing busily with a pen, as though composing an answer.

No one looked at the speaker. All eyes were riveted on the plates before them, and the hush of embarrassment drifted along the table. Howells looked around him, his face strained with horror.

Mark Twain's eyes roamed the crowd for a friendly face. He saw none.

He plunged on. The character who identified himself as Emerson claimed the authorship of "Barbara Frietchie."

That should bring a laugh.

No laugh.

He thrashed on to the end.

"I said to the miner, 'Why my dear sir, *these* were not the gracious singers to whom we and the world pay living reverence and homage; these were imposters.' "

"The miner investigated me with a calm eye for a while; then said he, 'Ah, imposters were they? Are you?' "

It was a very funny ending. It would have brought the house down in Hartford, or New York, or Philadelphia. But not in Boston. Mark Twain had invoked the names of local deities and had dared to spoof with them. Proper Boston—and Proper Boston was already in ascendance in the club—would have no trifling with those names. Mark Twain sat down in the roar of dead silence.

Howells somehow recovered enough to introduce the next speaker, the novelist William Henry Bishop, who arose white-faced and shaking.

The novelist started bravely enough. But the cold eye of the crowd was on him, too. He stammered, he tottered at the podium, and half-way through he collapsed and sank into his chair in a moist heap.

The next speaker did not even try.

Howells stumbled through a few sentences to put an end to the torture, and the crowd broke up, the diners keeping a safe distance from the speakers' table as they made their way to the cloakroom.

Charles Dudley Warner and Howells tried to comfort Mark Twain, but he was beyond assistance. They left him in his hotel room, sunk in a deep gloom. He remarked that after this, he guessed Howells would not want any more contributions from his pen. Howells was too anguished to reassure him.

Next morning an account of the speeches appeared in the newspapers. Everywhere but in Boston Mark Twain was congratulated for another masterful stroke of genius. But not in Boston. Boston would not forget and Boston would not forgive.

Mark Twain went back to Hartford in despair. He and Howells tried by correspondence to pick up the pieces. There really were no pieces to pick up: Emerson's head had been so high in the clouds he had not heard a word. When his daughter read the newspaper account to him the next day, he said it was very funny. Longfellow had thought it an amusing speech, and he told Howells he blamed the newspapers for making a mountain out of a molehill. Whittier, Longfellow said, had enjoyed the whole.

Dr. Holmes had really been writing notes to himself and he had not been upset. "It never occurred to me for a moment to take offense or to feel wounded by your playful use of my name."

But Boston, oh, how Boston continued on! At the dining tables and in the clubs the Mark Twain speech was debated endlessly, and those who had been there put down those who had only read the speech and found it funny.

"But not in that company . . ." was the shocked rejoinder almost every time. One did not associate Boston's literary gods "with the absurdly unlike personalities attributed to them . . ."

Mark Twain picked up his family and went to Germany. He did not come back for a whole year.

That's how bad it was that night in Boston.

CHAPTER

25

DR. HOLMES
TAKES HIS LAST BOW—
HE SAYS

THE WHITTIER DINNER FIASCO WAS A TOPIC OF CONVERSATION FOR A long time. Aside from wounding the sensitive Mark Twain, the affair indicated the extent of change that had come over Boston since Holmes's youth. Boston was Boston, and not prepared for humor from the Comstock lode. It never would be. That was what was happening to set Boston apart from all the rest of the United States, and it cost her the literary and moral leadership she had always taken as her birthright. Boston was becoming stuffy.

With the death of Francis Parkman came the end of Boston's leadership of the American historical school. Charles Eliot Norton, an old-fashioned Brahmin, member of the Saturday Club, backer of *The Nation* in New York, and public-spirited citizen, tried to interest Boston in buying the collection of Italian masters amassed by James Jackson Jarves. Boston did not need it. Boston wanted to stay as it was.

The Atlantic Monthly was doing well, and Howells was eager for contributions from Holmes. Holmes sent him rehashes—occasional poems for the most part, because he was writing little else. Holmes had many matters on his mind. One was the new Boston Medical Library. At a meeting in 1874, a group of doctors chose Holmes to be president of the promotional group. It had taken much of his time. In 1876, mindful of the city fathers' destruction of the Charles estuary, Holmes had allied himself with a citizens' group to press for a public parks system in Boston. That took more time and energy.

All the activity was a true indication of Holmes's position; he was an elder statesman.

When Holmes reached seventy, publisher Houghton decided to give him a celebration dinner similar to the dinner he had given for Whittier. Holmes's birthday was August 29, which was not at all a good time to hold a celebration, most of Boston having fled the city for country and seaside haunts during that overheated month. Holmes and Amelia, in fact, were in Beverly Farms, staying with the Turner Sargents. Little Amelia thus could help care for her mother, and Holmes could escape the cares of Boston and some of the honors and requests.

The celebration was held, then, on December 3 at the Brunswick at noon, in deference to Holmes's growing distaste for evening entertainment.

Dr. Holmes and Little Amelia met the guests, a hundred in all, and most of them intimate enough with the Holmeses not to have to ask about Big Amelia. Lowell was out of the country. Longfellow was sick. But the rest of Boston's literary lights were there: Mrs. Stowe, and Julia Ward Howe, and Emerson, and Whittier.

Champagne was served in the hotel's imposing reception room, where the guests talked for two hours—a good beginning for a Holmes party—before the crowd went into the dining room for brunch.

Whittier was supposed to read a poem of his own in honor of the Autocrat, but the party lasted too long for his frail health, and he had to leave, so James T. Fields read it for him.

Howells then spoke of Holmes, "who not only named, but who made *The Atlantic.*"

And then Mark Twain got up. It had been a stroke of genius for Howells to bring him there, this man who had so outraged Proper Boston two years earlier. Twain did not make the mistake of taking the literary god's name in vain this time. It was a humble speech, a literary speech, and he, Mark Twain, was the butt of the joke he told in it.

When Mark Twain's first book, *The Innocents Abroad*, was published, a friend had commented on the dedication.

"Very neat," said the friend.

"Yes," said Mark Twain, "*I* thought it was."

"I liked it almost as much as the first time I saw it."

"What do you mean? Where did you see it before?"

"Well, I saw it some years ago, as Doctor Holmes's dedication to his *Songs in Many Keys*."

"Of course my first impulse," said Mark Twain, "was to prepare this man's remains for burial, but upon reflection I said I would reprieve him for a moment or two, and give him a chance to prove his assertion if he could. We stepped into a bookstore and he did prove it. I had really stolen that dedication almost word for word. I could not imagine how . . ."

The solution: two years earlier Mark Twain had been laid up sick for two weeks in Hawaii, and he had read and reread Holmes's poems. The dedication had stuck in his mind, and that was how it had happened.

He had written Holmes, Mark Twain said, and Holmes had said it was all right, no harm done.

Holmes smiled and nodded in recollection.

That was all.

Mark Twain sat down to heavy applause, and with the feeling that the past had been at last wiped out for him. He could return unashamed to Boston.

J. W. Harper of the publishing firm located in New York City was there. Ten years before no New Yorker would have been invited to such a fête. But Harper was too important to leave out. And so were many others of the new breed: T. B. Aldrich and William Winter, J. T. Trowbridge and C. P. Crach, and Thomas Wentworth

Higginson, who went back to Holmes's day, but who was a late bloomer in literary affairs.

President Hayes sent a message, and John Holmes, the doctor's brother, did too. The President was detained by business in Washington. John Holmes was detained by an aloofness he had long felt about his brother. To be the brother of Dr. Oliver Wendell Holmes and live in the Boston area was to carry a heavy burden. Nor were the brothers very close, particularly after the old manse was sold, and John Holmes moved to a tiny house that belonged to his housekeeper, into rooms so small that he could not even hold a dinner party there. John Holmes had demurred, he said, because he felt the day should be his brother's alone. There was much more to it than that.

But that little shadow did not darken the occasion. A hundred attended and the list of those who sent messages was longer and impressive: Carl Schurz and George Bancroft, and Rebecca Harding Davis, and E. P. Whipple were among the regretful absentees. So was Frederick Douglass—the black advocate of civil rights. His letter was an indication that Holmes's fame and reputation had erased any memories of his anti-abolitionism of the past.

It was almost purely a literary festival, and as such it did not honor Holmes for his most lasting achievements, those in the field of medical education. That void was filled in part by the speech by President Eliot of Harvard about the doctor's professional life. The Eliot speech was reported in detail in the *Boston Medical and Surgical Journal,* but not in the newspapers. The world regarded Holmes now as a literary figure, and that was how he would largely be judged in later years.

That year Holmes published a biography of John Lothrop Motley in *The Atlantic.* It was really an extension of a sketch he had done for the Massachusetts Historical Society Proceedings and he regarded it as no more than an outline for a future biographer. Two other books were published in the next year or so—one was a collection of his medical essays. The other was *Pages from an Old Volume of Life*—a collection of his "non-series" essays for *The Atlantic.* The preparation kept him busy and close to his publishers.

In 1882, after thirty-five years as professor of anatomy at Harvard Medical School, Dr. Oliver Wendell Holmes decided to retire. His health was good, if his hair was white; he still took two turns around the common every evening when the weather was fine to clear his head after a few hours of writing, reading, or puttering with his microscope. But it was time to take life a little easier.

The big brick house was lonely. Wendell and Fanny Dixwell Holmes had moved as soon as Wendell had a connection with a Boston law firm. Wendell hated to be dependent on his father, and Holmes's egocentrism clashed with his own. Wendell would go on to a full Harvard professorship that year, 1882.

Dr. Holmes talked a good deal about his age. He considered himself a subject for a personal study of geriatrics. He was interested scientifically, and as a public figure he wanted to be sure that he knew the point at which he must stop public appearances, lest he appear a doddering fool.

But age was little more than the excuse for his resignation. The real reason was that he had received so tempting an offer from *The Atlantic* and the Houghton Company that he was persuaded to write more books. Age did play its role in his realization that he did not have the energy to undertake a brisk writing assignment and continue the medical lectures. The lectures had to end; he had been giving them for thirty-five years and that seemed to be enough. So in October 1882 Holmes announced to Dr. Eliot that he was going to retire in a month or two, and on November 28 he gave that final lecture. The last lecture was a valedictory; he spoke a bit about the past, and the growth of the school, and the evolution of medical science. The students presented him with a silver loving cup, and he posed for a photograph with the class in the amphitheater, surrounded by the cup and the huge floral pieces that had been sent in by well-wishers. And the university made him professor emeritus.

There was another turn in Holmes's life. He found himself heading to New York more often, for literary reasons. New York had established a Harvard Club, and it was growing into a powerful institution, to rival the club in Boston. The Century Association of New York also had literary pretensions that in a way rivaled those of the Saturday Club. The Century persuaded Holmes to come down to a celebration.

In April 1883 Holmes went down to New York for a week, a seven-day orgy he later called it. There was the dinner at the Century Association, a dinner at the Astors', a reception given by doctor friends, and a party at the Lotos Club. Then two hundred New York doctors gave him a mammoth dinner at Delmonico's—nine courses, five wines—the sort of treat the young men of the class of '29 had sometimes allowed themselves in their younger, non-dyspeptic days.

This sort of play was exhausting, even though it exhilarated Holmes, as it always did, to be the center of attention. Whitelaw Reid, the editor of the New York *Tribune*, called him "the prince of all writers." That, in particular, was pleasant for a reason Reid did not mention. Reid was successor to Horace Greeley, who had done his best a quarter century earlier to bring an end to Holmes's public career.

Holmes had one more official act to undertake for the Harvard Medical School. For several years he had assisted President Eliot in raising money to build a new building. It was finished and Holmes had been asked to give the dedication address.

That spring Governor Ben Butler was doing his best to achieve the national prominence he yearned for to set him on the road to the United States presidency. Always the demagogue, Butler had seized upon an issue he thought ought to bring him an enormous number of votes. He was investigating the Tewksbury Almshouse, with an eye to the Irish vote. He focused on the manner in which the dead bodies were disposed of—to Harvard Medical School, under an arrangement begun by Dr. Holmes.

At the statehouse hearings, Butler accused Harvard Medical School of playing fast and loose with the poor dead. Medical students bought bodies by the dozen, he indicated, and chopped them up in a most un-Christian way, poking fun at the viscera of the departed. Why, Dr. Holmes, for thirty-five years the professor of anatomy and chief dissectionist, was known for his anatomical humor, some of which could not be repeated in Boston drawing rooms. Did the public know, for example, that this same Dr. Holmes had possessed a piece of tanned human skin that he was accustomed to displaying to his classes? The investigators had it. How crass, how unfeeling, how un-Christian, how close to blasphemy!

The newspapers devoured the governor's charges; the uneducated readers writhed in horror and wrote angry letters attacking the processes of anatomical study. Some demanded that dissection of human bodies be discontinued.

The hysteria spread through Boston and grew so momentous that one day a mob marched threateningly on the medical school, and one night in May vandals entered and set fire to the new anatomical amphitheater. At least Holmes was certain that was the case, and he never changed his mind, although no one was caught, and the authorities did not pursue the matter in view of public opinion.

The opening of the new Boylston Street building was delayed. The building was made completely fireproof, or as completely so as possible, using steel, iron, and concrete. And in October it was ready for occupancy again.

But the argument over dissection still raged, and on the day of dedication, the faint hearts of the medical school locked up the anatomical dissection chambers. They were not to be shown to the public that would tour the building.

On the morning of October 17, Dr. Holmes and the other notables assembled at Huntington Hall of the Massachusetts Institute of Technology, a few doors away from the new building on Boylston Street. President Eliot was there. Mayor Palmer and former Mayor Green were there, but Governor Butler was not. Against a background of maroon drapery hung a portrait of Dr. Oliver Wendell Holmes. Holmes sat beneath it.

President Eliot opened the exercise at eleven with a brief message and an introduction of Dr. Holmes.

Holmes spoke of the first years of the medical school, of Dr. John Warren, and Dr. Benjamin Waterhouse, who had introduced vaccination to America. Then he leaped a hundred years to 1833 and Dr. Jackson and others of his teachers. He spoke of advancements in medicine. He braved the subject of women in medicine—he had always favored the admission of women. Why should they not be admitted to medicine?

"I myself followed a course of lectures given by the younger Madame La Chapelle in Paris, and if here and there an intrepid woman insists on taking by storm the fortress of medical education, I would have the gate flung open to her as if it were that of the citadel at Orléans and she were Joan of Arc returning from the field of Victory . . ."

Was that enough of a shock for the medical reformers who still so stoutly resisted women doctors? He went on. In many ways he felt women were superior to men in diagnosis in the sickroom, gifted with what he called a "natural clairvoyance." And "many a suicide would have been prevented if the doctor's wife had visited the victim the day before it happened."

There, that would give the reformers something to chew on.

But Holmes was not finished with them yet, not on this last day of his official connection with the school. He turned his attention to the anthropotomic laboratory—the dissecting room. He alluded to Ben Butler's campaign of hysteria. "Popular prejudice has made the study embarrassing and even dangerous to those engaged in it . . ." And it was the duty, he said, of "all intelligent members of the community to defend the anatomist and his place of labor against such appeals to ignorant passion as will interfere . . . above all, against such inflammatory representations as may be expected to lead to mid-day mobs or midnight incendiarism."

In his long career Holmes estimated that he had put two thousand students through the anatomy course, and in all that time had only twice felt impelled to rebuke individual students for unseemly levity in the treatment of the bodies with which they worked.

Let them remember, he said, "that for every lifeless body which served these experiments, a hundred or a thousand living fellow creatures have been saved from unutterable anguish, and many of them from premature death."

Holmes then turned once more on Butler and his political followers who had tried to savage the medical school for their political gain.

"There was formerly a small scrap, said to be human skin, which had been subject to the tanning process, and which was not the least interesting of the series. I have not seen it for a good while, and it may have disappeared as the cases might happen to be open while unscrupulous visitors were strolling through the museum."

While he was smiting the enemies of progress and the political hacks and their mob allies with dry adjective and wry humor, someone moved quietly out of Huntington Hall and down the street to the medical building. By the time the crowd arrived to inspect the premises, the doors to the dissecting room were unlocked and standing open.

26

DR. HOLMES
ENGAGES IN FARCE

IN 1883 THE EDITOR OF THE AMERICAN MEN OF LETTERS SERIES ASKED
Holmes to write a biography of Emerson; in the eyes of those who
knew Emerson well, no more unlikely person could have been
chosen. Emerson was as ethereal in his approach to life as Holmes
was briskly practical. Emerson was virtually humorless; Holmes bubbled over with joyous goodwill. When Henry Bowditch learned that
Holmes, an old friend, was going to write the biography of Emerson,
another old friend, he reared back his head and laughed aloud.

Holmes was not insensible to the anomaly. He wrote friends
whose opinions he respected in such serious matters, and asked them
if they believed he should do it. Enough of them encouraged him
that he decided to undertake the task. After all, he possessed Dr.
Johnson's two requisites for a biographer: he had seen Emerson in
his "official literary capacity," and he also had known Emerson from
the Saturday Club in his "unofficial person."

So Holmes outlined the book and sought help wherever help was to be found. He interviewed and corresponded with everyone he knew who had known the poet. He had to face a major problem: American opinion was divided about Emerson. Was he the transcendental figure his supporters claimed, whose name would rank high in literature for a thousand years? Or was he the product of a faddist society, overblown and overrated, whose reputation needed puncturing with a sharp needle?

Holmes ignored both those views. He wrote a book on Emerson that was faithful to his life, although less than inspired in its judgment of his work. But what means did Holmes have of understanding the metaphysics of Emerson? Holmes said just that. He had no mechanism that responded to Emerson in a way that would expose "the complete architecture of his intellectual system." That was the doctor, the scientist speaking, trying to dissect the Emerson mind, and failing. For twenty years Holmes had concerned himself with the psychology of the individual. For that same period and more, Emerson had concerned himself with the idealism of humanity and the highest flights of the soul.

When his *Emerson* was finished and published in 1884, even those friends who had held strong doubts that Holmes could pull it off congratulated him on the book.

Later biographers found they could use the Holmes book as little more than an outline for their own studies, except for the section on Emerson's poetry. For if Holmes was a student of any aspect of literature, it was poetry. He had examined English verse in the days when he was preparing the Lowell Institute lectures, and he had kept up his reading.

When Holmes finished the Emerson book he was tired. His brother John suggested that he "take a blow" and do nothing but read novels. But the advice was given too late, for Thomas Bailey Aldrich, Howells' successor in the editor's chair of *The Atlantic*, had been asking for three years for a new Holmes novel. Holmes had agreed. He was already writing the third of his psychological or "medicated" novels for *The Atlantic*. It was triggered by a remark of a middle-aged man—that he could never pass a tall hall clock without a feeling of terror. When the man was a baby, a heavy weight from one of those clocks had fallen near him with so loud a crash that it had created an indelible impression on his nervous system.

The novel, following the same psychology, was entitled *A Mortal Antipathy*.

The first chapter introduced the two female characters: Miss Lurida Vincent, large-headed, large-eyed, long-eyelashed, slender-necked, slightly-developed (which meant no bust to speak of). She was far better equipped with brain than muscles.

Lurida's foil was Miss Euthymia Tower, "of full womanly stature," whose dumbbells the other girls could not even lift. Holmes did not mention her I.Q., but the reader would gather that it was not high. Euthymia had something else—a swelling bust that threatened the buttons of her rowing jersey. She was captain of the eight-oared boat crew and pulled the stroke oar.

In chapter three, just as the reader had convinced himself that Dr. Holmes was writing pure farce, he introduced a conflict: "But far away, on the other side of the lake, a birchbark canoe was to be seen, in which sat a young man who paddled it skillfully and swiftly."

The young man was watching a race, a spectator observed, through an opera glass. The young man's opera glass was turned on the unbuttoned expanse of Miss Euthymia's close-fitting flannel suit. The fellow, the reader learned soon enough, was Maurice Kirkwood, Esquire. He was a strange fellow, said the old landlord's wife, "the solitariest human being that I ever came across."

The local doctor learned the dreadful truth: *Maurice had an antipathy to women!* They made him sick!

In chapter twenty-three Euthymia saved Maurice's life. Next day Euthymia came to bring him flowers. He held her hand. It didn't even make him sneeze. He was completely cured. But the doctor warned Euthymia—she had to come and see him every day, otherwise he might have a relapse. Then, God knew what would happen!

And that was that. In the last chapter, Lurida was writing to Euthymia, who was now Mrs. Maurice Kirkwood.

Dr. Holmes, tongue firmly in his cheek, said good-bye to his readers. This time it was not *auf Wiedersehen*, but *sayonara*.

CHAPTER

27

THE AUTOCRAT PUTS
ON THE PRESIDENT'S HAT

THE ODDEST ASPECT OF *A Mortal Antipathy* IS THAT OVER THE YEARS critics have labeled it "the least" of Holmes's books. If it is considered as a novel, that judgment is sound enough; but Holmes was not trying to write a novel. That much is obvious now and was obvious then to *Atlantic* readers. He used the novel form and broke out of it as he pleased; his characters were not believable and were not meant to be; no youth was ever so fair or put-upon as Maurice; even the powerful Katrinka of comic-strip fame in another century had not the staying power of Euthymia; Mme. Curie could not hold a candle to the spark of genius that rested beneath the shallow breast of Lurida; no doctor was ever so plain and hearty as Dr. Butts; no louts outside Shakespeare ever behaved so true to form as Holmes's villagers. But it was all in fun, except the serious overtone of Holmes's discussion of neurosis. If seen that way, *A Mortal Antipathy* was first-class amusement.

But for critics who insisted on taking the work seriously, the flaws were so numerous that they had to be cataloged. Thus cataloged, the work went down like lead in the sea of criticism.

Holmes had been tired when he finished the Emerson biography. By the time he wrote the last lines of *A Mortal Antipathy* he was near exhaustion. It had been a bad year all around. His second son, Edward Jackson Holmes, had died in 1884, leaving his wife and Holmes's single grandchild, Edward Jackson Holmes, Jr. Amelia was so far gone that she did not recognize most people, and it was impossible for her to attend any public functions. His world was falling rapidly around him; one symbol was the destruction of the old house at 8 Montgomery Place. He passed by one day on his walk and saw the workmen tearing it down—that house where he and Amelia had been so happy for eighteen years, where all the children had been born. Soon it was rubble, and then just another memory to diminish him.

Were his family burdens not enough, the demands on Holmes by an adoring public had become almost intolerable. One day, out for a constitutional on the Common, he was spied by a whole group of tourists who recognized the slight old-fashioned figure in the long coat and beaver hat. They moved toward him, obviously overflowing with requests for autographs, and Lord knew what else! Some might even have had manuscripts under their arms.

Holmes quickened his pace and hurried back toward Beacon Street. The group continued to follow him. He doubled his step, until he was nearly running. Being younger they gained ground.

He turned up the tall stone staircase, half in a panic, and took the steps two at a time, with his short legs flying until he reached the top.

There they were, down at the bottom, the leader with her foot on the step.

Holmes peered down anxiously.

"Don't come up. I've got it—and it's catching."

He turned, opened the door with his latchkey, stepped inside, and shut the big oak door decisively behind him.

To deal with his admiring public he had hired a secretary who used a typewriter; still there was too much for them to do. But he could not reject Charles Francis Adams, who wanted him to read his *New England Episodes* "with pencil in hand." And he had to answer John William Forbes and his old friend Dr. Hedge when they wrote on literary matters. He writhed under the burden until finally in despair he wrote "A Cry From the Study," an article for *The Atlantic*, pleading with his public to let him alone. But Holmes was too much a public figure for that. If anything, the flow increased.

For several years a number of Holmes's literary acquaintances and some personal friends had been pressing him to come to England. Lady Harcourt, who was Motley's daughter, was one. Lowell, who was serving as minister to England just then, was another. The death in 1885 of Turner Sargent, his son-in-law, left Little Amelia quite alone. He decided then to take the trip to England and take Little Amelia with him. It was inconceivable that Amelia could go there, or anywhere. Wendell, now a justice of the Massachusetts Supreme Court, and his wife Fanny, would look after Amelia while they were gone.

At the end of April 1886, Holmes and Amelia left Boston aboard the *Cephalonia*, fortified with baskets of champagne, grapes, oranges, half a barrel of oysters and a brand-new patented Star safety razor, Amelia's maid Emily, and a courier maid to attend them on the voyage. Holmes discovered a number of cousins and acquaintances aboard, and together they made a big table. He did not miss a meal all the way across, although he did suffer from his asthma during the voyage.

He suffered more when the *Cephalonia* reached the Irish coast at Queenstown on the afternoon of May 8; a tug came alongside, bringing thirty letters and telegrams for Holmes. They included invitations to tea, lunch, dinner, and engagements to make speeches.

Holmes was dismayed. He was even more distressed when the ship docked at Liverpool and he was met by the American consul, the vice-consul, and several representatives of English friends. They wanted to lay on entertainments, but Holmes begged off, and he and Amelia sneaked off to Chester for a few days. They visited Eaton Hall, the seat of the Duke of Westminster, who was reputed to be the richest man in the world; at least he owned most of London, it seemed. The duke was a horse breeder, a man after Holmes's own heart, for the doctor had long fancied himself an expert on horseflesh and had many useless betting stubs to attest to the unduly optimistic nature of his choices. They were shown Bec d'Or, a Derby winner of days past, and the other prides of the duke's stable.

They went to London then on the train, in a compartment festooned with flowers and gifts from well-wishers. Holmes gazed with pleasure on England's green landscape, but he was disappointed in the trees—not a one worth measuring!

In London they stayed at MacKellar's Hotel near Bond Street and Piccadilly Circus. The invitations began to arrive.

That night they went to dinner at Lady Harcourt's. It was a dazzling display of noble splendor, a dinner for twenty. Then came a grand reception for scores who wanted to shake the hand of the Autocrat.

That night when they returned to the hotel, the stack of invitations warned Holmes that something had to be done to protect themselves from well-wishers. He hired an efficient young woman named Adelaide Bush to write all the letters that had to be written.

"Dr. Holmes and Mrs. Sargent regret, but . . ."

"Dr. Holmes is extremely sorry to say that . . ."

He had several formulas, and she worked them out. One evening Miss Bush sat at her writing table until eleven o'clock rejecting invitations.

Holmes had come to London to see the sights. He found the tables turned on him; he had arrived at the height of the London "season," and he was as interesting to Londoners as Westminster Abbey was to him. They were busy, with breakfasts, luncheons, dinners, teas, receptions "two, three and four deep of an evening," and in their free moments they received company at the hotel.

They went to visit Mrs. Mildmay, Motley's second daughter. They went to Mrs. Bloomfield Moore's for luncheon, where they met Robert Browning and saw Oscar Wilde, whom Holmes had met at the Saturday Club. That evening they had another dinner and then a reception at Lady Granville's, where a thousand people assembled to meet them.

For a month that is how it went. Church at Westminster Abbey on Sunday, the theater where Ellen Terry was playing, and more than a score of other grand entertainments.

Having seen the sire of the Duke of Westminster's Derby entry, Holmes was determined to go to the Derby, and he did, on the train of the Prince of Wales. Ormonde, the duke's horse, won, but Holmes had not bet that day, except to enter one pool where he drew a blank. Back in London, Lady Dalhousie entertained him, and so did Lady Rothschild, and Sir James Paget, and dozens of others. Holmes was invited to No. 10 Downing Street by Mrs. Gladstone, and there he saw Prince Albert Victor.

They visited Windsor Castle and the Houses of Parliament. Anywhere there was to go that season they went, or could have gone, for London was opened to them in a way it had almost never been for an American.

Holmes was taken to the Literary Club, which reminded him of the Saturday Club, and that same evening went to Parliament to hear Prime Minister Gladstone speak on the Irish Question.

The dinner had been long and pleasant, filled with toasts and laughter. When Holmes and his party arrived at the House of Commons, they found the seats for distinguished visitors were all taken. Holmes took the seat of the Russian ambassador, and then was evicted, but he sat on the steps happily enough, until two o'clock in the morning; and then he had to walk home, for a cab was nowhere to be found.

Lowell was still in London, and he gave a party for his old friend. Henry James, the son of another of Holmes's old friends, was there, and George du Maurier, and a number of other writers. He visited Lord Tennyson on the Isle of Wight, and they talked of trees, to Holmes's delight.

On June 17 Holmes was honored by Cambridge University with the Doctor of Letters degree. He remained there for two days of entertainment. He was to go to Oxford next. He caught cold and was miserable, "too much occupation and excitement." Even so, his interest was aroused by some trees in the grounds of Magdalen College that were certainly worth measuring. Indeed, he insisted on measuring one Oldwych elm—twenty-five feet six inches, a good foot and a half bigger than the old Springfield elm, the largest tree Holmes had ever measured in America.

He, Amelia, and a party of friends then went to Edinburgh, where the university gave him an LL.D. degree in a ceremony much like that at Cambridge. Then it was back to Oxford for another degree, more luncheons, dinners, and receptions, until Holmes was reminded of a Chinese torture that consisted simply of keeping the subject awake. With all due gratitude to his hosts, that was how he felt at the end of the Oxford visit.

There were other excursions. They went to Stratford-on-Avon to pay homage to Shakespeare and were entertained by the Marquis of Northampton. They went to Great Malvern to rest, and Holmes was given a room at the Foley Arms that looked out on the shop of an apothecary. There in the shop was a plaster bust of Samuel Hahnemann, the apostle of homeopathy!

Holmes got his room changed.

They took a "four-wheeler" for a drive around the precipitous territory of the town, and their driver started up so steep a hill that Holmes was reduced to a Latin quotation to keep his nerve up.

"Facilis ascensus," he said to himself, *"sed revocare gradum."* ("It's easy to get up, but how do you get down?")

Their guide took them along a road that ran close to the edge of a cliff, so steep that Holmes kept curling his fingers and toes like claws to help the horse hold on. But they made it back and Holmes remarked that he felt like Mark Twain ascending the Riffelberg.

From the window of his new room in the Foley Arms, Holmes could see the abbey church of Malvern, a distinctly finer view than the one he had had before. They enjoyed every moment there; they were free for a time of well-wishers, and could rest and relax on long drives in the countryside.

They went from Great Malvern to Bath to stay at the Grand Pump Room Hotel, to Salisbury, Stonehenge, Brighton, where they stayed a week, and then back to London to MacKellar's Hotel once more.

They found London "deserted," which meant Parliament was out of session and the fashionable people had gone to the country. Nothing could have pleased Holmes more. Now he could do as he pleased and not be pleasing others. They drove to Chelsea to see the place where Thomas Carlyle had lived. He found Cheyne Walk dingy and run down; only an inscription told that the English writer had lived forty-seven years at No. 24. But Holmes routed around and found a middle-aged woman who recalled Carlyle—could remember his putting out bread for the birds, she said. "He hated to see living things wasted, poor dear."

Holmes treasured that scrap of information—it was all his own, something to add to the pack rat's nest.

St. Paul's, the National Gallery, the Royal Academy, the British Museum, the Temple, the haunts of Goldsmith and Dr. Johnson—they visited them all, in blessed tranquillity.

And then they went to Paris.

They stayed at the Hôtel d'Orient on the Rue Daunou, near the Place Vendôme. It was August, which meant that all Parisians who could in any way escape had left the city for the seashore or the mountains. Even their hotel was affected: August was the month for renovation before the autumn season began, and the scrubbing, painting, and hammering made the place "as unpresentable as a moulting fowl."

They knew no one, nor did anyone know they were coming. Holmes liked anonymity, but perhaps not quite so much of it. Their only companions were the people at the hotel and the fiacre drivers. In desperation, Holmes called on the American minister, Robert Milligan McLane, but he was following the Parisian fashion and was out of town.

Amelia and the maid went off to the shops. Holmes wandered about renewing old memories. He went to 55, rue Monsieur-le-Prince. There was the house he had lived in; the ground floor had been turned into a shop, but it was otherwise unchanged. He thought of going to the Hôpital de la Pitié, but he held back. M. Louis was long gone; nothing would be the same; Paris was no longer even the center of modern medicine. And Holmes was not a modern medical man either. He had not been in a hospital ward for many years, and he knew the sights and smells would affect him as desperately as they had that first time he set foot in Massachusetts General Hospital.

He visited churches, and the Café Procope, where he had breakfasted so often in those hectic student years, and had a cup of coffee for old times' sake. He went to the Louvre and found it all confusingly rearranged.

There was only one person in France he really wanted to see, and he did. Without a letter, without any introduction at all, he called at the Pasteur Institute for M. Louis Pasteur. Pasteur greeted the American physician, whose name meant nothing to him. They shook hands and spoke a few pleasantries. All Holmes had wanted to do was look into the face "of one of the truest benefactors of his race."

The weather was hot. Holmes and Amelia strolled the streets in the evening. Holmes was tired and did not care to go to the theater. They took a drive up the Champs-Élysées and into the Bois de Boulogne, where Holmes was surprised and pleased to see how the trees had grown. Nothing worth measuring, but still . . .

They returned to London after the week, and engaged passage for New York aboard the *Aurania*. The last person to see them in London was Lady Harcourt, and then they were off to Liverpool, where Holmes held a reception to apologize to the kind people who had offered him so much when he arrived.

They sailed, and arrived in New York on August 29. It was Holmes's seventy-seventh birthday, and friends had had a party on the ship, with a huge cake to celebrate the occasion. The next day they took the train home to Boston.

They had cut their visit short, actually, because Wendell had informed them that Amelia was ill and not doing well. They hastened to Beverly Farms, the Holmes's summer residence those days. They found Amelia there, or the physical Amelia. Her whole world was disconnected.

Holmes took Amelia home to Boston. Little Amelia came too—someone had to manage the ménage at 296 Beacon Street; father and daughter needed one another now more than they had for many years.

Holmes had kept a meticulous record of the European voyage, setting down the details of every entertainment and noting the names of all who had been kind to him. There were many letters to be written, and then the story for his publishers.

There was an unusually large stack of mail waiting, and it took weeks to wade through it all. Harvard was holding its two hundred fiftieth anniversary that year, and Holmes and Lowell were to provide poems. It was a labor of love, but the results were not very satisfactory. Holmes was too tired to rise above the mundane.

At about that time New England was swept by a new American literary craze—the author's reading. Holmes did some readings, but not for long. His eyes were beginning to bother him. He wrote one friend that he thought he had a *"cat*aract, in the kitten state."

Holmes made a book out of his European voyage. Most of it was travelogue, of interest to all who knew him and perhaps to some who knew England, but not showing much of the old verve and wit, except in a place or two. He wrote best when he was comparing London to Boston, Briton to American. His Republican spirit found it galling that he could not drive in a *numbered* hansom (which one rented by the hour), except in certain portions of Hyde Park. If he had enough money to rent a carriage by the week, he would get an unnumbered public hack and that was acceptable. He found the English system a little hard to take. But then he recalled an incident from the Pittsfield days, when he and Amelia and the children had been driving from the town to Canoe Meadow and came upon an oxcart that hogged the road ahead of them. They moved to pass. The men in the oxcart turned it obliquely across the road to stop them. They waited, and a little farther on tried again. The farmers ahead did the same thing. All the way home they had to walk the horse behind the lumbering oxcart because of the stubborn refusal of the cart men to yield the right of way.

"I could have wished I had been driving in Hyde Park," Holmes said all those years later, "where clowns and boors with their carts and oxen, do not find admittance. Exclusiveness has its convenience."

But when Holmes was wandering through Burlington Arcade one day and encountered his friend Abbott Lawrence, another Boston Brahmin, he really sparked, and out of the smoke emerged prose reminiscent of the Autocrat.

"There are," said Holmes, "three grades of recognition, entirely distinct from one another: the meeting of two persons of different countries who speak the same language—an American and an

Englishman for instance; the meeting of two Americans from different cities—as of a Bostonian and a New Yorker, or a Chicagonian [sic]; and the meeting for two from the same city—as of two Bostonians."

Holmes continued the comparison. For example, when an American and an Englishman meet in a foreign land, the Englishman mentions the fact that he has gained a bit of weight.

"How much is it now?"

"Fourteen stone. How much do you weigh?"

"Within four pounds of two hundred."

They have compared, and neither knows what the other is talking about. The same, said Holmes, is true in other matters.

"It is about as large a space as the Common," says the Boston man.

"It is as large as St. James's Park," says the Londoner.

"As high as the statehouse," says the Bostonian. "Or as tall as Bunker Hill monument, or about as big as the Frog Pond."

The Londoner would take St. Paul's, Nelson's Column, the Serpentine.

"What a marvelous field of corn," says the American about a sight he has seen, and the Englishman thinks of a field of soft, billowing wheat or rye or barley; while in the American's eye are the tall tasseled stalks "tossing their plumes and showing their silken epaulettes," of what the Englishman would call a field of maize.

And so, as Holmes said, "Conversation between two Londoners, two New Yorkers, two Bostonians, requires no footnotes, which is a great advantage to their intercourse."

There was, alas, very little of such discourse in *Our One Hundred Days in Europe*. There was talk about shopping and bookstores, and it was interesting travel talk, but more was about people and places than ideas, and it was in the realm of ideas and impressions that the Autocrat had sparked.

When it was finished, *The Atlantic* wanted him to start on something new. Was he not retired from teaching; did he not have more time for literature?

More time, perhaps, but less inclination. A literary lion is not allowed to stay cooped up in his lair. He must show himself and be shown; he must continue to remind the world that he is a lion. And so it was with Holmes. The demands were never-ending. He was asked to write additional stanzas to Joseph Hopkinson's song, "Hail Columbia!," and he did that in the summer of 1887, while he rested and relaxed at his daughter's house at Beverly Farms.

Holmes's asthma bothered him increasingly during these years. His eyes tired easily. His secretary got a new typewriter, but even that did not do enough to handle the correspondence, so he had a form printed up:

Edward Freiberger
_____

Chicago
_____

Dear Sir:
_____

    I am much obliged to you for your polite attention in sending me a copy of your poem, "To Elaine". I do not intend to read critically the great number of publications in prose and verse which I receive, but must content myself with my gratitude to my kind correspondents.

Yours very truly,
Oliver Wendell Holmes
_____

The secretary typed in the underlined information, and Holmes signed the letters by the dozens, scores, and hundreds. The books he gave away to libraries. The manuscripts he sent back. The gifts, and they were many, he consumed or donated or threw away. There was no stopping the flow, it seemed, even when he had another note printed up stating that he had impaired eyesight and could not answer any more letters.

At about that time, Holmes went down to Washington, D.C., for a visit. As always, he was honored at dinners and receptions, and at one of these affairs President Cleveland was also a guest. While all the other guests were in the drawing room, Holmes came quietly out into the hall. He did not see the little girl, daughter of the household, in her perch high on the stairs where she was allowed to sit and gather whatever glory she might from the laughter and scraps of conversation that drifted upward. Holmes walked to the cloakroom, and found President Cleveland's hat, a large and un-mistakable object. Solemnly, he picked it up, put it on his own head, and inspected himself in the mirror. Cleveland was six feet tall and weighed over two hundred and fifty pounds. The hat fell down over Holmes's ears. He removed it, hung it back on the hat rack, and got his own tall beaver, clapped it on his head, and jauntily strode out of the house.

There was plenty of life in the Autocrat yet.

CHAPTER

28

THE OLD BRANCH
BEGINS TO WITHER

The Atlantic WAS AFTER HOLMES AGAIN. EDITOR ALDRICH WANTED another series, another *Autocrat*, if that were possible.

What is possible when you are seventy-eight years old? The question had interested the scientist in Holmes for many years. He rather thought something *was* possible, if Aldrich did. He had given this new editor the same instructions he had given to Howells: if he found Holmes slipping into the ways of senility, warn the author before he made a fool of himself.

It had not happened. No evidence of weakness had appeared, Aldrich said; so Holmes undertook the new series.

The new group of articles to grace the pages of *The Atlantic* would be called "Over the Teacups." Holmes delivered the first of these essays at the end of 1887.

Holmes was not at all sure a new generation of *Atlantic* readers would be in the slightest bit interested in what he had to say.

". . . Nobody can blame the young people for preferring the thoughts and language of their own generation, with all its future before it, to those of their grandfathers' contemporaries."

Holmes then launched into one of his favorite areas of discussion: psychology and psychological oddities.

Holmes was already working on his next installment of "Over the Teacups," in February 1888, when Amelia died. That shock was intensified the same month by the death of James Freeman Clarke, his Harvard classmate and friendly poetic competitor of years past, but more recently his pastor and close friend. Two more important lights in Holmes's life had been snuffed out.

Holmes felt he could not continue the *Atlantic* series. There was the estate to be settled. Then, hardly had Little Amelia become established in the house, when she took sick. She seemed to recover, but the improvement was illusory; she died the next year. Holmes had just been getting ready to write again. Once more the process was stopped in midstream.

What was he to do?

This time the transition was more painful for all concerned. Wendell—the judge—and Fanny had no option under the moral code of nineteenth-century New England: they moved back into 296 Beacon Street, and Fanny took over the household. Judge Holmes was not so affected by it; he lived in a world of his own, largely untouched by the lesser emotions of family life, and he traveled a good deal to make speeches and to attend meetings. The burden of coping with the demands and problems of her father-in-law fell on Fanny. She never complained about the obligation, but performed in a manner that truly endeared her to Holmes.

Those deaths, emphasized by the constant trickling away of the lives of his acquaintances, gave Holmes a sense of living on borrowed time. People were forever asking him for "a few lines" in the volumes and papers he inscribed for them. He took to writing the last verse of "The Last Leaf":

> And if I should live to be
> The last leaf upon the tree
> In the spring,

Let them smile, as I do now,
At the old forsaken bough,
Where I cling.

New friends swept into his life to replace, in a measure, those he had lost. Little Amelia had taken him up to visit Mrs. Julia Dorr at Bar Harbor. Mrs. Dorr lived in Vermont during most of the year and wrote poetry. She had begun summering at the new resort of the wealthy merchants and businessmen who found Saratoga old-fashioned and Newport too glossy for their taste. She and Holmes corresponded regularly after Amelia's death, and Mrs. Dorr became very dear to Holmes. She tried to persuade Holmes to come up to Bar Harbor again in the summer of 1889, but he would not.

"I have no Amelia to talk it over and live it over with me," he protested. But the real reason was his growing weakness and his unwillingness to move from familiar surroundings. He was troubled by asthmatic attacks. And he felt very old, very tired, very much alone. "My son and his wife are doing all they can to make and keep me comfortable and cheerful, and I do my best—but the world cannot be what it has been for me."

Too many shocks had come too suddenly. The class of '29 assembled that year, and Holmes had a poem for them. But there were only six leaves left on the bough, and they all felt a little self-conscious. Who would go next? The question hung heavy in the air.

That summer Holmes was eighty years old. From Beverly Farms he was writing cheerful little notes to announce the fact, as though a new baby had come to the house. Fanny and Wendell had accompanied him to the Beverly Farms cottage for the summer. The area was growing and becoming a little pretentious. Next door to Beverly was the town of Manchester, and some of his acquaintances who lived there began giving names to their houses and calling their community Manchester-by-the-Sea. Holmes laughed and began heading his notes, "Beverly-by-the-Depot."

Whittier wrote him a poetic birthday tribute, and he was touched. He had hundreds of letters of congratulation.

By the beginning of the next year, although Holmes felt able to continue the Teacups series, he was tidying up his affairs. He gave his extensive medical library (one thousand volumes) to the Boston Medical Library Association. He spent many hours trying to persuade President Eliot to confer an honorary degree on classmate Samuel Francis Smith for "My Country, 'Tis of Thee." Eliot found that an insufficient reason for the granting of a Harvard LL.D., no matter how much he liked and respected Dr. Holmes.

Holmes had given up the boats, but the familiar figure in black broadcloth suit and coat and black beaver hat marched out every day for a stroll. Dr. Holmes was as much a part of the scenery as the trees that graced the grassy common. Nannies pointed him out to their charges, "See, there's Doctor Holmes." Schoolgirls who were studying his poems passed him open-mouthed; an artist came to sketch him and caught the figure, slightly bent, moving briskly along, in front of 296 Beacon Street.

Holmes admitted in the Teacups papers that he was preoccupied with old age. "The octogenarian loves to read about people ninety and over. He peers among the asterisks of the triennial catalogue of the University for the names of graduates who have been seventy years out of college and remain still unstarred . . ."

He seemed to make a game of it. He'd said to Longfellow years before at the Saturday Club that poets weren't long-lived. Longfellow had looked at him calmly and said he didn't believe a word of it. Next meeting, Longfellow handed Holmes a list of poets who had lived to ripe old age. Now Holmes drew up his own. "Bryant lived to be eighty-three years old, . . . Longfellow seventy-five . . . Halleck seventy-seven . . . Whittier, still living . . . eighty-two. Tennyson is still writing at eighty and Browning reached the age of seventy-seven . . ."

And Dr. Oliver Wendell Holmes was eighty-one and going like a house afire; well, still smoldering, anyhow.

Holmes raised the question of poetry: could an old man write poetry, with his "ossified" arteries? He answered with a poem:

> To the Eleven Ladies
> Who Presented Me with a Silver Loving Cup on the
> Twenty-ninth of August, M DCCC LXXXIX

It ended:

> Better love's perfume in the empty bowl
> Than wine's nepenthe for the aching soul,
> Sweeter than song that ever poet sung,
> It makes an old heart young!

The answer seemed to be *no*.

The Teacups papers were more personal than any of the other series had been. When Helen Keller, the deaf-blind woman who had conquered all those odds to learn to read braille and write, wrote him a letter, he included it in one of the Teacups papers. He put a poem at the end of one paper: "La Maison D'Or (Bar Harbor)." Julia Dorr knew what he meant.

He did not seem to care about the general reader.

He meandered along the road of his own life as he wrote, and many readers found that road duller than his past; his older readers found more to interest them by far than the younger ones. His continued popularity with the editors seems a little odd today. It must have been due to his position as "the living monument" of literary Boston.

The one real spark from Holmes was a poem that had much of the old-fashioned New England charm of "The Deacon's Masterpiece":

THE BROOMSTICK TRAIN, OR, THE RETURN OF THE WITCHES *

> Look out! Look out, boys! Clear the track!
> The witches are here! They've all come back!
> They hanged them high, —No use! No use!
> What cares a witch for a hangman's noose?
> They buried them deep, but they wouldn't lie still,

---

* This poem was suggested to Holmes by the coming of the electric railway, with its high wires and apparently magic method of propulsion (in the eyes of one born in 1809). The "broomsticks" of stanza nine were tall protrusions on each car, peculiar to the early electrified railroads—now long-since vanished. Although a modern reader has missed that era entirely, the poem had another charm: it was Holmes's celebration of the vast changes that had come to Massachusetts in his lifetime.

For cats and witches are hard to kill;
They swore they shouldn't and wouldn't die,—
Books said they did, but they lie! they lie!

—A couple of hundred years, or so,
They had knocked about in the world below,
When an Essex Deacon dropped in to call,
And a homesick feeling seized them all;
For he came from a place they knew full well,
And many a tale he had to tell.
They long to visit the haunts of men,
To see the old dwellings they knew again,
And ride on their broomsticks all around
Their wide domain of unhallowed ground.

Well did they know, those gray old wives,
The sights we see in our daily drives:
Shimmer of lake and shine of sea,
Brown's bare hill with its lonely tree,
(It wasn't then as we see it now,
With one scant scalp-lock to shade its brow;)
Dusky nooks in the Essex woods,
Dark, dim, Dante-like solitudes,
Where the tree-toad watches the sinuous snake
Glide through his forests of fern and brake;
Ipswich River; its old stone bridge;
Far off Andover's Indian Ridge,
And many a scene where history tells
Some shadow of bygone terror dwells,—
Of "Norman's Woe" with its tale of dread,
Of the Screeching Woman of Marblehead,
(The fearful story that turns men pale:
Don't bid me tell it, —my speech would fail.)

Who would not, will not, if he can,
Bathe in the breezes of fair Cape Ann,—
Rest in the bowers her bays enfold.
Loved by the sachems and squaws of old?

Home where the white magnolias bloom,
Sweet with the bayberry's chaste perfume,
Hugged by the woods and kissed by the sea!
Where is the Eden like to thee?

For that "couple of hundred years or so,"
There had been no peace in the world below;
The witches still grumbling, "It isn't fair;
Come, give us a taste of the upper air!
We've had enough of your sulphur springs,
And the evil odor that round them clings;
We long for a drink that is cool and nice,—
Great buckets of water with Wenham ice;
We've served you well upstairs, you know;
You're a good old—fellow—come, let us go!"

I don't feel sure of his being good,
But he happened to be in a pleasant mood,—
As fiends with their skins full sometimes are,—
(He'd been drinking with "roughs" at a Boston bar.)
So what does he do but up and shout
To a graybeard turnkey, "Let 'em out!"

To mind his orders was all he knew;
The gates swung open, and out they flew.
"Where are our broomsticks?" the beldams cried.
"Here are your broomsticks," an imp replied.
"They've been in—the place you know—so long
They smell of brimstone uncommon strong;
But they've gained by being left alone,—
Just look, and you'll see how tall they've grown."
—"And where is my cat?" a vixen squalled.
"Yes, where are our cats?" the witches bawled,
And began to call them all by name:
As fast as they called the cats, they came:
There was bob-tailed Tommy and long-tailed Tim,
And wall-eyed Jacky and green-eyed Jim,
And splay-foot Benny and slim-legged Bean,
And Skinny and Squally, and Jerry and Joe,

The driver may just unhitch his team,
We don't want horses, we don't want steam;
You may keep your old black cats to hug,
But the loaded train you've got to lug.

Since then on many a car you'll see
A broomstick plain as plain can be;
On every stick there's a witch astride,—
The string you see to her leg is tied.
She will do a mischief if she can,
But the string is held by a careful man,
And whenever the evil-minded witch
Would cut some caper, he gives a twitch.
As for the hag, you can't see her,
But hark! you can hear her black cat's purr
And now and then, as a car goes by,
You may catch a gleam from her wicked eye.
Often you've looked on a rushing train,
But just what moved it was not so plain.
It couldn't be those wires above,
For they could neither pull nor shove;
Where was the motor that made it go
You couldn't guess, *but now you know.*

Remember my rhymes when you ride again
On the rattling rail by the broomstick train!

Lowell wrote him in congratulation, almost Lowell's last letter.

In a way, Lowell's praise of the poem confirmed what Holmes suspected, that the rest of "Teacups" was not scintillating. He had grown too old, and was too far out of touch with the ideas of the 1890s.

"Over the Teacups" was concluded just before Lowell's death, at the end of 1890. In the last number Holmes announced that he would not write another series.

His Afterword was brighter than almost any of it. Holmes mentioned again his difficulties in keeping up with his fan mail. He made a joke of it in "my unwritten answers to correspondents," by an author driven to the wall by too much mail:

Answer 1. To the autograph hunter:

Want my autograph do you? And don't know how to spell my name. An *A* for an *E* in my middle name. Leave out the *L* in my last name. Do you know how people hate to have their names misspelled? What do you suppose are the sentiments entertained by the Thompsons with a *P* toward those who address them in writing as Thomson?

Answer 2. To the flatterer:

Think the lines you mention are by far the best I ever wrote, hey? Well, I didn't write those lines. What is more I think they are as detestable a string of rhymes as I could wish my worst enemy had written. A very pleasant frame of mind I am in for writing a letter, after reading yours!

Answer 3. To a pest who has named a child for the author:

I am glad to hear that my namesake, whom I never saw and never expect to see, has cut another tooth; but why write four pages on the strength of that . . .

Answer 4. To the eclectic critic:

You wish to correct an error in my Broomstick poem do you? You give me to understand that Wilmington is not in Essex County, but in Middlesex. Very well, but are they separated by *running water*? Because if they are not, what could hinder a witch from crossing the line that separates Wilmington from Andover, I should like to know?

He was tired, the reader need expect but little more from him in the future.

It was not quite a good-bye, but he was warning them; the last leaf was trembling on the bough.

29

THE LAST LEAF FALLS

HOLMES WATCHED THE OTHER WITHERED LEAVES FALL FROM THE bough. Dr. Henry Jacob Bigelow died in 1891, which removed Holmes's last link with the medical school. Lowell died a few weeks later—Lowell who was ten years younger—Lowell whom Holmes had confidently expected to long outlive him. That left only Holmes and John Greenleaf Whittier of the old bunch at the Saturday Club. Although Holmes and Whittier had never been close, they corresponded and visited one another.

Then in 1892, shortly after writing a poem in celebration of Holmes's eighty-third birthday, Whittier died.

From that time on, most of Holmes's close associations were with women. He leaned on Mrs. Dorr. Annie Fields came to take him driving. He drove himself at Beverly Farms in the summer, a small, neatly dressed, wrinkled figure who carried a parasol against the warm summer sun.

The class of '29 had so dwindled that there was no sense in trying to hold a meeting. They would not even fill a booth in a restaurant. First they were four and then they were three: Samuel

May, who had served for years as class secretary, Samuel F. Smith, and Holmes. Holmes had them to dinner at his house on reunion days. There were no more wines, no more songs, and very little food; they could not sing, and none of them ate much.

Holmes was deaf, but nothing like Sam Smith. Holmes said Sam was so deaf "you could drive a nail into his head and he would never find it out." Holmes's vision was dimming, but he could still read and still get about. His humor was undiminished.

He did publish *Before the Curfew,* a new volume of poems, but his major literary effort was the preparation of the Riverside Edition of his works for Houghton Mifflin. This involved correction of typographical errors, writing of new prefaces for old books, and separation of the poems he wanted to include and those he did not feel had stood well the abrasions of time.

Holmes was still a faithful member of the Saturday Club. He went almost every month to the meetings. But they were painful occasions, as he remarked one evening.

"This room is full of ghosts to me. I can see so many faces here that used to be here years ago . . ."

He might have written more. *The Atlantic* wanted more. But he could not bring himself to start another series of papers. No, Holmes said, ". . . you can not cheat old age." He would not start something new. He believed people would say, "Are you not rash at eighty years to write for young people who think a man old at forty?"

Holmes read a great deal— books that he had missed during the busy years of his life. He went to the Boston Symphony, and he always had two tickets. He took Mrs. Fields, or Elizabeth Stuart Phelps, or some other lady acquaintance. One night he fell asleep during the concert, and then was so embarrassed he would not go again.

He took to attending symphony rehearsals in the afternoons.

He was surrounded by relatives and "connections," and the ladies were pleased with his gentle company; it was also more than socially proper to be seen with him. He had once complained that he and Lowell and the others were in danger of being solidified in concrete as monuments; now he was, beyond doubt, a "wonder of the world" that must at least be seen by those who visited Boston.

In June he went to Beverly Farms, and in October he returned to Boston. He sat for his portrait, painted for the Philadelphia College of Physicians by Sarah Whitman. There was irony: the college had been a center of anti-Holmes sentiment in the days of the puerperal fever fight. All that was long forgotten. He had outlived even his critics.

Dr. Holmes was appointed chairman of the American Committee of Cooperation on a World Congress of Authors, a scheme that was to be brought to life in convention in Chicago during the summer of 1893. Charles Eliot Norton was the vice-chairman. C. Dudley Warner and Howells, and Colonel Higginson and Thomas B. Aldrich were members of the committee. They were all names with which Holmes was comfortable.

Holmes's last public appearance was on February 23, 1893, when he attended a luncheon given by the publishers Lee and Shepard at the Hotel Vendome, and a reception for members of the National Education Association. His works were then used in most of the American public schools. Houghton Mifflin had almost all of them in print. There were cheaper editions available, and several editions in England. The royalties kept coming in, especially from the *Autocrat*.

On April 23, the Reverend Phillips Brooks died. That was another shock, for Holmes had half planned that Brooks would bury him. It was to be the other way around. Annie Fields came that day and sat by the fire, and they had a long talk. Because of the mournful news, their conversation turned to hymns, and Holmes confessed that he did not like the modern hymns—no "saintliness" in them.

At church, when the preacher bored him, Holmes leaned forward in the pew and pulled out the hymnal from the back of the next seat. Then he would play a little game with himself. He would turn the pages looking for a hymn he liked. Next he would cover the name at the bottom with his hand and guess the name of the author. Almost always the hymns he preferred were those of Isaac Watts or Charles Wesley. There it was, the old Calvinist iron, still imbedded in that gentle soul.

He kept track of things. On June 14 he noted that he weighed 148¼ pounds. One day when he marched up two flights of stairs to see an acquaintance in bed, the maid looked at the little man and asked him if he was sure he could "make it."

"I'll have to climb a good many more than that before I see the angels."

In November 1893 he fell sick with the " 'flu," and the bout was a long and difficult one. Fanny and the maids and his secretary nursed him through, but when he recovered he was weak, and he went out to face the grim Boston winter less often than before. Few knew that he was not spry and healthy, because his memorial poem to Francis Parkman was published in *The Atlantic* the following February. There was Holmes again, in his accustomed place. That last leaf still seemed sturdily attached to the bough.

But in February as others read those lines about Parkman that one critic called "stately," Holmes was ill again with influenza. This time he was near to dying. The family brought in a nurse, Miss Ida O'Brien, and she fussed over him for eight long weeks before he was deemed by his doctor well enough again to be tended only by Fanny and the maids. It was April before Holmes was allowed out of the house, to walk only as far as Exeter Street. But on April 28 he managed to get to the Saturday Club!

He was, he said, the "vanishing American." His weight had fallen to 142½ pounds that spring. That summer he went out less often. His face had grown as wrinkled as a dried fruit, but not a prune: he smiled too often for that.

His eyes still twinkled and he was still capable of the grand gesture. One day in 1894 he read in the *Transcript* that actress Ellen Terry was in town. She was then the reigning queen of the theater on both sides of the Atlantic. Holmes sent her a little note:

> *Sur la scène*
> *Toujours la reine;*
> *Sans diadème*
> *Encore la mème.*

He could not go to see Ellen Terry's play because he could not sit through a long performance. But he was interested in her, just as he was interested in everything around him. Especially he was interested in himself, as a phenomenon of nature. From within the stately mansion of his soul, Dr. Oliver Wendell Holmes was watching the crumbling of the castle.

The summer of 1894 Holmes again went to Beverly Farms. But he returned to the city early. He had found it harder to write a letter even with the assistance of his secretary. Yet when he did write, as he did to Howells to thank him for a profile of himself that Howells was planning, the paper concealed the truth. He still quipped and made Latin jokes and seemed as spry as he had ever been.

One evening late in September he sat by the fire with Fanny and Wendell, half dozing in his chair. Fanny was knitting and the judge was reading. Suddenly, Holmes looked over at his son.

"Well, Wendell, what is it, King's Chapel?"

"Oh, yes, Father."

"All right, then, I am satisfied. That is all I am going to say about it."

And he said no more.

The days went by. On Sunday, October 7, he got up, had breakfast, and went to church at Kings, where he had been married and his children baptized. He came home and napped awhile in his chair. Sunday had always been a day of rest; the secretary was off on business of her own, and there was no thought of writing even so much as a letter. That evening at teatime, the little family assembled in the parlor by the fire. First frost had fallen, and the evening sky had that especially brilliant tone of New England autumn. In the dusk, Fanny and Wendell saw the doctor's head slip forward on his chest, as it did when he dropped off for a nap. Fanny said something to him. He did not reply. The sun went down, and Wendell went to awaken his father. But Dr. Holmes had already left.

NOTES

CHAPTER ONE

The best way to get a feeling for Dr. Holmes's place in Boston is to consult the collection of newspaper clippings in the Harvard University archives, particularly those published at the time of Holmes's death.

Most of the material about the death and burial of Dr. Holmes was found in the files of the various newspapers of the period. The Harvard archives have a collection of newspaper clippings related to the event from the Boston *Transcript, Globe,* and *Advertiser.* The reports from the foreign newspapers also come from those files. The observations of S. I. Hayakawa and Howard Mumford Jones come from their book, *Oliver Wendell Holmes* (New York: American Book Company, 1939). Edmund Wilson's findings come from his published letters. Helen Keller's reaction was noted by the *Transcript.* Holmes's interchange with William Winter's son comes from Holmes's paper in the Houghton Library. The report of the funeral is from the various contemporary newspapers.

CHAPTER TWO

Most of the notes about Holmes's earliest years are from John T. Morse, Jr.'s, biography of Holmes, *Life and Letters of Oliver Wendell Holmes* (Boston: Houghton Mifflin Co., 1939). Some are from Colonel Thomas Higginson's *Cambridge Days*. The genealogy comes from the Morse book and Holmes's miniature biographical sketch prepared for a publisher in his latter days. Holmes often wrote about the "old gambrel-roofed house," particularly in *Over the Teacups*, his very last book, published when he was in his eighties. Throughout his writings, and particularly in the three series of essays known as the Breakfast Table group, Holmes drew illustrations from his own life. Thus, while he never made more than a few notes for an autobiography, he was as acute an autobiographer as ever existed, and it would be possible to construct a sensible enough book with scissors and paste applied to his own writings. In fact, those potentialities were seen in 1915 by Caroline Ticknor, a descendant of one of Holmes's publishers, who edited a number of the doctor's long reminiscences of Boston into *Doctor Holmes's Boston*.

The tales of school days in Cambridge are from Morse, Holmes's own writings, and from Higginson and Richard Henry Dana, Jr.'s, reminiscences. *Perdidi Diem* comes from Morse. The observations about Holmes's religious inclinations are from his own writings and Morse. Holmes's Andover days are described frequently in his long correspondence with his schoolmate, Phineas Barnes.

CHAPTER THREE

The descriptions of Harvard in 1826 were drawn from the books of the corporation in the Harvard archives and from the histories of the classes of the period, also in the archives. The tale of "Charitable Ann" comes from a newspaper story about Holmes by an old family servant, published after Holmes's death. The stories of the class of

'29 come from the class book and from Holmes's reminiscences in later years, set down by Morse. The story of the struggle for control of the First Congregational Church of Cambridge, and of the Reverend Abiel Holmes's eventual departure, is told in an anonymous publication, *An Account of the Controversy in the First Parish in Cambridge*. At various times throughout his career, Holmes referred to the struggle, particularly when he was engaged in his battle with orthodox Calvinism in the late 1850s and 1860s.

Holmes's academic records are a part of the Harvard archives, and his activities are recorded therein and in his own reminiscences published as anecdotes or parts of lectures over the years. Samuel May, a particular friend of Holmes's from the class of '29, was class secretary, and his records have many insights into the behavior of this strange and in some ways misassembled group. Holmes later noted in a discussion recorded by Annie Fields, wife of his publisher, some of the memorable achievements of his class. They were a distinguished lot, jurists, literary figures, politicians, but Holmes was the most famous of them all.

Holmes's class poem in 1829—and the whole commencement exercise—were recorded by the *New England Palladium* and several other newspapers. The report of the class dinner was set down in detail by May.

CHAPTER FOUR

Very little is known about the philosophical decision that led Holmes to try the law before he entered medicine. He never explained why he chose the law, and only briefly and usually indirectly did he indicate that he found it too boring to continue. From that some have deduced that Holmes had no use for lawyers, and Catherine Drinker Bowen, in *Yankee from Olympus* (Boston: Atlantic Monthly Press, 1944), invented conversation in which Dr. Holmes indicated his contempt for lawyers. But Mark DeWolfe Howe, in his later biography, *Justice Oliver Wendell Holmes, The Shaping Years, 1841–1870* (Cambridge: Belknap Press, 1957), said flatly that the younger Holmes was pushed into the legal profession by his father, and that seems much more in character. As a Brahmin,

Holmes had utmost respect for the profession; he was married to the daughter of a distinguished judge, and his brother John and many of his friends were lawyers and judges.

I have included several of the poems Holmes wrote in the early 1830s, because these are among his most successful, and certainly "Old Ironsides" is the most famous. Holmes's energy and growing ability to deal with poetic theme seems apparent here, culminating in "The Last Leaf," which he wrote shortly before embarking on the medical studies that would demand his total concentration for the next five years. Had Holmes continued as he was going in "The Last Leaf," he might have become the important poet that Edgar Allan Poe, for one, already then thought him to be.

CHAPTER FIVE

Holmes himself is the source of the material about his early medical studies. He wrote his friend Phineas Barnes about his change in status, and gave a little picture of his life in the boarding-house—which was to become the source for his later Breakfast Table essays. Eleanor M. Tilton's *Amiable Autocrat, A Biography of Dr. Oliver Wendell Holmes* (New York: Henry Schuman, 1947), made exhaustive inquiries into the medical scene in Boston in that period, and from that emerges the picture of Holmes's medical course under Dr. Jackson and his colleagues. Holmes's letters home and to Phineas Barnes, many of them in the Houghton collection, are the sources for some of this chapter. Morse uses much of the material, but not all. Fellow student Thomas Appleton's letters home, recorded in Susan Hale's *Life and Letters of Thomas Gold Appleton* (New York: D. Appleton Co., 1885), are also a source for some stories, especially the tale of the night out in Paris and Holmes's early visits to the Louvre. Holmes obviously had some amorous adventures in Paris, too, but he was totally discreet about them as far as one can ascertain. There was never a mention of a young lady or any sort of sexual encounter. Holmes told part of the story of the Independence Day celebration in Paris in 1833; and Appleton told the rest. Holmes's reminiscences of his Paris teachers, later the subject of general and medical lectures, provided many of the insights here. His running battle with his family over money and his stay in Europe are faithfully recorded by Morse from the letters home.

CHAPTER SIX

The source here is again primarily Holmes himself, through his letters and later reminiscences and observations about his Paris student days. Ms. Tilton has explored this admirably in medical terms, but not so well in human terms, a fault I tried to remedy in the account of Holmes's student life and travels. I am much indebted to the librarians of the Holmes collection at the Boston Medical Library for a number of favors and some observations about Holmes and his place in medicine and the literature of medicine.

CHAPTER SEVEN

The details of Holmes's first days at home come from his own writings, from Morse, and other biographies of Holmes: William Sloane Kennedy's *Oliver Wendell Holmes: Poet, Litterateur, Scientist* (Boston: S. E. Cassino and Co., 1883), which has the virtue of contemporary account; E. E. Brown's *Life of Oliver Wendell Holmes* (Akron, Ohio: Saalfield Publishing Co., 1903), published nearly a decade after Holmes's death, which contains first-hand recollections by contemporaries; Samuel McChord Crothers' *The Autocrat and His Fellow Boarders* (Boston: Houghton Mifflin Co., 1909), a slender essay of a laudatory nature; Miriam Rossiter Small's *Oliver Wendell Holmes* (New York: Twayne Publishers, 1962), one of the Twayne United States Authors series, which concentrates on the literary figure; and M. A. DeWolfe Howe's *Holmes of the Breakfast Table* (London: Oxford University Press, 1939), which places Holmes in his times and in the affairs of men much more accurately than all the others.

The trouble with Morse's work, from a reader's point of view, is that it is largely a collection of letters and Holmes's own observations, with almost none of the personal recollection and evaluation one might have expected from Holmes's nephew, his wife's sister's son. Morse spent many days at the Holmes house in his boyhood; he and Oliver Wendell Holmes, Jr., were the best of friends. From him we might have had a good look inside that house, and particularly a far more anecdotal and revealing study of the two Amelias, Holmes's wife and daughter. Rather, there is almost nothing, and whatever I have been able to reconstruct about wife and daughter and the household has come almost entirely from bits, pieces, and suggestions by Holmes himself in letters and essays, and from outside sources that mention the Holmeses only peripherally. Morse was far too close to Judge Holmes, his cousin, to want to embarrass him in any way, which is a tribute to his Victorian gentility, but not to his skill as a biographer.

Holmes told the story of his encounter with Park Benjamin over his poem "The Last Reader," which Benjamin had the temerity to touch up. He expounded on this theme later in the Breakfast Table essays. By that time everybody who knew Holmes was aware of his fussiness about reading proofs. The newspapers that printed his poems at times gave him enormous pain with typographical errors, until he insisted on trotting down to the editorial offices of the *Transcript* and other papers to read proof before edition time, if they wanted to print anything he had written. His care and insistence on absolute accuracy made him the terror of *The Atlantic*'s offices in Lowell's day and thereafter, under editors Fields, Howells, Aldrich, and Scudder.

Over the years, the poetic competition between Holmes and the Reverend James Freeman Clarke grew, flowered, and then subsided, as Holmes became known as a major literary figure and Clarke became famous in New England for his sermons in King's Chapel.

The Bartlett story is largely from Reginald Fitz's study of Holmes, the doctor, "My Dr. Oliver Wendell Homes," which appeared in the *Bulletin of the New York Academy of Medicine,* Vol. 19 (1943).

CHAPTER EIGHT

The material on the Boston Dispensary years comes from *The History of the Boston Dispensary* (1859) and from Tilton. The study of the Boylston Prizes of 1837 comes from the Holmes collection in the Houghton Library. The material about Holmes's life comes from Morse, the Houghton collection of letters, James and Annie Fields's *Authors and Friends* (reprinted by AMS, New York, 1969); and Justin Winsor's *Memorial History of Boston* (Boston: J. R. Osgood & Co., 1887). Information on the Tremont Medical School is from Holmes's own recollections in the Houghton collection, and from Tilton. The Dartmouth story comes from the Houghton collection. The story of Holmes's flirtation with Baltimore and the University of Maryland School of Medicine comes from a series of letters reproduced in an article by George E. Gifford, Jr., in the *Bulletin of the History of Medicine*, Vol. XXXVIII (1964).

CHAPTER NINE

The story of Holmes's early years of marriage comes from his later writings and from letters in the Houghton collection. The tribute to Holmes as a medical scientist "a hundred years ahead of his time" was made by Fitz in the study already cited. The tales about quackery and medical delusions are from Holmes's lectures. The homeopathy story is described in his paper on homeopathy, and the puerperal fever stories are from Holmes's works and papers. His findings on puerperal fever were one of the major contributions he made to scientific medicine, although through an unfortunate combination of events, they were generally ignored by the American medical profession for at least a decade.

CHAPTER TEN

The Dickens tales came from James Fields's *Yesterdays with Authors* (Boston: Houghton Mifflin Co., 1899), and from James C. Austin's biography of Fields, *Fields of the Atlantic Monthly* (San Marino, Calif.: The Huntington Library, 1953), except for the Bartlett story, which comes from a letter Bartlett wrote to Holmes. My conclusions about Holmes as the physician were drawn from his carefully written case histories, found in the Houghton collection.

The Holmes-Lowell argument over morality is probably too well known to need elucidation here. Lowell's letter has been lost, but Holmes's reply survives in Morse and the Houghton papers, and reconstruction of the issues is easy enough, in view of the events of Lowell's life at that time.

CHAPTER ELEVEN

The analysis of the Harvard medical faculty is from Fitz's paper. The Harriot K. Hunt incident comes from Holmes's papers and the files of Harvard College. The study of Holmes as a medical lecturer comes from Dr. David Cheever's observations after many years as his demonstrator, and from Thomas E. and Eleanor A. Hunt's article on Holmes, "Dr. Oliver Wendell Holmes, Teacher and Microscopist," in the *Alabama Journal of Medical Science* (January 1966).

CHAPTER TWELVE

The notes about the Berkshire Festival and Holmes's occasional poetry at this time are from his own works and the collection of his letters at the Houghton Library of Harvard University. The sources for the observations about Holmes's activities in Pittsfield that summer are letters in the Houghton collection, which were printed in Morse's *Life and Letters of Oliver Wendell Holmes*, which is most valuable for its letters.

The observations about Holmes and his basic profession—medicine—come from many sources. The first person really to deal exhaustively with Holmes as a medical man was Eleanor Tilton in her *Amiable Autocrat*, a Ph.D. thesis that was later published. The note about the Wednesday Evening Club of 1777 comes from the history of that club. The anecdote about Holmes and his dissertation on the female reproductive anatomy comes from a newspaper clipping in the Houghton Library files. The other recollections of his medical lectures are largely from Fitz's study of Dr. Holmes that appeared in the *Bulletin of the New York Academy of Medicine*.

The story of Dr. Webster's murder of Dr. Parkman comes from George Dilnot's *The Trial of Professor John White Webster* (London: Geoffrey Bles, 1960), and from Dr. Orville T. Bailey's article,

"Brahma, Parkman and Webster," in the *Journal of the American Medical Association* (April 1972). Holmes's appearance at the trial was part of the court record.

CHAPTER THIRTEEN

The Dickens story is from Holmes's papers in the Houghton Library. Ms. Tilton made an exhaustive study of Holmes's lecturing dates over the years. His lectures and notes on them appear scattered throughout his papers.

The basic source for the tale of Dr. Holmes, Nathaniel Hawthorne, Herman Melville, and publisher James T. Fields at the Berkshire picnic comes from the August and September 1850 issues of the *Literary World,* a New York magazine published by Evert Duyckinck and his brother, George. Cornelius Mathews, a writer for the magazine, was one of the guests, and he wrote the story in a flowery, even soupy style that was not uncommon in the period. Holmes was called "The Town Wit," Melville was "New Neptune," Hawthorne was "Noble Melancholy," and publisher Fields was "Mr. Greenfield." There are other sources. Hawthorne mentions the outing in his reminiscences, and Fields speaks of it in his *Yesterdays with Authors.* Holmes had a sidelong reference or two in various essays and lectures.

Observations about Holmes's dress and his appearance come from many sources. He always dressed in either a dark suit or a black coat and gray trousers, always wore a linen shirt and collar and necktie. The tidbit about the patented India-rubber bag is from Mathews. I was drawn to the anecdote particularly in a conversation with Harvey Meyerson, who has been working on a biography of Melville for many years.

CHAPTER FOURTEEN

The report of the 1850 meeting of the class of '29 is part of the class record kept by secretary May. The source for the material about Holmes and the children is Mark Howe's biography of Oliver Wendell Holmes, Jr.

Holmes's literary perambulations that summer are from Fields and Hawthorne's reminiscences. Anyone who doubts Holmes's position in Pittsfield need only consult the pages of the local newspaper. The account of the dedication of the Pittsfield cemetery was the major news story of the week.

Holmes got one hundred dollars from publisher Fields for "Astrea," which pleased the author mightily.

Miss Hunt's troubles about medical education are told in the Hunt article in the *Alabama Journal of Medical Science*.

The story of the three young blacks is told in two biographical studies of Martin Robinson Delany, one by Dorothy Sterling, called *The Making of an Afro-American, Martin Robinson Delany* (New York: Doubleday & Co., 1952), and the other from the *Journal of the National Medical Association,* May 1952, and from the Harvard College records in the archives.

CHAPTER FIFTEEN

Holmes on the lecture circuit comes from Morse, Tilton, the Boston newspapers of the period as noted and quoted, and Holmes's papers. The stories of literary Boston come from various lives of Emerson, Longfellow, and Fields, and Austin's book on Fields. Also, Edward Waldo Emerson's *The Early Years of the Saturday Club* (Boston: Houghton Mifflin Co., 1918) was useful here. Holmes's recollections of the lecturer's art and tribulations come from the Breakfast Table essays, where from time to time he related a vignette of some aspect of the Lyceum circuit.

The material on the class of '29 comes from the class records. Holmes's reissue of his puerperal fever paper was a turning point in the history of medical science. The evidence of the quarrel with Horace Greeley can be found in the pages of the New York *Tribune*. The story of the Harvard legacy that was refused is in the Harvard archives. The announcement that Holmes would sell his house was made to friends in letters. Not for many years would he admit publicly the wrench of this decision. Even Oliver Wendell Holmes, Jr., whose perceptions were more coldly legal than warmly emotional, would recall with a sad nostalgia the pleasant summers in Pittsfield, as he was emerging into puberty.

CHAPTER SIXTEEN

The story of the founding of *The Atlantic* comes from Horace Scudder's *James Russell Lowell* (New York: AMS Press, 1901), and Edward Emerson's *The Early Years of the Saturday Club*. Thomas Higginson's recollection of his interchange with editor Underwood comes from his own reminiscences. The pages of *The Atlantic* for the period tell much of the story of the success of the magazine. When I asked Leon Edel, the biographer of Henry James, how he would place Holmes in the land of letters, he said that Holmes was not a literary man at all, but "an amateur." Not really. Dilettante, yes. Amateur, no. And particularly as a writer, Holmes was probably the most hardheaded professional of all those who began in *The Atlantic*. He was a strict taskmaster with himself and with his editors. And if he felt that he was being underpaid for any effort, he never hesitated to say so, even to hint that he was ready to take his wares elsewhere.

CHAPTER SEVENTEEN

Holmes acquired and retained the position as preeminent literary figure of New England (and of America) for so many years that most readers are quite unaware of the manner in which he acquired the fame. *The Atlantic* made him, and he made it. Even *The Early Years of the Saturday Club* does not indicate very clearly Holmes's junior position to Emerson, Longfellow, and the rest at the beginning of the 1860s. It was a more formal period than today, but Holmes's letters and papers indicate that he was not on a first-name basis with any but Lowell during this period. It was Dr. Agassiz and Mr. Emerson, and that was largely how it would remain.

Holmes's letters to most of the world, although cordial in tone, were also very formal. Only in the later stages of "the club" did he begin to relax. I have traced the poignant story of Holmes's emergence into the limelight and the growth of the Saturday Club from a number of sources—histories of Boston, Edward Emerson's works, and biographies and reminiscences of all the major participants whose lives touched on Holmes's own: Lowell, John Holmes, Emerson, Longfellow, Dana, Judge Hoar, Whittier, Hawthorne, Fields, Thomas Appleton, Dr. Agassiz, etc.

CHAPTER EIGHTEEN

In the 1970s it is difficult to assess the impact of Holmes's lecture, "The Chief End of Man," unless one is a student of comparative theology or the history of Calvinism in the United States. At that time one either accepted the old stern tenets of the puritan, with the view that man's life on earth was no more than preparation for eternity—or one was damned by the orthodox thinkers. Thus, Holmes, with his easygoing deism, was damned. And because the Calvinists felt themselves losing ground at the time, and because none is more hated than the apostate, Holmes was damned all the more fervently.

Holmes's novel *Elsie Venner* can still start arguments around a dinner table, but not, now, the arguments of his day. The question raised by this book—and reinforced by his other two novels —is over the claims of Holmes's medical admirers that he was a forerunner of Sigmund Freud. I would not make so broad a claim, as did Rose Alexander in her article, "Oliver Wendell Holmes— Psychiatrist," in the *Medical Record* (July 5, 1939), or C. P. Oberndorf in his book, *The Psychiatric Novels of Oliver Wendell Holmes*, published in 1943. But it seems evident that Holmes was leading the pack, and bringing to the public through his immense prestige an appreciation of the inner man and the framework of the study that had no name in his day, but would be called psychiatry.

Holmes's invention of the term and concept of Brahminism was typical of the man's curiosity and analytical approach to life. He gave a name to pain-killing drugs—*anesthesia*. He gave the name to *The Atlantic Monthly*. He also gave other names that did not stick, such as anthropology to what we now know as psychology.

CHAPTER NINETEEN

Holmes's position as a popular writer has been forgotten over the years, but it is illustrative to say that in the late 1850s *The Atlantic* had a larger circulation than it has in the 1970s, 400,000 copies sold each month in a nation of 31 million people as compared to today's 220 million. Many copies were sold on the other side of the Atlantic Ocean, but the impact of this mushrooming magazine is still readily discernible in the figures. And among the writers for that publication, famous names in literature for the most part, Holmes led them all in popularity. He was a New England writer, but New England was accepted as the cultural center of the United States. After the publication of *The Autocrat of the Breakfast Table*, Holmes was perhaps the most popular writer in the English language.

The publication of *The Professor at the Breakfast Table* had brought some adverse reactions, particularly in the orthodox puritan community. There had been other negative reactions from literary critics outside of New England. So Holmes did not achieve his earlier prominence again until the golden years, when as the surviving literary figure of Boston he could do no wrong, and actually was doing nothing at all.

There was nothing remarkable in Holmes's apparent *volte-face* in relation to the South and slavery. His position in the hottest days of the abolitionist fire had been that the Union must be saved. So when the Confederacy was formed, he backed Abraham Lincoln's decision to save the Union by force of arms. "A Voice of the Loyal North," his poetic plea for Southern restraint, was composed for the 1861 reunion of the class of '29, but was really written for the nation at large, Holmes knowing all the while that *The Atlantic* or the Boston *Transcript* would print anything he wrote and that it would receive international attention.

There has been a good deal of speculation over the years (much of it engendered by Mrs. Bowen's *Yankee from Olympus*) about the father-son relationship between Dr. Holmes and Mr. Justice Holmes. The Holmeses' activity in the first few months of 1861 indicates that the family tie that binds was not any more strained in the Holmes family than it was in any American family. The generation gap was as real and as recognized among families of the puritan and Victorian eras as it would be in the twentieth century.

In Holmes's generation reasonable people accepted the differences, but maintained the strength of the family. Holmes *knew* he was a hard man to live with, and not the sort of father that could be "pals" with his boys. But he was fully behind them in their enterprises and never let either boy down. When Wendell decided to enlist on the eve of commencement, Holmes did not utter a chiding word, but interceded with Harvard's faculty, where many such words were being spoken. Holmes protected young Wendell from Harvard's full wrath, and spent much of his time that spring and summer of 1861 attempting to secure Wendell's commission in the Union forces.

Mark D. Howe's biography of Oliver Wendell Holmes, Jr., is useful in establishing the relations of father and son. It is not very revealing about Holmes's homelife, but then, except for glimpses in Dr. Holmes's writings, not much about the Holmeses is revealing. They were a very private Brahmin family.

The difficulties of Wendell, Jr., and Harvard are shown in the Harvard archives. Holmes's papers indicate—through his letters—how seriously he worried about Wendell and how he tried to intercede with his old friend, President Felton. The denial of a part in commencement to his son was a hard blow—but Holmes never complained of it.

CHAPTER TWENTY

Several articles in medical journals have described Dr. Holmes's inventions and adaptations. Fitz is particularly informative. The stories of the wartime experiences of the Holmes family in *Yankee from Olympus* make fascinating reading. I wish that either Mark DeWolfe Howe or I had been able to document more of them. But they certainly are in character—the bustling little doctor trying to see to every detail and, in so doing, embarrassing the twenty-year-old son.

Holmes the writer was never more clearly exposed than in the emotionalism of the war years. His reporting of the "home front" in *The Atlantic* makes excellent reading even today, and ought to be required for social historians who seek to know "how it was" in Union cities between 1861 and 1865. The entire Holmes family was involved in the effort. Amelia came out of her shell for the first time since her marriage to run the Boston Sanitary Commission. Little Amelia helped with the Sanitary Commission. Dr. Holmes lectured to the civilian workers and made many speeches. These were notable in part because (even afterward) the doctor was not known as an orator. Poet and lecturer, yes, but orator, no.

CHAPTER TWENTY-ONE

During the Civil War years, Holmes was at his peak. The demands of his society taxed his abilities, but he managed to meet them in science, teaching, public service, and a flow of articles and poems for magazine and lectern.

The Saturday Club was not as homogeneous a group as may have been believed. Holmes knew most of the members as "Mr. So and So." Some of them were not friends of his at all, although he never went so far as Richard Henry Dana, who was so incorrigible a blackballer that Holmes and the others continued to withhold nominations to membership until days when Dana was absent. And there were other frictions. Emerson, for example, did not like Hawthorne. But Holmes managed to remain aloof from these difficulties and was probably the most popular member of the club.

CHAPTER TWENTY-TWO

William Dean Howells arrived in Boston to be assistant editor of *The Atlantic* at the zenith of Boston's literary years. Never had the concentration of American literary men and celebrities been greater. New York was already threatening. Boston's literary elm was rotting, but the leaves were never more lustrous, and Holmes's bough was strongest and brightest of them all.

In the late 1850s and early 1860s, Holmes was at a peak of his own. He was interested in everything around him. When Wendell came home after his *Wanderjahr* with some English luggage that sported a new sort of clasp, Holmes made a drawing of it so he could have some for himself. Holmes remained in close touch with a number of members of the class of '29, although he was closest to the Boston group.

His relations—literary and personal—with publisher Fields were as intimate as they could be. When Fields went abroad he asked Holmes and Lowell to befriend young Howells, and they did.

CHAPTER TWENTY-THREE

Dr. Holmes's quarrel with the city fathers of Boston was reported in the newspapers. The issue of the development of the Charles River estuary occupied him and many others for months, but there was no gainsaying "progress." The new rich needed a place to live, and Back Bay it would be.

Once the Civil War was over, Holmes retreated to his previous position of ignoring most affairs of the day. His letter of January 4, 1868, to Alexander Porter Morse, is an indication of his refusal to let the sectional issue dominate and impinge upon his personal relationships. Morse was the son of his old schoolmate, Isaac Morse, and also editor of a Southern literary journal. Holmes addressed him in both capacities, suggesting that the South ought to try and heal the wounds left by the war, even as Oliver Wendell Holmes, Jr., had healed the three wounds given him by Southern soldiers. Had young Morse or his brother been one of the marksmen? "I forgive you if either of you did it . . ."

He was interested in the careers of his friends Lowell and Motley, both of whom served as diplomats. He corresponded with them regularly, and in that sense discussed public affairs. He once wrote President Grover Cleveland suggesting that he ought to keep Lowell in office as minister to England, although Lowell was an appointee of Republican Presidents Hayes, Garfield, and Arthur.

His relations with Harvard in these years were those of an elder statesman. President Eliot firmly refused to be pushed by Holmes into bestowing honorary degrees that Holmes would have liked to have seen, but Holmes was so much a Harvard fixture that on his death the president sent out black-edged cards to announce the fact.

In *The Poet at the Breakfast Table*, Holmes showed (not for the first or last time) how conscious he was of the ephemeral nature of literary fame. It would not have surprised him to awaken in 1979 and find that of his works only a small handful have "survived," and that most universities lump his writings into American literary survey courses.

CHAPTER TWENTY-FOUR

Even the deep tragedy of Amelia's weakening and increasing inability to cope with the outside world never really escaped beyond the bonds of family. Close friends knew that Amelia was not well in the 1870s, but the Holmeses simply did not discuss the matter, and while Holmes might wax loquacious and even descend to bathos in his lionization of Wendell, Jr., the hero son, he never wrote about Amelia in the later years. It was a matter so private that no clear picture of Amelia Holmes has come down.

The 1870s were the years in which New York came to Boston (E. L. Godkin and Howells among the leaders) and wrested the literary leadership of America away from *The Atlantic* crowd on its own grounds. Holmes saw it happening, although the change never affected him or his position in the literary world. Indeed, in the later years there was virtually no negative criticism of anything he wrote.

The story of Mark Twain's "disgrace" comes from several sources, most important of them Albert Bigelow Paine's biography, *Mark Twain* (New York: Harper & Bros., 1912), and Holmes and Howells' recollections.

CHAPTER TWENTY-FIVE

M. A. DeWolfe Howe's *Memories of a Hostess* (Boston: Atlantic Monthly Press, 1922), set the scene of literary Boston in the 1870s and 1880s. *The Atlantic* literary breakfast to honor Holmes on his seventieth birthday was exhaustively reported in the Boston press. The Paine biography is useful in reporting Mark Twain's reactions.

Holmes's last lecture (1882) to the Harvard Medical School was widely heralded, as indeed was everything Holmes did in this period of his life. His trip to New York was a "seven-day wonder" in the Boston and New York press. His speech opening the Boylston Street medical building was fully reported in the *Transcript*, *Globe*, and other newspapers.

CHAPTER TWENTY-SIX

I have taken seriously the Holmes biography of Emerson, within its own limitations, which were those of the author. He admitted that and plowed on. Critically speaking, then, the biography is authoritative only in discussions of Emerson's poetry, and Holmes would be the first to agree to that.

I have taken more seriously than most students of Holmes the "medicated novels," for it seems to me many have missed the point that these were written as magazine serial stories, primarily, and their main purpose was to entertain. Holmes pursued his thoughts and tracks on his own, but he was not the only person in America thinking about the psychology of humanity, and trying to separate life from religion. Also, in *A Mortal Antipathy*, Holmes set out to poke fun at various puffed-up elements of society, including suffragism (the precursor of women's liberation), small-town New England, and snobbism. To my mind he succeeded admirably, although most critics (especially Hayakawa and Jones) call it Holmes's "least successful work," because it was least reminiscent of the Breakfast Table series.

Holmes's feeling for Dr. Johnson emerged a number of times in his life and writings. He liked to compare his own life to that great English literary figure's career, and with more than a touch of vanity in the comparison. But after the Civil War Holmes had no doubt about his position as a "literary giant," although his New England common sense told him it would never last. And he was vain enough. Once, at one of the dinners given by *The Atlantic* so often that the "Atlantic Club" was often confused with the Saturday Club, he espied *Atlantic* author John Townsend Trowbridge and went to sit next to him, announcing with considerable indignation that the critic of one of the literary magazines had said that Trowbridge wrote better than Holmes did.

What did Trowbridge think of that? The Holmes chin was thrust out and the Holmes eyes flashed.

Trowbridge felt the anger, and thought fast. Perhaps, he replied, but there was another critic who said Edmund Kirke could write better than Trowbridge.

Then Holmes laughed. "If you can write better than I, and Kirke can write better than you, then Kirke is the man. We know where we are!"

His good humor was restored, and then he was off on a flight of words.

CHAPTER TWENTY-SEVEN

In the last years the people who disliked Holmes, such as Francis Underwood, were reduced to misquoting him in their books on other literary figures. He was so compelling a figure himself that he often said he felt like a walking monument, and while his ego was flattered by the attention, the story of his walk on the Common and then the flight from a pack of admirers was typical of his struggle to retain some right of privacy. His letters to friends during the period complain peevishly of the manuscripts and books and blessings heaped upon him by people he did not know, would not ever know, and did not want to know.

CHAPTER TWENTY-EIGHT

Holmes's perennial popularity is given credence by editor T. B. Aldrich's request of him, when he was nearly eighty years old, to write another series for *The Atlantic*. That series, *Over the Teacups*, could have a renewed meaning in the last quarter of the twentieth century, as American eyes turn to the aging processes, and the aging are so many among us. For Holmes never lost his scientific eye for the phenomena of nature, just as he never lost his sensuousness. Up to the last he went to concerts, and then to rehearsals when the formality of concert-going grew too much for him. He loved the pleasures of the table, although he had long since quit smoking because of his asthma, and drank virtually nothing in these last years. His poem, "The Broomstick Train," was a recognition of the collision between the old (Holmes's world) and the new (the world of his son). But much of what he wrote was timeless, as his colloquy on the irritation of the writer and public figure who is bedeviled by a loving public.

CHAPTER TWENTY-NINE

Holmes outlived almost everyone he knew among his contemporaries. The last years were a study of old age, growing weakness, but even in this period Holmes showed the old resiliency. He set out to read things he had missed through the years, and he occupied himself with that task fervently. He kept track of old friends, Annie Fields and others—most of them women, because the women outlived their men. But near the end he sensed that this last leaf was withering on the bough, and soon must fall, and he said as much to his son Wendell that night a few days before he died. With the Brahmin's sense of time and place, he warned them, so that all would be as it should be right to the last.

ACKNOWLEDGMENTS

I AM DEEPLY INDEBTED TO THE LIBRARIANS AT HARVARD UNIVERSITY'S
Houghton Library, and especially to Marte Shaw, curator of the
reading room, for help far beyond the call of duty. John Lanham
of the Widener Library was also extremely helpful in arranging for
me to have the use of many volumes. Richard J. Wolfe of the Harvard Medical Library spent a good deal of time and effort on my
researches into Holmes's medical career.

I am also indebted to John Harris of the Boston *Globe* and to
Russell M. Jones, late of Westminster College in Fulton, Missouri,
for information about Holmes at various periods.

The University of Hawaii libraries were most gracious in allowing me the lengthy use of a number of volumes by and about Dr.
Holmes.

Honolulu
October 1978

INDEX